Measuring Business Excellence

In recent years, changes in business activities suggest that a shift in market capitalization is taking place. Share prices of many large companies have severely corroded, and stakeholders are demanding that company chairmen take urgent steps to achieve profitability through Business Excellence (BE).

BE and Total Quality Management (TQM) models provide a means of measuring the satisfaction of customers, employers and shareholders simultaneously. A number of such models currently exist, but, the author argues, none of these address all dimensions of TQM.

This book introduces the principles of TQM, and establishes their use in measuring BE in an organizational environment. It comparatively evaluates various TQM and BE models (including the European Foundation for Quality Management (EFQM) model), and discusses the complexities of measuring success.

The author also provides a new comprehensive model, based on theoretical and empirical research, which draws together the diverse principles of established models. This model provides critical organizational success factors, and also details the most effective methods for measuring these factors.

Presenting important, innovative work by one of the most eminent scholars in the field, this book will be essential reading for both academics and professionals working in quality management.

Gopal K. Kanji, Professor of Applied Statistics at Sheffield Hallam University and director of Kanji Quality Culture is a founder–editor of two international journals, *Journal of Applied Statistics* and *Total Quality Management.* His career has spanned more than thirty-five years in the field of statistics and quality, and along with his teaching and research activities he has published more then 70 papers and 8 books. Recently, he has been appointed president of The European Society for Organizational Excellence (ESOE) and vice-president of the International Foundation for Customer Focus (IFCF). He is also a fellow of the American Society for Quality (ASQ) and an Academician of the International Academy for Quality (IAQ).

Routledge advances in management and business studies

University of Stirling Library, FK9 4LA
Tel: 01786 467220

POPULAR LOAN

This item is likely to be in heavy demand.
Please **RETURN** or **RENEW**
no later than the date on the receipt

Measuring Business Excellence

Gopal K. Kanji

London and New York

First published 2002
by Routledge
11 New Fetter Lane, London EC4P 4EE

Simultaneously published in the USA and Canada
by Routledge
29 West 35th Street, New York, NY 10001

Routledge is an imprint of the Taylor & Francis Group

Typeset in 10/12 pt Baskerville by
Newgen Imaging Systems (P) Ltd., Chennai, India
Printed and bound in Great Britain by Biddles Ltd., Guildford and King's Lynn

British Library Cataloguing in Publication Data
A catalogue record for this book is available
from the British Library

Library of Congress Cataloging in Publication Data
Kanji, Gopal K.
  Measuring business excellence / Gopal K. Kanji.
    p. cm.
  Includes bibliographical references and index.
    1. Total quality management – Evaluation.   2. Industrial management – Evaluation.
    3. Industrial productivity – Evaluation. 4. Organizational effectiveness – Evaluation.   I. Title.

HD62.15 .K364 2002
658.4'.013–dc21   2001041993

ISBN 0-415-25822-7 (alk. paper)

Contents

Figures

Tables

Preface

In recent years the changing face of business activities suggests that a paradigm shift of market capitalization among various businesses is taking place. Share prices of many large companies have corroded severely and stakeholders are demanding that the Company Chairman should take urgent steps to achieve profitability through Business Excellence (BE).

BE is a means of measuring customers', employers' and shareholders' satisfaction simultaneously within an organization. Here, BE can be used to measure how well the different areas of an organization are performing using various quality dimensions.

For many companies, to remain a leader in a dynamic and unpredictable marketplace it is necessary to achieve BE in four key areas of enterprise. They need to:

1   Maximize stakeholder value
2   Achieve process excellence
3   Improve organizational learning
4   Delight the customer

They also need to ensure that their achievements in these areas feed off each other to form a cycle of continuous improvement, so that:

- Delighting the stakeholders helps to generate revenue and satisfactory returns for the investor.
- Increased revenue helps fund investments in processes and learning.
- Better processes and learning help people to delight the stakeholders and create BE.

Therefore, to achieve BE, it is necessary for the organization to give equal weight to all four areas of enterprise rather than concentrating exclusively on the financial perspective.

For BE, it is also necessary for the organization to follow a suitable generic Total Quality Management (TQM) model which provides various principles and core concepts. In order to create a quality culture, the organization must understand the quality dimensions. However, there are various pitfalls directly related to the organization for the implementation of TQM that must be looked at carefully.

This book provides a unique development of the Business Excellence Model (BEM) and measurement of organizational performance through TQM principles. By addressing prime, principles and core concepts of TQM the author creates a structural BEM in order to provide organizational Critical Success Factors (CSFs) and their measurement. By addressing key issues at the forefront of BE, the author demonstrates methods whereby principles of TQM can be applied to various stages of organizational development. The novelty of the BEM is that it is made up of a conceptual network of CSFs that have been validated by empirical data.

The eight chapters of this book aim to introduce the understanding of TQM principles within the organizational setting in order to measure BE. It provides various steps of BE and its complexity of measurement. The required quality culture for achieving BE through CSFs has also been presented. It has also taken a closer look at the various measurements of CSFs in an organizational setting.

The aims and objectives of the book are therefore,

1 To evaluate various TQM and BEMs;
2 To understand Kanji's Business Excellence Models (KBEMs);
3 To examine the relationships between various BEMs;
4 To analyse the:

   (a) model's components, that is, CSFs and BE;
   (b) model's approach in obtaining measurements of CSFs and BE;
   (c) measurement results, interpret them and make recommendations for continuous improvement;
   (d) methodology to measure the performance of the organization.

The ideas of TQM provided by TQM gurus represent fragments of the TQM dimensions and the author believes that the new BEM captures all these ideas. Consequently, the areas covered in the book are consistent with other books on TQM. However, the BEM, is also a special type of TQM model because it incorporates a structural modelling approach for measuring an organization's performance (i.e. BE). Finally, this book provides a comprehensive model that captures the essence of all established models proposed by quality experts and some new models for leadership excellence and business scorecard.

Acknowledgements

I would like to acknowledge my gratitude to many people who contributed to my understanding of business excellence as it has been outlined in this book. I would specially like to acknowledge my sincere thanks to Mr. Per-Gunner Andersson, Dr. Abdul-Malik Tambi, and Ms. Patericia Moura e sa for their contribution in the preparation of this book. My thanks also due to Dr. Osama Arif, who has helped me to prepare the manuscript for this book. Finally, I thank my wife Valerie, for her enormous and continuing tolerance and support.

Gopal K. Kanji

1 Review of business excellence

Introduction

Every sound organization strives for Business Excellence (BE) and thereby company, customer and employee satisfaction. Several Business Excellence Models (BEMs) are applied in organizations throughout the world. But what do the models accomplish? What can, the leading organization in every area, benefit from using these models? An organization is a very complex object to measure. Organizations are different in many aspects, for example, size, complexity and types of customer. Some people argue that what you really want to know about an organization is impossible to measure. I believe, or rather hope, that this is not true. The fact that most organizations do measure their performance, and, in my view, should continue to do so, means that there must be substance in organizational performance measurements. This book aims to reveal whether today's models are used to their full potential or if there is room for improvement.

What is business excellence?

Over the last ten years the term 'business' or 'organizational' excellence has become frequently used in quality and management literature. BE, as used by many authors of quality management literature, has the same or similar meaning as Total Quality Management (TQM).

Business Excellence $\cong$ Total Quality Management

BE is an evolution of TQM since it is built on the same values.

Total Quality Management

It is well known that in general about 85 per cent of the common problems of manufacturing and service industries are related to the management and system and only 15 per cent are specific to the operation and connected with technology. TQM principles and practices have had a significant impact in helping organizations to overcome these problems.

Over the centuries understanding of quality has developed from inspection to TQM. To our knowledge, the Egyptians were the first to use inspection when building the pyramids. During the Second World War, when aircraft technology became more complex, inspection was unacceptable due to the cost in people and equipment. Here inspection developed into Quality Control (QC) where quality manuals, document control, self-inspection, product testing and use of statistics became the control systems used to assure product quality. The following stage was to go from QC where focus is solely on product quality, to Quality Assurance (QA) or Quality Management (QM) where focus is on the quality of the system where system audits, process control, cost of poor quality and non-production operations are used. Understanding of quality then developed into TQM, where quality is managed through principles and practices in all parts and operations of the business.

Throughout the development of understanding quality, statistical theories have been central and, in statistical understanding, variation is fundamental. Variation exists in every event or process. If the variation is not known, you can neither predict nor manage the outcome of a process correctly. TQM is a philosophy applied throughout the world in all kinds of organizations, for example, hotels, stores, car manufacturers and telecoms. Since the philosophy of TQM is so fundamental to business, it is applicable to all organizations. However, the definitions of TQM vary slightly from country to country, or from culture to culture. Still, you will find that some elements of TQM are too fundamental to be switched off, which will be outlined next. Here follows a definition of TQM which is very much based on Kanji's (1990) definition:

Total Quality Management is a *management philosophy* that fosters an organizational *culture* committed to *customer satisfaction* through *continuous improvement.*

The fundamentals in the definition are *management philosophy, culture, customer satisfaction* and *continuous improvement,* which can easily be applied to all kinds of organizations. TQM is built on a philosophy where individuals, teams and organizations can improve their performance at all times. To guide organizations in their journey to BE, TQM models are often used. Hundreds of different models are applied around the world; some are generic and also used by a variety of different organizations. One comprehensive model is Kanji's pyramid model shown in Figure 1.1, which has been accepted and applied in organizations, for example, in Europe and Asia. This model, among other BEMs, will be analysed in-depth later in various chapters. The fact that Kanji is using the same model for TQM as for BE further strengthens the argument for the two being synonymous.

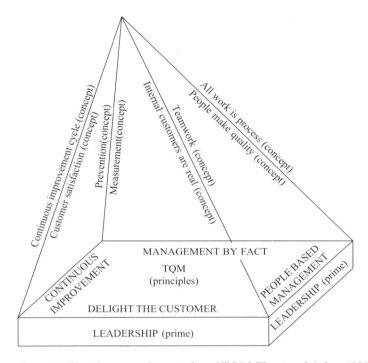

Figure 1.1 Kanji's pyramid principles of TQM (Kanji and Asher 1993).

The pyramid is a generic model made up of five principles and eight core concepts. Except for leadership, the principles are translated into practice by applying two core concepts for each principle. The five principles with their respective core concepts are:

- Leadership (Prime)
- Delight the customer – *Customer satisfaction* and *Internal customers are real*
- Continuous improvement – *Continuous improvement cycle* and *Prevention*
- Management by facts – *All work is process* and *Measurement*
- People-based management – *Team work* and *People make quality*

Leadership

Leadership is a prerequisite for putting TQM principles and core concepts into practice. Management at all levels must understand TQM in-depth and show their commitment through outlining quality goals, policies, principles and plans. In order for management to plan for quality improvements, one must first know where they are at this moment. Then you can start planning where you want to be and how to get there. An efficient way of finding out where you are, is to apply self-assessment, based on a BEM.

Delight the customer

'Delight the customer' focuses on how to satisfy the external customer. This implies understanding the needs of both products and services, tangible and intangible, according to Kanji and Asher (1993). The two core concepts, 'customer satisfaction' and 'internal customers are real' are related to this principle, as seen in Figure 1.1. The internal customer is the next operation, department or user in the value-chain and should be regarded as a true customer and the reason why your operation or department exists. Within an organization there are a number of customer–supplier relationships, which have to be managed. A typical example is between design and production.

A chain is never stronger than the weakest link. This applies to the value-chain as well. Figure 1.2 illustrates typical customer–supplier relationships starting and finishing at the external customer. The figure shows that the customer is also regarded as a supplier, supplying information about its requirements. Marketing receives customer information and writes requirements from R&D department, which in this case is the internal customer of the requirements. The same procedure is used from R&D to production, production to sales, and finally from sales back to the external customer.

Continuous improvement

According to Oakland (1993), 'never ending or continuous improvement is probably the most powerful principle to guide management.' The two core concepts related to continuous improvement are 'continuous improvement cycle' and 'prevention'. Prevention is derived form the fact that the cost for a fault increases exponentially over time, which means that, the later a fault

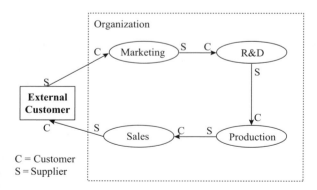

Figure 1.2 Customer–supplier relationship.

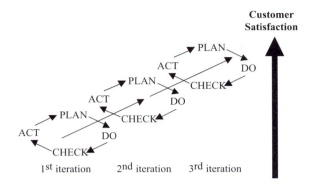

Figure 1.3 Deming's Plan-Do-Check-Act cycle.

is found, the more expensive it is to correct it. By preventing faults you can dramatically increase profit since a penny saved is a penny earned, whereas a penny in sales normally is around 30 per cent of a penny earned. By following a continuous improvement cycle it means that you never stop learning and improving, both internally and towards the external customer. Deming's Plan-Do-Check-Act cycle, shown in Figure 1.3, is one widely used tool for continuous improvement.

Management by facts

To be able to improve one must first know the current performance. When managing the business, decisions should be based on facts rather than 'gut feeling'. By facts I mean measurements, both hard and soft. Hard measurements are tangible, for example, profit, yield, lead-time. Soft measurements are less tangible and often more difficult to measure, for example, customer and employee satisfaction. The two core concepts related to management by facts are 'all work is process' and 'measurement'. As the concept says – all work is process – a TQM organization must be process-oriented. Process-oriented means that you focus on *how* you are working, not only on the result. The importance of process orientation is clearly shown in some of the BEMs described later. By focusing on measurement it does not mean watching over ones shoulder. The philosophy of TQM is built on measuring the process in order to find the cause of a failure early in the process. Actions to correct the fault should be focused on changing the process, not blaming individuals. This is an important feature of TQM.

People-based management

For most companies today the people are the company. Therefore, it is obvious that you must use and manage the most important resource in order to achieve customer satisfaction. The two core concepts 'team work' and 'people make quality' underline the need for cooperation between people and that excellence cannot be achieved only through standards, technology and processes. People must be encouraged to produce quality. This should be done through clear goals (what to do and achieve), processes (how to do it) and feedback on the performance (how well or poor it was done). People want and need to learn, and since organizational learning cannot exist if individuals do not learn, organizations must foster a culture where learning is natural.

Business excellence

By experience and learning from organizations doing well, it has been found that most long-term successful organizations have several things in common. TQM and BE have developed their philosophy from these good experiences.

As for TQM, statistical thinking is central in BE. By learning about variation of organizational attributes, such as leadership and people satisfaction, we can analyse cause and effect relationships in an organization. We learn that people in most cases work better in teams than individually. We learn that strong leadership in most case helps people to do a better job. In other words, we know, or at least have some idea about its variation and probability. These theories are as of today not very scientific or specific. Today we might *not* be able to say that it is statistically proven that, for instance, strong leadership has a strong impact on BE, but in future, we might, by using more sophisticated BEMs.

Why do we change from TQM to BE? Why do we not stick with TQM models, levels and indexes and develop these further? Some negative things about TQM have recently been printed in newspapers, articles and in management literature. Ackoff (1994) presents some problems associated with TQM in his book '*The Democratic Corporation*'. He argues that in some aspects TQM has become 'total', such as focus on customers, both internal and external. But TQM, in his opinion, is not total enough. Total quality should apply to the expectations, not only to customers, but to all those who are affected by what an organization does, that is, all its stakeholders (suppliers, employees, consultants, stockholders, bankers, etc.). He also says, continuous improvement focuses too much on getting rid of what is wrong instead of how it should be, and that TQM planning is based on getting on from where one is to where one wants to go instead of from where one wants to be to where one is. This means backward planning. In my view Ackoff has a valid point that an organization cannot only focus on the customer. Some TQM processes do have a broader scope than customer satisfaction, but in general I agree with Ackoff that TQM should have a more total approach with focus on all stakeholders' expectations.

BEMs have started to apply the same thinking that Ackoff represents. The stakeholder perspective is apparent in the European Foundation for Quality Management (EFQM) Excellence Model and Malcolm Baldrige

National Quality Award (MBNQA), which will be presented in various chapters. EFQM and European Organization for Quality define Organizational Excellence as 'The way of working which enables an organization to achieve balanced stakeholder satisfaction (i.e. customer, employee, society and shareholder) so increasing the probability of long-term success'. This definition proves the broadening of TQM to also include stakeholders other than customers.

Why measure business excellence?

How can you even come up with the idea of measuring the BE of an organization? Just look at the complexity. Mills (1995) issues a warning with regard to measuring BE. He says – 'you must be sure of what you measure. TQM is potentially very complex, so beware of unknown or unseen interactions between some of the large amount of measures you may have'. He brings up three aspects, namely, complexity, unknown interactions and unseen interactions. The organization or system, which I will come back to, consists of people interacting, often with different cultures and conditions.

For instance, pick a person in the street and try to understand how he or she would react in a given situation. Ask the person what 'quality' means to him or her. How would the person respond? You probably do not know. However, it is easier to understand people through 1000 individuals than through one. This means that if you ask 1000 people what quality means to them, you would probably be able to say something about how people think of quality. The question about what quality means would probably not get the same response in Germany as it would get in China. Cultures differ not only between individuals but also within and between organizations, which affects how BE should be measured. Moreover, the majority of organizations do not operate in static environments, and therefore the parameters affecting the organization are also changing. Accordingly parameters outside the organization must be identified and measured. Deming (1994) states 'A system cannot understand itself'. What he means is that you have to gain knowledge from outside the system, for example, through measuring customer satisfaction.

It is complex and difficult to measure the performance of an organization, nevertheless it is crucial for an organization to do so. A well-known saying is – 'What you don't measure, you don't know. What you don't know, you can't manage. When you can't manage you are at the mercy of chance.' We must measure, to be able to take the right actions. Today too many management decisions are based on 'gut feeling'. What is vital to the organization should be measured, with both hard and soft measurements. According to Deming (1994) the results of most activities are not measurable. For example, in education we know the cost, but not the benefit and result. In my opinion we are able to measure the benefit, not by hard measures but by soft. The same goes for customer and employee satisfaction.

Fundamental prerequisites for measuring business excellence

It is fruitless to discuss how to measure an organization unless you define what an organization is. In my opinion an organization is best described and viewed as a system. In other words, we are about to measure a system, or more precisely, the performance of the system. A basic principle of measuring BE is to view the organization as a system, then model the organization and finally define the kind of information needed and how to collect it.

Viewing the organization as a system

The basic principle of the 'new' approach, system thinking, is to gain knowledge about the whole relevant system before looking at the parts. This is contrary to how most managers think and act today.

Most organizations are divided into divisions, departments, sections, etc. Individual managers tend to perceive their own part of the organization as the whole and consequently strive for its improvement and optimization. Sub-optimization often causes more damage than improvement. Optimization is when you find the best balance for the whole system or organization, whereas sub-optimization is when you optimize a subset of the system with no guarantees for an improved whole.

In systems thinking the relationships within an organization and between the organization and the environment is central. One must therefore know the main inputs, processes, outputs, and feedback loops. The main inputs (e.g. people, material and equipment and money) are to be processed into main outputs (e.g. products and services, pollution and waste). And all this has to be coordinated and managed through policy deployment, measurements, decisions and actions. The system and its environment will be described more in detail in later chapters.

Building a model

The terms system and model are sometimes used as if they were interchangeable, but they are not. A model is a made-up picture of reality, which contains the most important elements of a true system. A model is an abstraction and often offers a simplified view of the reality. The purpose of building a model is to understand reality. It is important to remember that a model only *represents* reality, it *is not* the reality. It is very complex to make a model of an organization, especially since an organization has to adapt to a continuously changing environment. When building a model the most important elements inside and outside the system that have an effect on the system must be included.

Using the model for understanding

Once we have a model of the organization, it is time to start using the model to learn about how the organization responds to different stimuli. This is where measurement of BE enters the scene. With a model including all elements of importance, we can look at each element's performance and interactions between elements. Only by understanding the whole system are you able to take correct actions at all times. Customer and employee satisfactions are two examples of important elements to measure in an organization.

A measurement system has to be applied to the model. A customer satisfaction rating on the organization is an example of how to measure an element. The EFQM uses a measurement system called RADAR where elements such as people satisfaction, customer satisfaction, processes, and leadership are given an individual score which together add up to a BE score between 0 and 1000. This specific measurement system will be explained in a later chapter.

Systems approach

In the areas of product development and production, QM has applied system thinking for decades. For example, in reliability engineering, design of experiments and in regression analysis you view the product, service or production line as a system. But during the 1990s, the system thinking approach also began to be applied to organizations as a whole, QM developed into TQM. TQM applies QM in all operations and view the organization as a system that interacts with its customers, suppliers and to some extent also society (laws, governments, universities, etc.).

An organization can and should be thought of as a system and, therefore, when modelling and measuring it, system theories have to be applied. Nevertheless, it is important to be aware of the fact that not all organizations qualify as a system. Some organizations are a subset of independent systems that form an aggregation, for instance, conglomerates and holding companies. When modelling an organization it is crucial not to oversimplify or, in the words of Senge (1993), 'The art of system thinking lies in seeing through complexity to the underlying structures generating change. System thinking does not mean ignoring complexity. Rather, it means organizing complexity into a coherent story that illuminates the causes of problems and how they can be remedied in enduring ways.' One of the great benefits of system thinking is that you will be able to understand the many interrelationships between parts of the system, and thereby improve the goal setting, policy deployment and the organizational structure. Last, but not least, this makes it possible to evaluate organizational performance in a realistic manner, that is, to get realistic measurements of BE.

Definition of a system

The system concept has been adopted from the exact sciences, specifically from physics, where exact laws lead to exact measurements. However, the methods of the exact sciences are of little or no use for the social sciences, since these often deal with more complex and multidimensional systems.

Though it is non-mathematical, the definition given below is quite precise and commonly accepted.

A system is a set of *objects* together with *relationships* between the objects and between their *attributes* related to each other and to their *environment* so as to form a whole.

Schoderbek *et al.* (1990)

The key concepts, underlined here, will be explained and analysed in this chapter.

The well-known QM guru Deming has made major contributions to TQM, especially through his approach to systems thinking. Deming defines a system thus:

A system is *network* of *interdependent components* that work together to try to accomplish the aim of a system. A system must have an aim. Without an aim, there is no system.

Deming (1994)

What Deming adds to the former definition is that the system must have an identified aim. This definitely applies for an organization. An organization without an aim is in most cases an organization in chaos, which stresses the importance of leadership, as outlined in Chapter 4.

Another important contributor, not specifically to TQM, but to system thinking is Ackoff who offers the following definition of a system.

A system is a whole that contains two or more parts that satisfy the following five conditions.

1   The whole has one or more defining functions.
2   Each part in the set can affect the behaviour or properties of the whole.
3   There is a subset of parts that is sufficient in one or more environments for carrying out the defining function of the whole; each of these parts is separately necessary but insufficient for carrying out this defining function.
4   The way that the behaviour or properties of each part of a system affects its behaviour or properties depends on the behaviour or properties of at least one other part of the system.
5   The effect of any subset of parts on the system as a whole depends on the behaviour of at least one other subset.

Ackoff (1994)

Ackoff's definition is much more complex than the former two. But, who said this was going to be easy? What Ackoff adds to the former two definitions is a description of what interaction between the parts of a system means. Ackoff's 'defining function' is an equivalent of Deming's 'aim'.

Social systems

When dealing with organizations, we are not dealing with mechanical or biological systems, but with social systems. According to Peters (1997) organizational systems are 5 per cent technology and 95 per cent psychology and attitudes. Ackoff (1994) also pictures the enterprise, or organization, as a social system in which people individually and collectively play the major roles. How complex is a social system? Boulding classifies different systems into nine levels of complexity (see Schoderbek *et al.* (1990) and Figure 1.4). The first three levels are physical and mechanical systems and the next three levels deal with biological systems. The last three levels of humans, social organizations, and transcendental (unknowable) systems are the most complex systems to understand and manage, and hence a major challenge in BE measurements.

Ackoff (1994) describes social systems as 'systems that have purposes of their own, are made up of parts that have purposes of their own, and are parts of larger systems that also have purposes of their own, and these larger

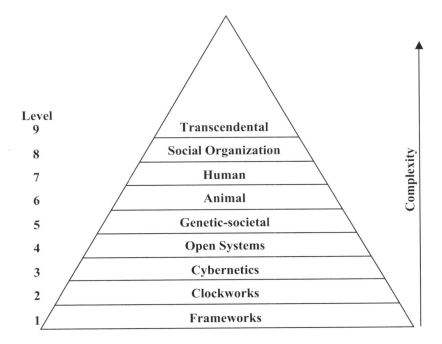

Figure 1.4 Boulding's ordering of systems by complexity.

containing systems include other systems that have purposes of their own.' These aspects are important to consider when measuring an organization in order to measure the right things, especially when looking at interactions, and all the purposes must be recognized as relevant by those who manage an organization.

System components

The components of a system are parts, elements or functions. In BE, the functioning of the components, rather than the parts in themselves, is crucial. From a functional viewpoint there are three types of components: inputs, processes and outputs. An example of these three component types is when printing a paper on a printer. You need input (document file, paper and a printer) that you process by a printing-programme, and the output is a printout.

System attributes

A system's attributes are the properties of both objects (parts) and relationships (interactions between parts), see Schoderbek *et al.* (1990). As an example, if you picture a car as a system the attributes are maximum speed, horsepower, fuel consumption, comfort, colour, etc. Attributes for an organization would be, for example, productivity, responsiveness, customer satisfaction, leadership and number of improvements. When measuring BE the attributes of the system are in focus. When the system performance is measured, attributes should be treated in the same way as parts or elements of a system. This means that customer satisfaction does interrelate with employee satisfaction, and that they both have impact on the organization's or system's goals.

System interaction

Ackoff (1994) says 'Improving the performance of the parts of a system taken separately may not, and often does not, improve the performance of the system taken as a whole.' Does this match today's management practices? In my opinion it does not, since improvement of parts, do not indicate how they interact and the system is focused upon. Managers are normally looking for culprits, but it is unusual that management is blamed for neglecting to pay attention to interactions, which in my opinion is one of their most important responsibilities.

Social interactions or relationships are complex to understand. For example, look at a 'simple' social system with only two parts, a married couple. Would you say the interactions are easy to understand? I would not. Normally, we cannot say how well two people get on with each other by looking at them separately. Not until we see them together can we get some idea about how well they will get on. This goes for marriage, co-workers, doubles partners in

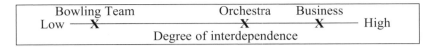

Figure 1.5 Degree of interdependence.

tennis, etc. Another example is a football team. Purchasing the best players in the world is no guarantee for getting the best playing team. When looking at organizations, we know that a huge number of complex interactions exist that managers are unaware of. According to Deming (1994), 'The components need not all be clearly defined and documented: people may merely do what needs to be done. Management of a system therefore requires knowledge of the interrelationships between all the components within the system and of the people that work in it.' Deming offers the following guidance to managers: focus on interactions, rather than parts or subsystems since people normally know how to perform their part. In *The New Economics* Deming (1994) illustrates different degrees of interdependence for different groups of people, see Figure 1.5. Business is high in the scale. Even though all business organizations are not alike, most business organizations would end up to the right in the figure.

An anecdote from the sports world shows the importance of social interactions. A Swedish reporter asked Sven-Göran Eriksson, the current manager of the England football team (previously Lazio, Italy), how he had developed as a coach since he moved from Swedish to Italian football. He replied that he focused more on the individual, instead of the most effective football system. Sven-Göran Eriksson has been and still is very successful in what he is doing. In my view what makes him successful, is that by focusing on the individual he focuses on how well the individual will interact with the rest of the team. There is more to working together than playing for 90 min every weekend, since training and other social occasions are important too. You must see a system as a whole with complex relationships between its components.

System environment

The system environment is the surrounding of an organization. Everything that is external to the organization and not included in the system, as defined above, can be viewed as the system environment. If you look at a football team, the fans, opponents, police, and even the weather can be viewed as components of the external environment, whereas the players and the coach are internal parts of the system. Environmental factors differ between organizations. A company, for instance, operates in a complex and dynamic environment and has to adapt to the continuously changing business situation. Duncan's model illustrates four different environmental patterns for organizations, see Schoderbek *et al.* (1990).

The environment's characteristics, among other aspects, determine how the measuring of an organization should be done. Environmental parameters are of different importance to different organizations. For instance, impact on society is normally of major importance for a large company in a small town, whereas for a small company in a large town it is generally less important. The impact on society can be described in terms of how well the organization is seen in the media, its importance for and impact on the area where the company is located. The environment is outside the organization's *complete* control, but in many ways the environment determines the organization's performance. We can control it to some extent, but never completely. This must not keep us from monitoring the environment though. Measuring BE means measuring the excellence of how the organization performs its business, and this does not include any consideration of whether the environment is helping. In other words, we should focus on the systematic and controllable environmental parameters *only* when measuring BE, not on all environmental factors.

We should focus on the *systematic and controllable environmental parameters* only when measuring BE.

This does not mean that we should stop measuring customer satisfaction, impact on society, vendor satisfaction, etc. But, measurements should focus on *how well* the organization achieves high customer satisfaction, positive impact on society, high vendor satisfaction, etc.

What components are systemic and what are environmental? Earlier in this chapter, I accounted for the prerequisites that have to be fulfilled for something to be considered part of a system. When these prerequisites are not fulfilled, a parameter is either environmental or of no importance for the organization. Churchman (1968) suggests the following two questions when deciding whether a component is systemic or environmental: Is the factor related to the objective of the system? Can I do anything about it? Figure 1.6 explains the difference between being part of a system and being a part of the environment.

Most parameters are not 100 per cent controllable but the factors that the organization can control and do something about should be considered when measuring a system. Schoderbek *et al.* (1990) have made a model of a typical organization with its environmental parameters, some more controllable than others.

His model shows that labour, material and equipment, capital and land are highly controllable by the organization, whereas ecology, government, general public and competitors are only controllable to a small extent. Customers and technology are somewhere in-between the two groupings. The

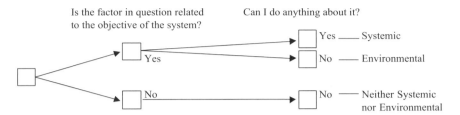

Figure 1.6 Determination of environmental factors.

figure also shows that organizations can influence, and to some extent control, a number of environmental parameters. And, since the environmental parameters have an impact on the organization's performance and thereby on its BE, it is crucial for the benefit of the organization that it is able to control and manage these parameters.

The system boundary demarcates the environment from the system. It is vital to clearly define what is within and what is outside the system in order to focus the measurement on the right parameters.

Analytic (element) vs systematic (whole) approach

Senge (1993) stresses the importance of looking at the whole as 'You can only understand the system of a rainstorm by contemplating the whole, not any individual part of the pattern. Business and other human endeavours are also systems.' A similar example in business would be to analyse BE by only looking at policy deployment. Policy deployment of course has an impact on BE, but by analysing policy deployment only, you will not be able to understand the organizational performance. In order to understand an organization's performance you must look at the entire system including all main elements and their interactions within the system and towards their environmental parameters at the same time.

Open vs closed systems

An open system interacts with its environment, whereas a closed system does not take in or give out anything to its environment. All social systems, for example, organizations, should be regarded as open systems. According to Schoderbek *et al.* (1990), some theorists even doubt that closed systems exist outside the mind. Problem solving by business executives is often carried out in a quasi-closed system in order to simplify and get a rough picture of the situation. One of the dangers associated with treating an open system as if it were closed is that the environmental impact that is actually there is easily neglected. As mentioned earlier, BE measurements should focus on both systematic and controllable environmental parameters. And again, organizations should always be regarded as open systems.

Business excellence models

There are different views on how organizational performance should be measured. The philosophy of TQM offers guidelines on what is important in order to achieve excellence. Examples of models are:

- Kanji's Business Excellence Model (KBEM)
- Deming Prize
- EFQM Excellence Model
- MBNQA
- Ericsson Business Excellence Model (EBEM)
- Balanced Scorecard (BSC)
- Lynch and Cross' Performance Pyramid
- ISO 9000
- Capability Maturity Model (CMM)

These models provide a tool for measuring and evaluating organizational performance and guide organizations to focus their improvement efforts on the right areas. To a large extent, these models are based on theories of TQM but they differ in scope and approach. Some models are more result-oriented whereas others are more process-oriented. Three of the models are also awards, namely the Deming Prize, the MBNQA, and the European Quality Award (EQA). Some models require third-party assessment whereas others can be used for self-assessment. The models will be compared further in other chapters.

Requirements on a business excellence model

Poorly defined performance meaurement systems can seriously impede an organization's ability to adapt successfully to changes in a competitive environment. Oakland states that appropriate performance measurements play the following roles in quality and productivity improvements:

- To ensure customer requirements have been met.
- To be able to set sensible objectives and comply with them.
- To provide standards for establishing comparisons.
- To provide visibility and provide a 'score-board' for people to monitor their own performance levels.
- To highlight quality problems and determine which areas require priority attention.
- To give an indication of the cost of poor quality.

- To justify use of resources.
- To provide feedback for driving the improvement effort.

Some of these roles will be discussed in the later chapters.

Complexity

A model should be simple to use; at least some immediate understanding is required before a model is chosen in favour of other models. By simple I do not mean that it measures what is easy to measure. I mean that a clear structure, approach, set of questions, understandable results, among other things, that increase usability should characterize the model.

Flexibility

Different organizations act in different environments and therefore different performance indicators are required. A model of BE should be able to measure small companies, large corporations, service organizations, manufacturing organizations, non-profit organizations, etc. In other words, a model must be flexible in order to adapt to various organizational requirements.

Cost

Cost is to some extent related to complexity. If a model is simple you will need less help from consultants. The cost also depends on whether or not the model can be used for self-assessment.

Validity

The model should measure what it is intended to measure, in the same way as a yardstick should measure length. The validity of different models is difficult to analyse in the short term. You can use the model over a period of time and by statistical methods verify that what has been measured has actually happened. The principles of TQM have lived long enough to show that there is some correlation between the principles and business results, but how strong the correlation is has not yet been fully determined. The validity of a model is important but difficult to verify.

Reliability

How much can you trust the measurement results? Wrong measurement can be very dangerous to the business. The model should somehow be able to verify the reliability of the measures.

Systems approach

An organization is a social system and has to be treated as such. It is often not the parts of a system but their interaction that makes a difference. And it is just as important that the relationship between cause and effect is visible in a model. This will offer exceptional knowledge about which areas to improve.

Coverage of TQM principles

It is crucial that the TQM principles are sufficiently represented in a model. If not, areas that have proved to have a major impact on an organization's performance will be forfeited. Craig (1994) illustrates the extent to which different BEMs fulfil the TQM principles. KBEM, the EFQM Excellence Model and EBEM are in the same area as Deming prize and MBNQA.

Coverage of stakeholders

As mentioned in earlier part of this chapter about system approach, it is important to focus on all stakeholders, that is, not on the customers alone. An organization can control those parts of the environment that affect it and this opportunity should be utilized in the best possible way. Ackoff (1994) defines stakeholders as those who directly influence or are influenced by the organization. Customers, suppliers, debtors, shareholders, employees, partners and society are examples of stakeholders. The role of as many stakeholders as possible should be included and considered in a BEM.

Process orientation

Process orientation means to focus on *how* to achieve excellence. Examples are process management, teamwork and policy deployment.

Result orientation

Result orientation means to focus on the outcome of processes. Examples are return on investment, employee satisfaction and market shares.

Benchmarking

Benchmarking is a smooth way for organizations to compare their results with the results of other organizations, preferably competitors. Benchmarking also can and should be used within an organization, which means comparing the performance of, for example, divisions with each other.

Trends

In order to get a feeling about the temperature of the organization, top management often wants to be able to see the organization's performance in a small number of understandable key measures. These measures should be reported on a regular basis in order to notice improvements and deterioration. Trend analysis is therefore an important feature of BEMs.

Criticism of BEMs

Crosby (1996), who is pessimistic about the usefulness of BEMs, makes the following critical remarks:

> The C.E.O. picks up the criteria for the Baldrige or NASA or some similar award, hands it to someone, and instructs that person to "go do this." Several dozen pages long and full of proper-sounding verbiage, the criteria gives the impression of containing the wisdom necessary to install quality management. Actually the material represents what was being done in the quality assurance days of the 1960s and 1970s. Those were the golden days when acceptable quality levels were standard and nothing worked well at all. These systems didn't work then and there is no reason to suspect that they will do so now. The only result will be a few books full of procedures, which will sit on the credenza of selected managers.

In my opinion, Crosby's critical remarks should be directed at managers rather than at quality awards and models. If a BEM is used in the wrong way, of course it will not help the organization.

Crosby (1996) states the following about ISO 9000 and Baldrige: 'It is only to provide a living for consultants who certify companies and quality professionals who do not want to think for themselves.'

Deming who is a well-known QM guru argues that the MBNQA focuses too much on results and neglects the important principles of TQM. Juran, also a well-known QM guru, is more enthusiastic and sees MBNQA as the most powerful tool for quality development he has seen in his career.

Self-assessment

Self-assessment is a comprehensive, systematic and regular review of an organization's activities and results against a model of excellence. It offers organizations the opportunity to learn about its strengths and areas for improvement; what TQM means when applied to the organization; and where the organization is on the road to quality (see Crosby 1996). Self-assessment is about continuous improvement. Organizations often use BEMs for regular reviews of their quality improvement status. The ultimate goal of BEMs is to help organizations to continuously improve their quality performance rather than to receive a quality award.

Presentation of business excellence models

In this section some well-known models will be compared with KBEM, which represents a holistic view of TQM.

Kanji's Business Excellence Model

KBEM is based on his pyramid model described earlier. A highly developed measurement system has been combined with the pyramid model.

The purpose of KBEM is to apply statistical concepts to measuring the organizational excellence. This will enable us, for the first time, to analyse interactions between quality dimensions such as leadership, customer satisfaction and employee satisfaction. KBEM has just begun to be used by companies in Europe and Asia and sufficient evidence does exist that validates reliability of its theories, which will be outlined next.

Presentation and analysis of the model

Kanji's pyramid model (Figure 1.7) has been used for over ten years and the statistical methods applied are no news for statisticians. The theories behind the model are not new in themselves; it is the specific combination of different scientific areas that is new and so far unique. Other models have, to some extent, used system theories but Kanji's model represents a comprehensive systems approach and interactions are analysed as well. And again, interaction is the most critical area to address in a system.

KBEM represents a completely new concept, which is applied in the pyramid model, but might as well be applied using other BEMS, or in areas such as supply chain and production, see Kanji and Wong (1999). It depends on how you define the system being measured. You can view supply chain management as a subsystem to the complete company and thereby get new system approach and new areas of interest.

KBEM is not just another model, it is a *completely new concept.*

The pyramid model outlined as Kanji's Business Excellence Structural Model is shown in Figure 1.8 where you see the main causal relationships between the prime, principles, core concepts and business results. The model (see Figure 1.8) does not intend to cover all interactions, only the most important for BE. In reality, there are many more relationships between the variables.

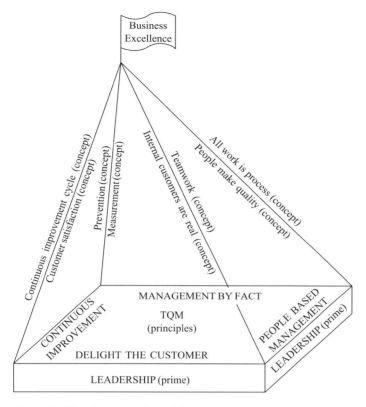

Figure 1.7 Kanji's pyramid model.

Kanji argues that most models in use (e.g. Deming, EFQM, MBNQA) are indicative models, whereas this model is an improvement model. By using the most common models mentioned above, you would be able to know how far you have come in the TQM implementation and benchmark against other organizations. This is possible with KBEM as well. But, the main purpose for an organization is to find areas that will have the most positive impact on BE and business result. By measuring the cause and effect, it is possible to analyse to what extent a variable affects the result. The statistical method used is called latent variable partial least squares, and is presented in more detail in a later chapter.

In KBEM there is a set of between two and six questions for each principle and core concept, based on Kanji's pyramid model. The questions are flexible, and should be unique for each company or any specific measurement.

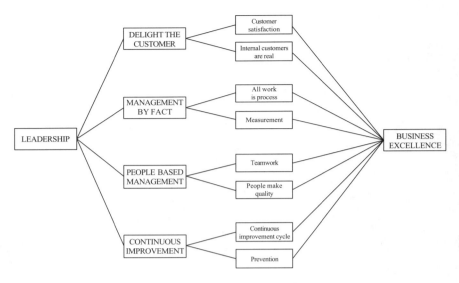

Figure 1.8 Kanji's Business Excellence Structural Model.

For every new measurement the reliability of the questions asked is calculated. Kanji uses Cronbach's coefficient alpha (α) to do this. Nunnally (1978) states that 'Coefficient alpha is the basic formula for determining the reliability based on internal consistency. It should be applied to all new measurement methods. If it proves to be low, either the test is too short or the items have very little in common.' Nunnally (1978) also says that the major source of measurement error is due to the sampling of content. What coefficient alpha really tells us is that the questions used in the model are related and that the test is long enough.

The questions are answered on a scale between 1 and 10, which makes it very easy to analyse the data. Nunnally (1978) states that 'As the number of scale steps is increased from 2–20, the increase in reliability is very rapid at first. It tends to level off at about 7, and after about 11 steps there is little gain in reliability from increasing the number of steps.' Based on this it is clear that the use of a ten-step scale should provide reliable data.

Each box in Figure 1.8, representing the prime, principles, core concepts and business results in KBEM, is a variable. All these variables are scored based on the average score on their respective questions. This average is useful when analysing how well a certain area is performed in an organization, which is displayed in Figure 1.9.

BE is not the total average of all the variables, the Business Excellence Index (BEI) is based on how well all other areas are performed. BEI is dependent on how the variables correlate and thereby achieves BE.

Business Excellence

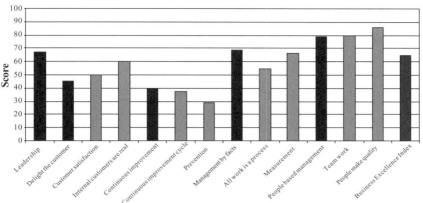

Figure 1.9 Presentation diagram of Business Excellence (BE) measurements.

The strengths and weaknesses of Kanji's model are presented below.

Strengths	Weaknesses
Strong systems approach, where interactions are measured	Not as established and well known as MBNQA, Deming, EQA
Adaptable to company needs – high flexibility	
Strong focuses on the core principles of TQM and not only result oriented	
Extremely cost and time efficient, easy to use	
Applies comprehensive statistical analysis	
Strong focus on improvements rather than status of the organization's quality management scheme	

Deming prizes

In honour of Dr W. E. Deming's contribution to the development of industrial quality control in Japan, the Japanese Union of Science and Engineering (JUSE) instituted the Deming Prize in 1951. There are three categories of Deming prizes: the 'Deming Prize', awarded to individuals; the 'Deming Application Prize', awarded to companies; and the 'Deming Factory Prize'. Since 1984 there is also the 'Deming Application Prize for overseas

Company'. The Deming prizes' main purpose is to increase the knowledge and practice of Total Quality Control (TQC). In TQC the use of statistical control tools is central.

Presentation and analysis of the model

In Table 1.1 the audit checklist for Deming's Application Prize is presented.

The Deming Application Prize criteria listed in Table 1.1 cover the company's internal efficiency and interfaces towards vendors and customers. Company Wide Quality Control (CWQC) is central in the evaluation of a company, which means that you systematically and economically fulfil the customers' requirements and expectations all the time, throughout the company. Every division, department, team and individual in the company should apply the principles and areas listed above. The Deming Application Prize has a positive impact on the applying companies, not only the winners, since the evaluation phase normally takes years and brings improvement areas to light. JUSE recommends companies to work with their consultants for a few years before applying for the prize.

The criteria for the Deming Application Prize are not intended to be used as a tool for self-assessment. Rather JUSE wants to be involved and advise the company throughout the application process. This is of course an obstacle since it implies a 'huge' initial cost, compared to self-assessment. In my view though, this work should be thought of as an investment for the future rather than a cost; nevertheless there will be a significant cost initially.

We all know about the 'Japanese wonder' where the industry in Japan from having major problems after the Second World War, improved their efficiency and product quality to become the world's leading economy in the 1980s. It has been understood that the Deming Prize contributed to this achievement.

The Deming Prize has been criticized for focusing too much on manufacturing organizations and thereby overlooking service organizations. In the beginning of the 1990s only 3 out of 59 award winners were service organizations.

Although the relationships in some of the areas are complex, Kanji's pyramid model and the Deming Application Prize correspond well, as seen in Figure 1.10.

From the comparison you can see that, except for 'for the future', all areas in the Deming Application Prize are covered in Kanji's model. 'for the future' focuses on knowing the strengths and weaknesses and it also requires plans for the TQC program and information on how these plans relate to the corporate policy, which to some extent is covered in Kanji's model. What the Deming Application Prize lacks compared to Kanji's model is the focus on the 'internal customers are real', 'prevention', and comparison with competitors and best-in-class organizations. The strengths and weaknesses of Deming's model are presented below.

Table 1.1 Checklist for Deming Application Prize (Imai 1986)

1. Corporate policy	What is the corporate policy? What goals and measures are employed in order to plan, design, produce, sell and assure good products or services? How successful is it, and how is it checked? (Policy formation, deployment, implementation, and audit)
2. Organization and administration	What kind of organization is employed to carry out and administer Statistical Quality Control (SQC)? Other issues to be studied include clarity in authority and responsibility and coordination among divisions, committee activities, and small-group activities. (Cross-functional organization)
3. Education and extension	What kind of education programs is routinely provided, such as seminars on SQC, both within and without the company? To what extent are the concepts and methods of SQC understood? How is the effectiveness of these programs confirmed? What education is provided to vendors and subcontractors? How is the suggestion system carried out?
4. Implementation	What kind of activities are conducted to assure TQC in such fields as R&D, design, purchasing, manufacturing, inspection, and sales? For instance, the following must be checked: profit management, cost control, purchasing and inventory control, production-process control, facility management, instrumentation control, personnel administration, labour relations, education programs, new-product development, research management, vendor relations, grievance procedures, use of customer information, QA, customer service, and customer relations.
(a) Collection and use of quality information	How is the information transmitted from the head office and distributed among plants, sales office, and departments?
(b) Analysis	How are important quality problems defined, and how are statistical methods used for problem solving?
(c) Standardization	How are standards established, used, and revised? How is standardization maintained, and how is consistency maintained among standards?
(d) Control	How are control points established? How are counter measures adopted? What is the control system for emergency measures, and how is it administrated? How are various tools such as control charts used? Are the production processes under control?
(e) Quality assurance	How is the QA system administrated and diagnosed? What is the system for new-product development? How are quality functions deployed? What preventive measures exist in the safety and product liability areas? What measures are employed for process control and improvement? How are process capabilities managed?
5. Effect	What impact has TQC's introduction had on product quality? What impact has it had on service, delivery, cost, profits, safety, and the environment? Does the company manufacture and sell top quality products? What tangible benefits has it gained?
6. For the future	Does the company recognize its current strengths and weaknesses? Are there plans to carry the TQC program forward? How do these plans, if any, relate to the long-range corporate policy?

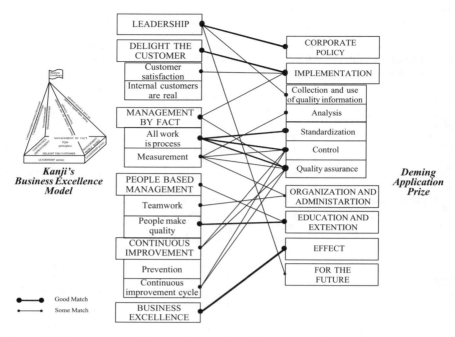

Figure 1.10 Comparison of Kanji's Business Excellence Model (**KBEM**) and Deming Application Prize.

Strengths	Weaknesses
Strong record of companies that have good experiences from applying for the award	Not as established and well known as MBNQA and EQA in Europe and USA
Strong focus on statistical and quantitative methods	No self-assessment tool
Strong focus on leadership and motivation	Not a comprehensive systems approach, focus is only on customers and suppliers outside the company
Process-oriented approach	High cost
	Not flexible for adaptations to individual organizations and not suited for service organizations
	Benchmarking against other companies not easy
	No evidence can be shown that high score leads to good business results
	Interactions between criteria are not shown

Malcolm Baldrige National Quality Award

In 1987 Ronald Reagan instituted the MBNQA to increase the knowledge of QM among American companies. The award winning companies are obliged to spread information about their success in the quality area to other American companies through papers and seminars, etc. The award is inspired by the Deming Prize and is similar in its principles and evaluation criteria. The MBNQA award is given in three categories: production companies, service companies, and small companies with up to 500 employees.

Presentation and analysis of the model

The MBNQA (Figure 1.11) is based on seven criteria: leadership (125), strategic planning (85), customer and market focus (85), information and analysis (85), human resource focus (85), process management (85), and business results (450). MBNQA uses a scoring system where each criterion is 'worth' a pre-set value (see values within brackets). All together the criteria add up to 1000 points. The seven criteria are subdivided into nineteen items that consist of one or more areas that should be evaluated in the organization. Each item is assigned a score based on the MBNQA scoring guidelines. The scoring of items is based on three evaluation dimensions: approach, deployment, and results. This means that the company must have approaches to all MBNQA items, fully deployed with follow-up and analysis of their results in order to get high scores.

There is no separate criterion for continuous improvement as in KBEM. But since MBNQA evaluates the approach, deployment, and results, continuous improvement must be applied to all areas in order to get high scores. MBNQA has been criticized and debated, especially in USA. An article by Garvin (1991) in the *Harvard Business Review* started an exciting

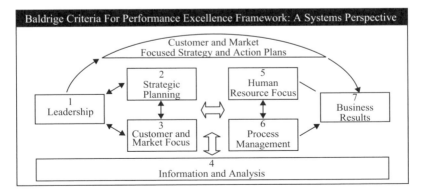

Figure 1.11 Baldrige criteria for performance excellence framework (NIST 1999).

debate. Critics argued that MBNQA is static and does not assure product and service quality; in Crosby's (1996) opinion MBNQA has trivialized quality management into a do-it-yourself kit that could be more destructive than helpful; Garvin argued that MBNQA is dynamic, and in fact it has changed over the years. Moreover, MBNQA is not only measuring product and service quality and thereby no guarantees can be given that a high score equals high product and service quality. Finally, MBNQA is a framework for quality management, and should be used as a guide for organizations, not as a law that you follow step-by-step without questioning the content.

The model is a very useful self-assessment tool. A lot of companies use the award criteria without any thoughts about applying for the award.

In comparison with KBEM, it is clear that the correspondence between the two is very good (see Figure 1.12).

All criteria have a one-to-one map, except for 'strategic planning', which to a large extent is included in Kanji's 'leadership' but not as visible as in MBNQA. Like the Deming Application Prize, MBNQA lacks a clear focus on 'internal customers are real' and 'prevention'. As mentioned before, continuous improvement is not a separate criterion, but in part

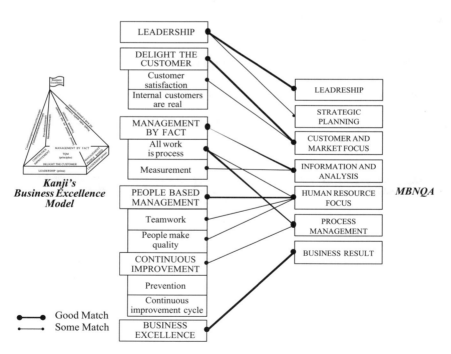

Figure 1.12 Comparison of KBEM and Malcolm Baldrige National Quality Award (MBNQA).

Kanji's 'continuous improvement cycle' is covered by MBNQA's 'process management'. Finally, strengths and weaknesses of the model are presented below.

Strengths	Weaknesses
Well-established model in USA, with strong history	Not flexible for adaptations to individual organizations
Useful as a self-assessment tool	Not a comprehensive systems approach, focus is only on customers and suppliers outside the company
Benchmarking against other companies and trend analysis easy to do	No evidence can be shown that high score leads to good business results
Good balance between result and process orientation	Interactions between criteria are not shown
	Must follow a strict scoring mechanism in order to benchmark

European Foundation for Quality Management Excellence Model

History and purpose

Rank Xerox received the first EQA in 1992. Since then several companies have been awarded. The model was developed by the non-profit organization European Foundation for Quality Management, founded in 1988.

The EFQM Excellence Model helps organizations to know how far they have come in their journey to BE.

Presentation and analysis of the model

The EFQM Excellence Model (Figure 1.13) is easy to understand and serves as practical tool enabling companies to assess all their business processes against the BE principles.

It is based on nine criteria. Five of these are 'Enablers' and four are 'Results' (see Figure 1.13). The 'Enabler' criteria cover what an organization does. The 'Results' criteria cover what an organization achieves. 'Enablers' cause 'Results'.

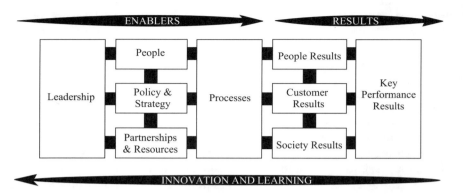

Figure 1.13 ® The European Foundation for Quality Management (© EFQM) Excellence Model.

Each criterion has a percentage: Leadership 10 per cent, People 9 per cent, Policy and Strategy 8 per cent, Partnerships and Resources 9 per cent, Processes 14 per cent, People Results 9 per cent, Customer Results 20 per cent, Society Results 6 per cent, Key Performance Results 15 per cent. The evaluation of an organization is done through what EFQM calls RADAR (Result, Approach, Deployment, Assessment and Review). The first element, Result, is used for evaluation of the 'Result' criteria. Approach, Deployment, Assessment and Review are used for evaluation of the 'Enablers' criteria. From the RADAR evaluation a percentage results for each criterion. This percentage is multiplied with a given number in the model. The maximum scoring when all the criteria are summarized is 1000. Award winners normally score around 700. The EFQM Excellence Model is a well-respected model throughout Europe. Several national quality awards and companies throughout Europe use the model or a similar adaptation of it. The structure of this model is also very attractive, with its Enablers and Results criteria.

The coverages of the two models are very similar, though their structures differ (see Figure 1.14). The criterion 'Society Results' in EFQM does not have an equivalent in Kanji's model. 'Society Results' includes items such as ecology, security, and cooperation with the local community. This is a development in the right direction towards better system thinking. The EFQM Excellence Model lacks focus on 'teamwork' and 'prevention' compared to Kanji's model. Teamwork is a powerful feature for an organization when working with quality management and its impact should not be neglected. Prevention is also a cornerstone in TQM and has been a major principle in cost-saving projects. Processes should be designed to prevent failures from reaching the customers.

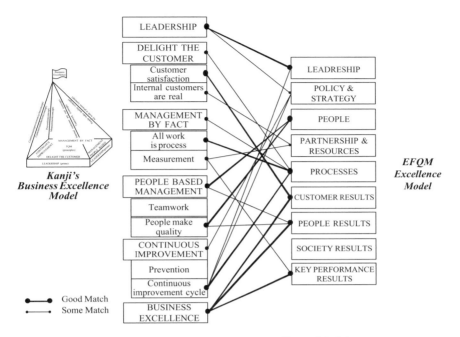

Figure 1.14 Comparison of KBEM and EFQM Excellence Model.

Finally, strengths and weaknesses of the model are presented below.

Strengths	Weaknesses
Well-established model in Europe with strong history	Not flexible for adaptations to individual organizations
Simple and useful self-assessment tool	Not a comprehensive systems approach, focus is only on customers and suppliers outside the company
Benchmarking against other companies and trend analysis easy to do	No evidence can be shown that high score leads to good business results
Good balance between result and process orientation	Interactions between criteria are not shown
Clear and visible split between Enablers and Results	Must follow a strict scoring mechanism in order to benchmark
Includes importance of handling technology, facilities and partnerships of all kinds	

Ericsson Business Excellence Model

EBEM is to be seen as an ideal framework for Ericsson's business operations. The purpose of having a model specific to Ericsson is to have a flexible tool for Ericsson's own needs.

Presentation and analysis of the model

The model is derived from EFQM Excellence Model and consists of twelve criteria grouped into three categories; Opportunities, Enablers and Results (see Figure 1.15).

Since the model is based on EFQM, I will only focus on what has been changed or added. With opportunities, three criteria are added: Technology, Products and Services, and Markets and Competition. Ericsson lives on leading the technology race and to be first on the market with new products and services. It is therefore vital to measure Ericsson's performance on utilizing opportunities in these three areas.

Another difference, compared to EFQM, is the evaluation of the criteria. The EBEM uses a five-level step-by-step maturity model. The evolution of an organization progresses from being internal and product-oriented to external and society-oriented organization. The five levels of maturity are the following:

Level 1. Product-oriented – Focus is on 'deliver products, solve problem and handle customer complaints'.

Level 2. Process-oriented – Focus is on 'product and service realization process' and on 'measure process' to identify problem areas.

Level 3. System-oriented – Focus on the entire system including support processes and their control. This control considers both the internal and external customers. Trend measurements lead to preventive actions.

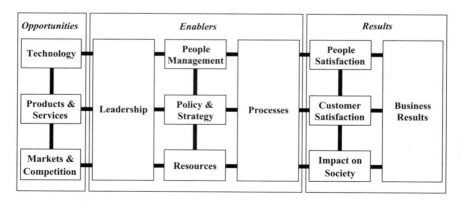

Figure 1.15 Ericsson Business Excellence Model (based on EFQM model).

Level 4. Focus on 'win-win situation for the whole chain in cooperation with customers and suppliers'. Competence is used efficiently in the product service realization process. Organization is becoming a learning organization. Excellent results compared to competition.

Level 5. Vision and management of the organization is based on the responsibilities of all stakeholders: customers, suppliers, partners, owners, employees and society. Continuous improvement is embedded in all operations. The organization has learned how to change and accelerate change. The organization is able to adapt faster to external triggers than others are. Results are excellent compared to best-in-class.

The maturity approach is similar to RADAR, which is used in EFQM and the equivalents of levels 1–5 are more or less found in RADAR. A possible difference is that the dimension where chasing faults gradually changes to prevention, which is much more obvious in the maturity grid than in the RADAR model. Finally, strengths and weaknesses of the model are presented below.

Strengths	*Weaknesses*
Simple and useful self-assessment tool	Interactions between criteria are not shown
Includes importance of handling technology, facilities and partnerships of all kinds	Not a comprehensive systems approach, focus is only on customers and suppliers outside the company
Good balance between result and process orientation	No evidence can be shown that high score leads to good business results
Clear and visible split between Opportunities, Enablers and Results	Separate scoring mechanism which makes benchmarking against other organizations difficult
Focus on external opportunities	

Balanced Scorecard

Presentation and analysis of the model

BSC is a performance measurement system focused on results. It is flexible and possible to apply differently in different organizations. In general, there are no directives on which performance is to be measured. BSC only provides guidance (see Figure 1.16). The application of BSC should be unique to each organization and to levels in the organization. One should of course be careful when using different models at different levels of management to avoid confusion in the interpretation of the results.

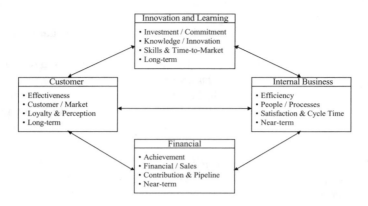

Figure 1.16 Balanced Scorecard (BSC).

The criterion 'Innovation and Learning' focuses on developing competence, supporting innovation and on keeping employees motivated and committed to the work.

'Internal Business' focuses on utilizing resources and competence in the most efficient way through processes and systems. 'Internal Business' is measured on short-term basis.

The 'Financial' criterion, which is also for short term, focuses on sales, returns on investment, cash flow, contribution and other financial measures.

And finally, the criterion 'Customer' focuses on the external customer, for example, market situation, customer satisfaction and customer loyalty is in focus. If this criterion is used for all stakeholders, suppliers, society, partnerships are also likely to be measured.

From the comparison in Figure 1.17 it is obvious that BSC covers the principles of TQM quite well. The comparison is very general and since BSC is different for every organization there is no guarantee that this comparison is valid. Finally, strengths and weaknesses of the model are presented below.

Strengths	Weaknesses
Flexibility	Interactions between criteria are not shown
Strong focus on customer and market	Not a comprehensive systems approach, focus is only on customers (varies between organizations)
Easy to use	Only focus on results

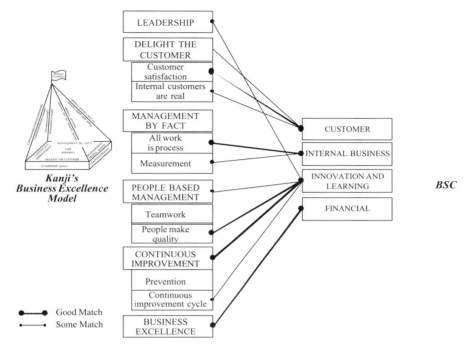

Figure 1.17 Comparison of KBEM and BSC.

Other quality models and awards

There are other models that normally are not directly associated with BE. Nevertheless, they are all used for optimizing the organizational performance, based on quality principles, and guide organizations in their management of quality improvements. Examples of these models are:

- ISO 9000 – quality standard used worldwide, often by third-party certification.
- Lynch and Cross's Performance Pyramid – Visualize the linkage in performance measurements from corporate vision down to individual performance indicators.
- Crosby's Quality Management Process Maturity Grid – Crosby's grid guides organizations through the following of five maturity levels: uncertainty, awakening, enlightenment, wisdom and certainty.
- CMM is focused on the software development process and not the complete organization as TQM does. The model is based on the same principles as Crosby's Quality Management Process Maturity Grid with five maturity levels. For organizations developing software, CMM is

an excellent complement to BEMs, especially for internal efficiency measurements.

National quality awards

The spin-off from EQA and MBNQA has been tremendous in USA and Europe. More than 60 different countries have their own quality awards originating from EQA and MBNQA. All these national quality awards have spread the message of TQM and increased the knowledge about quality principles and practices around the world.

Comparison between different BEMs

In this comparison the design tool House of Quality (HoQ) is used, see Figure 1.18. The six models compared are: KBEM, Deming Prize, EFQM Excellence Model, MBNQA, EBEM, and BSC. To the left in the HoQ there is a list of requirements of a BEM. The compared models are listed at the top, under the correlation 'roof' of the HoQ. The correlation 'roof' shows when it is an advantage to combine two models. Each requirement is graded with an importance value (I). In the matrix the models are evaluated against the requirements with a relationship value (R). Strong relationship is 5, medium is 3, and weak is 1. All three levels are positive ratings and represent how well the model fulfils the requirements. For each model a total score is calculated through summarizing the products of relationship (R) and importance (I).

Figure 1.18 shows that KBEM is the best, based on the requirements listed. But, no model is the best in all areas, for example, in benchmarking EFQM and MBNQA are best. All models will now be compared based on the twelve requirements listed in Figure 1.18.

Complexity

Kanji's model is outstanding in terms of ease of use, whereas the other models need some kind of training prior to use. BSC is also easy to use but it is not fully comparable since it is not a model with a set of questions to evaluate. The Deming Prize is the most complex model to use and the organization needs help from external consultants in order to use it for evaluation.

Flexibility

Flexibility is about the ability to adapt to the situation. Kanji's model and the BSC are the most flexible tools since they are adapted to each organization's needs. EFQM and MBNQA are general models that have adaptations for small companies, service companies and large corporations. The Deming

Requirements (R)	Importance (I)	Kanji's	Deming prize	MBNQA	EFQM	Ericsson EM	BSC
Complexity	4	⊙		△	○	○	⊙
Flexibility	3	⊙		△	△	△	⊙
Cost	2	⊙		△	△	○	⊙
Validity	3	○	○	○	○	○	△
Reliability	4	○	○	△	△	△	
Systems Approach	4	⊙	△	△	△	△	
Coverage TQM Principles	4	⊙	⊙	⊙	⊙	⊙	△
Coverage Stakeholders	4	△	△	△	○	○	○
Process Orientation	3	⊙	⊙	○	○	○	△
Result Orientation	3	○	△	○	○	○	⊙
Benchmarking	3	△	△	⊙	⊙	△	△
Trends	4	⊙	○	⊙	⊙	⊙	⊙
Total score Σ **(I*R)**		157	82	103	119	111	101

+ Positive Correlation

⊙ Strong Relationship (R=5)   ○ Medium Relationship (R=3)

△ Weak Relationship (R=1)

Figure 1.18 Comparison between different business excellence models.

Prize and the EBEM do not have adaptations at all. The Deming Prize has also been criticized for not being suitable for service organizations.

Cost

Kanji's model and BSC are the two models with the least cost involved. The major cost when applying models are consultant costs and time spent for employees on interviews and questionnaires. Since Ericsson already has the knowledge of the EBEM internally, the cost is lower than for EFQM and MBNQA. Deming is the most expensive model since it works differently and, as said before, JUSE recommends companies to use consultants for a few years before an evaluation of the company is done.

Validity

It is difficult to evaluate the validity of the different models. What is known, however, is that by using, for example, MBNQA and the Deming Prize, companies have improved their performance. Since EFQM, EBEM, and Kanji's model are based on the same principles, they should be somewhat similar in terms of their validity. Hopefully, the future will show that Kanji's model provides more valid measurements, but it is too early to say. BSC is rated lower since it is not as strongly tied to TQM principles as the other models.

Reliability

Kanji's model and the Deming Prize are the best in reliability. For Kanji's model this is so because reliability actually is measured for each application, and in the case of Deming Prize because measurements are done over a longer period of time. For EFQM, EBEM and MBNQA the reliability is sufficient due to the guidelines they use for measurements. BSC is less reliable as a model, since little guidance about how to measure is given.

Systems approach

An organization should not get high scores, for example, for process performance alone, unless other attributes of the system is working since 'the performance of a system is not the sum of the performance of its parts taken separately, but the product of their interactions.' One should not overlook the danger of not paying attention to interactions. BSC does not look at interactions at all. Deming Prize, MBNQA, EBEM, and EFQM deal with cause and effect relationships but the models are not able to verify any correlation of parameters. In a way, Kanji's model more or less originates from this lack of system approach in existing models. It provides a structured model which shows correlation between variables and cause and effect structure from leadership to BE (see Figure 1.8).

Coverage of TQM principles

All BEMs originate from TQM and therefore cover the principles and concepts well. Since BSC is flexible and result-oriented, some of the TQM principles are not guaranteed. BSC may cover TQM principles, but this is more dependent on how it is applied, which is the reason for low ratings. Kanji measures external stackeholders using his business scorecard (see Chapter 6) methodology.

Coverage of stakeholders

In general, all BEMs should improve in this area. From the earlier discussion it is evident that you should measure all stakeholders. EFQM, EBEM and BSC do this best today. For example, they include partnership and impact on society, which the other models do not. However, KBEM and BSC will provide BE for all the stakeholders.

Process orientation

Should the criteria be more process-oriented or more business-oriented? In my view a balance between the two is best. By focusing only on the business result you overlook the principles of TQM, and the point of using TQM as the guide towards BE is lost. The process orientation is very high for the Deming Prize and Kanji's models, whereas MBNQA, EFQM and EBEM are somewhat less process oriented. MBNQA and EFQM both give about 50 per cent of the scoring on process-oriented criteria and 50 per cent on result-oriented criteria. BSC has some focus on processes, but is in general focused on result.

Result orientation

BSC is strong on result orientation. Kanji's model, MBNQA, EFQM and EBEM are about equal in result coverage. Kanji's model might be better than the other three, but the rating is the same. The Deming Prize is much more process-oriented than result-oriented and is behind the other models in this area.

Benchmarking

The more standardized a model is, the easier it is to benchmark against other organizations. MBNQA and EFQM are both excellent for benchmarking. The other models are all behind, mainly since those models are adapted to each organization. However, Kanji's Business Excellence Index (KBEI) can be used for national and international Benchmarking.

Trends

All models, except for the Deming Prize, are excellent in trend analysis. Their scoring systems make it easy to see trends. For BSC the result measurements are also good for trend analysis. The Deming Prize does not have an official scoring system that can be used by an organization to evaluate its improvements. This is normally done with help from consultants.

Having indicated that KBEM scores higher than the other existing models, the forces of excellence in Kanji's model will be discussed in the following chapter.

2 Forces of excellence in Kanji's Business Excellence Model

Introduction

Forces of excellence are transforming the way we work with low cost opportunities to quickly expand markets globally and deliver better, more personalized customer service. The challenge for Business Excellence (BE) today is to turn the organization's vision into reality. The task is to build a highly and well integrated Total Quality Management (TQM) base in order to utilize the Critical Success Factors (CSFs) of the organization.

Organizations that have achieved a higher level of BE have demonstrated very high growth in their customer base, thus improving overall profitability and stakeholders values.

Whatever their size, the time has come for organizations to make real sense of BE. Here, the BE approach will depend on its competitive landscape, strategy, objectives and resources. The forces of excellence will guide them in the right direction to achieve excellence.

In this chapter, the author discusses KBEM as an index and provides the route to BE through TQM framework.

Getting started...

- *TQM* and *BM* became very popular ideas during the last decade. However, when trying to measure their overall performance, to identify strengths and areas for improvement and to prioritize efforts, organizations still face considerable difficulties and problems.
- *Organizations need a framework* that is comprehensive, flexible and easy to adopt. Since success clearly depends on a combination of factors that are interrelated, the approach must be holistic, highlighting at the same time the impact that any change in one of the components will have on the overall system.
- *Providing organizations* with such a framework and describing its main principles and concepts is our main purpose.
- Even believing that these principles are universally valid and their adoption potentially leads to sustainable *Organizational Success*, the route to *BE*

must be specifically tailored for each organization, depending on its particular starting point, its own system of beliefs and values and its assets in terms of competencies and core processes.

Kanji's Business Excellence Model

Kanji's Business Excellence Model (KBEM) (see Figure 2.1), based on Kanji's pyramid principles of TQM, links together the prime (Leadership) the four principles (Delight the customer, Management by fact, People-based management and Continuous improvement) and the eight core concepts to provide forces of excellence in an organization. A structural model has been used for this purpose.

What does Kanji's Business Excellence Index (KBEI) measure?

The Business Excellence Index (BEI) is a means of measuring customers', employees' and shareholders' (i.e. stakeholders) satisfaction simultaneously within an organization in order to obtain a comprehensive evaluation of the organizational performance.

KBEM can be used to measure BEI in order to show how well different areas of the organization, that is, leadership, continuous improvement and other TQM principles, are performing.

It has been constructed in such a way so as to allow direct comparison across each area while at the same time being able to compare the same business in

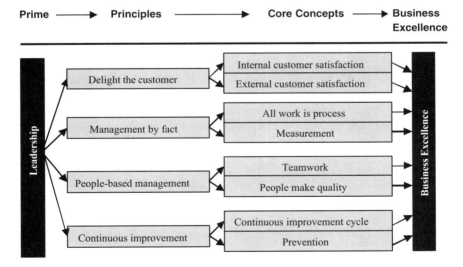

Figure 2.1 Kanji's Business Excellence Model.

different geographical areas. The BEI also allows a particular business to be measured over time.

The BEI is therefore a measurement of the complex interaction between TQM principles and BE of the organization at a certain point.

Leadership: the 'Prime' for BE

'Top management is actively involved in creating a Total Quality Culture (TQC) and has a vision'.

Leadership is the fundamental driver of BE. It is the role of leadership:

- to define a mission, vision and goals that promote a quality culture;
- to establish a set of shared values;
- to define a quality strategy;
- to better coordinate the use of resources in order to improve financial performance;
- to establish goals and systems to enhance customer satisfaction;
- to establish effective information systems (I/S) and to use objective data in the decision process;
- to promote the development of the human resources, investing on training and education and to recognize quality achievements;
- to communicate, define and motivate continuous improvement.

What does the 'Leadership' show?

It shows the extent to which ...

- top management assumes responsibility for quality performance;
- the organization's quality goals are clearly defined;
- the organization's quality values are adopted and reinforced throughout the organization;
- top management has a vision and a long-term strategy that encourages continuous improvement;
- leadership allocates quality initiatives and the necessary resources;
- fulfils the stakeholders values for the organization;
- promotes a quality culture within the organization.

An integrated approach to BE

A closer look at the integrated processes for prime, principle, core concepts and BE follows.

TM Integrated Process (ONE)

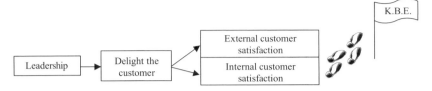

To achieve BE, leadership must have a clear customer focus.

Delight the Customer

Delight the Customer means:

> 'Exceeding customers' expectations in what matters most to them'.

What am I supposed to do?

- Place customer satisfaction at the top of the agenda.
- Establish goals and systems that enhance customer satisfaction.
- Take into consideration the needs and expectations of both external and internal customers.
- Monitor changes in customer preferences and, to some extent, anticipate them.

What does 'Delight the Customer' show?

It shows the extent to which the organization . . .

- listens to its customers;
- determines current and future customer requirements and expectations;
- uses feedback from customers to improve its products and services.

Delight the Customer is translated into practice by two *core concepts: External Customer Satisfaction* and *Internal Customer Satisfaction.*

External Customer Satisfaction (ECS)

Quality must be incorporated into all activities with a clear customer focus. Customers usually compare perceptions of what they actually received from the organization with their expectations (what they were expecting to get from the organization). Customer delight arises when perceptions exceed expectations.

What does 'External Customer Satisfaction' show?

It shows the extent to which the organization . . .

- uses methods for determining and monitoring external customer's perceived quality and value;
- uses customer feedback to improve product/service quality;
- handles complaints, resolves them, and uses complaint information for quality improvement and prevention of recurrence of problems;
- measures performance against customer targets;
- compares its customer satisfaction results with those of main competitors.

Internal Customer Satisfaction (ICS)

Getting the internal relationships working is essential if external customers are to be satisfied. Every single person in the organization has an effect on the external customers. Internal cooperation needs to be stimulated to enhance organizational performance. The most effective leadership style tends to give high importance to teams and employee participation.

What does 'Internal Customer Satisfaction' show?

It shows the extent to which the organization . . .

- uses methods for improving coordination of interdependent tasks;
- makes people aware of the fact that they all have customers and suppliers;
- has a strong employee interaction with customers and suppliers;
- focuses on external customers when tasks are being performed.

Why follow this process?

- By delighting the customer you can turn satisfied customers into loyal customers. Loyalty generates repeated purchases and increased revenues, thus leading to organizational excellence.
- Employee satisfaction is needed to support continuous improvement and external customer satisfaction. Delighted employees who feel proud of their work have an outstanding performance, thus having a positive impact on BE.

^{TM} Integrated Process (TWO)

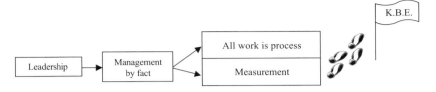

To achieve BE, *leadership* decisions must be based on facts. Knowing the current performance levels is essential to measuring the organization's improvement.

Management by Fact (MBF)

Management by Fact means:

> 'Having the facts (objective data and necessary tools) to manage the business at all levels'.

What am I supposed to do?

- Collect and analyse information about customer needs, operational problems and the success of improvement efforts.
- Look at the organization as a set of interrelated processes.
- Identify critical areas/variables and control points where measurement should take place.

What does 'Management by Fact' show?

It shows the extent to which the organization . . .

- has a performance measurement system that evaluates its quality improvement processes;
- disseminates performance measurements throughout the organization;
- uses the performance measurements to improve its products and processes.

Management by Fact is translated into practice by two *core concepts*: *All Work is Process* and *Measurement*.

All Work is Process (AWP)

Every organization is a complex network of processes. A process is a combination of inputs and steps to follow to produce outputs. All processes contain inherent variability. One of the main ideas of Quality Management is to progressively reduce variation.

What does the 'All Work is Process' show?

It shows the extent to which the organization . . .

- has processes that are designed to meet the quality requirements;
- assesses the quality of its processes;
- determines which are the critical processes and selects adequate control points;
- applies appropriate statistical methods to control its processes;
- uses assessment results and benchmarking to enhance knowledge about processes.

Measurement (M)

Having a measure of how well the organization is doing is essential to choose among different improvement initiatives and assess the effectiveness of quality efforts.

What does 'Measurement' show?

The extent to which the organization . . .

- collects a wide range of complete and accurate performance indicators;
- develops an appropriate methodology for assessing quality;
- compares current performance with past performance and with that of competitors and *best-in-practice* organizations.

Why follow this process?

- Only by collecting relevant data and establishing the facts, you can make reasonable decisions based on facts. Knowing what went wrong and what was effective will make you use your resources better, hence contributing to BE.

- Understanding interdependencies will enhance cooperation. Looking at your organization as a network of processes is the foundation of performance improvement.

™ Integrated Process (THREE)

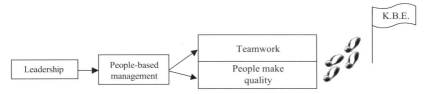

In an organization striving for excellence, *leadership* places a high priority on human resource development with quality orientation.

People-Based Management

People-Based Management means:

> 'Giving people the knowledge, skills and encouragement to take responsibility for the quality of their own work'.

What am I supposed to do?

- Help employees to reach their full potential.
- Break down barriers between departments, allowing people to work together in teams.
- Institute programmes of ongoing training and education.
- Make employees feel they contribute to the organization's achievements and that their contribution is highly valued.

What does 'People-Based Management' show?

It shows the extent to which . . .

- human resource management supports quality, by providing people with the knowledge and skills they need to do a good job;
- feedback is provided to employees on their performance;
- means are available for all employees to contribute effectively to meeting the organization's quality objectives.

People-Based Management is translated into practice by two *core concepts*: *Teamwork* and *People Make Quality*.

Teamwork

Providing people with an opportunity to work together in the pursuit of total quality helps to remove internal barriers, makes people aware of their interdependent tasks and improves communication. Through the use of teams people clearly understand the consequences of poor quality.

What does 'Teamwork' show?

It shows the extent to which the organization . . .

- uses teams to solve cross-functional problems;
- explores teams as platforms for change;
- brings people together to improve communication;
- develops teams for everyone's participation.

People Make Quality

Systems, standards and technology themselves will not mean quality. People need to be equipped with the knowledge and skills for the job, and be informed about how well they are doing so that they become encouraged and responsible for their jobs. Involvement and commitment to customer satisfaction are key factors.

What does 'People Make Quality' show?

It shows the extent to which . . .

- quality related training is given both to managers and employees;
- managers remove the barriers that prevent people from improving quality (i.e. lack of training, poorly defined jobs, etc.);
- the organization empowers individuals by creating a collaborative and risk-taking environment.

Why follow this process?

- Most organizational problems demand an interdepartmental cooperation that can be more effectively achieved through the use of teams.
- Training and education make people embrace a continuous process of learning that is essential to BE.
- Motivated and knowledgeable employees will effectively solve problems when they occur, making the organization save considerable amounts of money without recurrent failures.

^{TM} Integrated Process (FOUR)

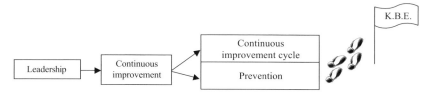

To achieve BE, *leadership* has to lead the quest for improvement. Continuous improvement results from process management practices that bring forth incremental improvements and innovations in processes, products and services.

Continuous Improvement

Continuous Improvement means:

> 'However much we may improve, it will be necessary to do even better next time'.

What am I supposed to do?

- Identify and establish improvement projects.
- Foster a culture of continuous improvement.
- Monitor changes in customer demands.
- Benchmark against best-in-class.
- Make incremental change as the aim of all who work in the organization.

What does 'Continuous Improvement' show?

It shows the extent to which . . .

- the organization continually searches opportunities for improvement;
- the organization reacts to changes in customer satisfaction indicators;
- quality improvement methods are used to improve all products, services and processes;
- the organization compares current quality levels of service with those of competitors.

Continuous Improvement is translated into practice by two *core concepts*: *Continuous Improvement Cycle* and *Prevention*.

> ## Continuous Improvement Cycle
>
> The continuous cycle of establishing customer requirements, meeting those requirements, measuring success and keep improving can be used to fuel the engine of continuous improvement.

What does 'Continuous Improvement Cycle' show?

It shows the extent to which the organization . . .

- has a quality culture of continuous improvement;
- continuously identifies small, incremental improvements in the way internal and external customers are satisfied.

> ## Prevention
>
> The fundamental idea of prevention is causing problems not to happen. There are essentially two ways to attain this: first, by concentrating on the design of the product itself, and second, by working on the production process.

What does 'Prevention' show?

It shows the extent to which . . .

- improved customer services are introduced to drive out failures;
- processes are designed to prevent potential problems.

Why follow this process?

- BE is a moving target. Only by a culture of continuous improvement and by celebrating incremental changes can BE be effectively pursued.
- Prevention is a crucial way to move towards continuous improvement. The continual process of driving possible failure out of the system can breed a culture of continuous improvement that is essential to BE.

BE – the final aim

It is very important that you apply *simultaneously all the FOUR integrated processes* described above if you want to achieve BE.

'The BEI is a means of measuring customers', employees' and shareholders' satisfaction simultaneously within an organization in order to obtain a comprehensive evaluation of the organizational performance'

What does 'BE' show?

It shows the extent to which the organization ...

- has strong financial performance;
- has high customer demand;
- has been able to recruit and maintain outstanding staff;
- achieves its goals;
- compares its current performance with that of competitors' and best-in-class;
- fulfils stakeholders values;
- has good supply chain management process;
- has both short-term and long-term strategy for every aspect of the organization.

Good reasons to use KBEM

- It is SIMPLE in terms of concepts and relationships presented.
- It is EASY TO USE – all parameters can be estimated using a proper software and it produces a single index that allows comparisons among different areas of the business (both directly and over time) and with other organizations (as well as across industries).
- It is GENERIC – it can be applied in different contexts.
- It is ROBUST – it efficiently yields different outputs when inputs are changed.
- It is COMPLETE – it includes all TQM factors and utilizes a measurement instrument that can be adjusted to different situations.
- It is VALID – its validity has been statistically proven.
- It is EFFECTIVE – is able to measure all critical factors and their contribution to BE, thus giving a clear indication where improvement efforts should be focused on.

What do you need to start KBEM?

- To have suitable *Leadership* committed to do continuous improvement and to create quality culture.
- To administer a concise and *structured questionnaire* that can be tailored to your organization. Each principle and core concept described above

is represented by a set of indicators or measurement items in that questionnaire.
- To use a *KW special software package* that calculates all the parameters of the model and the final BE score.
- For various 'stakeholders' use business scorecard of *KBEM.*

How to measure KBEI?

The BEI is obtained using a structural equation model that simultaneously measures the impact of all the variables on BE. This software easily calculates the values of all parameters in the model and the final score of BE. The same software additionally helps to prioritize improvement efforts, by simulating the necessary changes in each of the CSFs to reach a particular BEI, subjected to existing constraints (Excellence Seeker's Approach).

KW management package

What does it do?   It calculates the structural coefficients of KBEM, the scores achieved by the company in each organizational area and the resulting KBEI, (see Figure 2.2 for a condensed model). In addition, the package includes an algorithm that allows you to identify how much you have to improve in each area in order to achieve a targeted BEI.

It also provides the company with a range of statistical measures and graphs that may be easily incorporated in your management report.

How?   KBEM is based on a structural equation modelling (SEM) technique which combines aspects of multiple regression and factor analysis to estimate a series of interrelated dependence relationships simultaneously. The software essentially uses the PLS method in the simultaneous estimation of the weights of the constructs of the model. It calculates these weights in a way that maximizes the goodness-of-fit of the model and, thus, the ability to explain BE as the ultimate endogenous variable.

When?   You can use the program at any time, providing you have the necessary data from the questionnaires. Regular use of the software allows you to monitor the impact of any changes and improvement efforts on the KBEI.

Who?   It is not necessary to have any particular expertise to work with the software package. Anyone within the organization who feels comfortable working with Windows, the usual software program, will soon become familiar with this package.

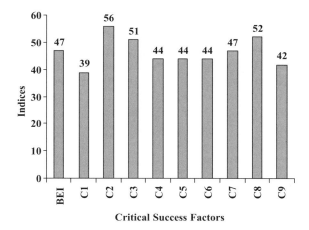

Figure 2.2 Kanji's Business Excellence Index (KBEI) for a condensed model.

Notes: C1. Leadership; C2. Delight the customer; C3. Customer focus; C4. Management by fact; C5. Process improvement; C6. People-based management; C7. People performance; C8. Continous improvement; C9. Improvement culture; BEI. Business Excellence Index.

KW Management Software

How does the software work? The package consists of a questionnaire, an Excel spreadsheet and the dedicated KW management software. Data from completed questionnaires is input into the spreadsheet. The KW management software takes this data, computes the statistics and posts them back to the spreadsheet. You then incorporate these results into your own reports.

Where 'KBEM' has been applied?

Educational sector (higher education) It has been applied on 183 higher educational institutes in three different countries, USA, UK and Malaysia.

UK (51): 20 university colleges, 18 old universities, 13 new universities.

USA (72): 51 public institutions, 21 private institutions.

Malaysia(60): 11 public institutions, 49 private institutions.

Retail banking This includes several branches of set Retail Banks in Hong Kong.

European organizations This includes various manufacturing and service industries.

Hotel industries This includes 64 hotels in Hong Kong.

Supply chain management This includes 139 organizations in Hong Kong.

Conclusions

One of the most important benefits of the presented method of KBEI is that it is applicable to both manufacturing and service industries and allows organizations to compare themselves against different organizations with whom they are competing. This is of particular benefit to organizations that are not performing as well as they might, as it will give them an incentive to do something about their failings. Besides being able to incorporate organizations within the same sector, because the index is a single number it is possible for them to compare across industries, and how well they are doing against the national index (when calculated).

Organizations can use the data from the index to assess the contribution by the various CSFs of the organizations, identify potential barriers to entry within markets, predict return on investments and pinpoint areas in which customers are not being satisfied.

Following the discussion of forces of excellence in Kanji's model, the next chapter will present the understanding and pitfalls of the BEMs.

3 Understanding and pitfalls of business excellence

Introduction

Total Quality Management (TQM) has emerged as a field based on the recognition of the work of several major leaders of the quality movement, namely Edward Deming (1981), Joseph M. Juran (1986), Philip Crosby (1979), Kaoru Ishikawa (1985), Garvin (1988), Feigenbaum (1991), and Genichi Taguchi (Taguchi *et al.* 1988).

Crosby (1979) was known for his five absolutes of quality and the fourteen-point plan for quality improvement. While Deming was more concerned with management philosophy, Crosby was concerned with implementation issues. Crosby's definition of quality is conformance to requirements.

Deming (1981) is remembered for his fourteen points of thinking about quality management, the Deming cycle and seven deadly diseases. Deming had a particular appreciation of statistics and taught the Japanese statistical process of control in the 1950s. Deming's definition of quality is fitness for purpose.

Juran (1986) describes a quality trilogy of quality planning, quality control, and quality improvement. Juran also derived the concept of the internal customer that relates to an organization with more than one person. Juran was the first person to point out that the Pareto principle could be applied to quality improvement. Juran also introduced the development of the quality council, that is, a body that manages the quality activities of an organization. Juran was also involved with developing the concept of statistical process control. Juran's definition of quality is fitness for use.

Ishikawa (1985) is recognized for contributing to the emergence of quality circles, where workers meet to discuss suggestions for improvements. Ishikawa developed the fishbone diagram and the employment of seven old tools of quality that provided grass-root capability in the use of problem-solving techniques.

Garvin (1991) developed what are known as the eight dimensions of quality: performance, features, reliability, conformance, durability, serviceability, aesthetics, and perceived quality. Garvin also introduced the notion of five quality bases: transcendent, product, user, manufacturing, and value.

Feigenbaum (1991) became known for his work in quality control. He originated the industrial cycle – the development of a product from concept to market launch and beyond. Feigenbaum also introduced the concept of the hidden plant which implies that waste lowered the real capacity of the plant because of rework and not actually getting it right the first time.

Taguchi's major contribution is on the effective quality of design (Taguchi *et al.* 1988). Essentially, Taguchi's methods focus on determining the cost of not meeting the specified targeted value. This is in contrast with traditional quality management practices, in that, as long as products meet the specification limits set for a given product and process (tolerance), then the product is acceptable. Consequently, he developed the loss function that calculates the reduction in utility as a function of the distance from the target value of a product or characteristic results – which is the loss to the society in terms of cost.

Kanji and Asher (1993) define TQM as a process of satisfying agreed customer requirements continually at low cost, by involving everyone's daily commitment. According to Kanji (1990), quality is not a programme or a project, but it is a management process that recognizes the fact that, however much an organization may improve, its competitors will continue to improve and its customers will expect more.

Based on the TQM concepts proposed by these and other researchers, many TQM models have been developed. The models can be divided into conceptual models, which isolate TQM processes into several key areas, and measurement models, which measure the performance of the key areas. Examples of conceptual models are the Kanji's pyramid model (Kanji 1996) and Oakland's TQM model (1989). Examples of measurement models are Motorola's Six Sigma Signals Quality model (Smith 1993), award models such as European Foundation for Quality Management (EFQM) Excellence model (EFQM 1999), Malcolm Baldrige National Quality Award (MBNQA) (NIST 1994), Deming Prize model, SERVQUAL (Parasuraman *et al.* 1988), INTQUAL (Caruana and Pitt 1997), and Critical Success Factors (CSFs) measurement model by Saraph *et al.* (1989).

While many existing TQM models are generic such as those already mentioned, others are in-house models that were developed by individual organizations specifically for their own TQM processes. Examples of manufacturing organizations that have developed TQM models are Rank Xerox, IBM, Hewlett Packard, and Toyota. For service organizations, examples are represented by police departments (Wells 1998), the leisure industry (Tawse and Keogh 1998) and the education sector (Rowlands 1998; Spanbauer 1989; Seymour 1993; De Cosmo *et al.* 1991; Coate 1993; Geddes 1993; Doherty 1993; Clayton 1995).

The in-house models are regarded as special-purposed models because they are custom-designed for the TQM processes in the organizations. One distinct feature of these models is that they do not include all principles and concepts of TQM. For example, the TQM process at South Bank University is mainly concerned with improving the customer–supplier chain process in providing a high quality of service to students (Geddes 1993).

One of the objectives of the section is to find a generic TQM model that is applicable to the organization's processes and to provide CSFs for the performance measurement.

The achievement of BE is at the core of the implementation process of TQM (Porter and Tanner 1998). We have also mentioned earlier that TQM requires measurement and understanding of business performance and therefore understanding of assessing BE is an essential part of any TQM process.

In the following section we will start by describing and discussing the benefits and shortfalls of the MBNQA model and the EFQM Excellence Model in assessing BE for an organization.

The diffusion of these models is closely related to the quality awards which are given, to publicly recognize the achievements of the organizations which have successfully adopted the concepts of TQM. The winners serve as useful role models for other organizations intent on adopting TQM practices (Ghobadian and Woo 1996).

A number of factors have encouraged many countries to introduce local, national, or transnational quality awards. It is important to mention that the first award programme – the Deming Prize – was launched in 1951 in Japan. The Deming Prize is not based on an underlying framework linking concepts, activities, processes and results together. It simply provides a list of desirable or good quality-oriented management practices. The focus of the Deming Prize is mainly on the application of Statistical Quality Control (SQC) techniques with a view to improving process performance.

The broad aims of quality awards are to (Loomba and Johannessen 1997; Ghobadian and Woo 1996):

1   increase awareness of the importance of 'quality of offerings' and interest in 'quality management' because of their important contribution to superior competitiveness;
2   recognize the achievements of those companies that have superior quality and providing an example to others;
3   encourage systematic self-assessment against established criteria and market awareness simultaneously;
4   prompt cooperation between organizations on a wide range of non-commercially sensitive issues;
5   stimulate sharing and dissemination of information on successfully deployed quality strategies and on benefits derived from implementing these strategies;
6   promote understanding of the requirements for the attainment of 'quality excellence' and successful deployment of 'quality management';
7   stimulate organizations to introduce 'quality management' improvement process.

As we will address later, the models underpinning the quality awards, like most models, have limitations. Nevertheless, they provide a useful audit framework against which organizations can evaluate their quality management methods, establishing a benchmark from which future progress can be measured, and providing the businesses with improvement ideas.

Moreover, there is broad agreement that quality awards have succeeded in generating awareness and interest in the TQM concepts and provide a useful starting point.

However, it will become clear that these models have some important pitfalls in the measurement of BE. Thus, we will present at the end of the section an alternative BE framework – Kanji's Pyramid Model (1996) – which incorporates the main CSFs. This BEM can easily be validated by suitable data and appropriated statistical techniques.

The Malcolm Baldrige National Quality Award Model

As an attempt to promote quality excellence in the USA, the MBNQA programme was conceived in 1987.

The Baldrige award framework has four basic elements: driver, system, measures of progress and goal. As described by Porter and Tanner (1998), there exist dynamic relationships among the criteria. Senior executive leadership sets directions, creates the values, goals and expectations. The system consists of a set of well-defined and well-designed processes for meeting the company's customer and overall performance requirements. Measures of progress comprise the control elements of the model. The measures provide the basis for determining the types of actions required in the pursuit of the two primary goals of the model; customer and marketplace performance, and business performance.

The criteria (see Figure 1.11) are built upon a set of core values and concepts. These values and concepts are the embedded behaviours found in high performing organizations (NIST 2000):

- *Visionary leadership.* Senior leaders need to set directions and create a customer focus, clear and visible values, and high expectations. Leaders need to ensure the creation of strategies, systems and methods for achieving excellence, stimulating innovation, and building knowledge and capabilities. Through their ethical behaviour and personal roles in planning, communications, coaching, developing future leaders, review of organizational, and employee recognition, senior leaders should serve as role models, reinforcing values and expectations and building leadership, commitment, and initiative throughout the organization.
- *Customer driven.* Quality and performance are judged by an organization's customers. Being customer driven is a strategic concept. It is directed towards customer retention, market share gain, and growth. It demands constant sensitivity to changing and emerging customer and

market requirements, and the factors that drive customer satisfaction and retention.

- *Organizational and personal learning.* Organizational and personal learning is a goal of visionary leaders. The term organizational learning refers to continuous improvement of existing approaches and processes and adaptation to change, leading to new goals and/or approaches. Employee success depends increasingly on having opportunities for personal learning and practising new skills.
- *Valuing employees and partners.* An organization's success depends increasingly on the knowledge, skills, innovative creativity, and motivation of its employees and partners. Valuing employees means commitment to their satisfaction, development, and well-being. Increasingly, this involves more flexible, high-performance work practices tailored to employees with diverse workplace and home-life needs. Organizations need to build internal and external partnerships to better accomplish overall goals. Successful internal and external partnerships develop long-term objectives, thereby creating a basis for mutual investments and respect.
- *Agility.* Success in globally competitive markets demands creating a capacity for rapid change and flexibility. Businesses face ever-shorter cycles for introductions of new or improved products and services. All aspects of time performance are becoming increasingly important and should be among your key process measures.
- *Focus on the future.* Pursuit of sustainable growth and market leadership require a strong future orientation and a willingness to make long-term commitments to key stakeholders. Major components of a future focus include developing employees and suppliers, seeking opportunities for innovation and fulfilling public responsibilities.
- *Managing for innovation.* Innovation should focus on leading the organization to new dimensions of performance. Organizations should be structured in a way that innovation becomes part of the culture and daily work.
- *Management by fact.* Organizations depend upon the measurement and analysis of performance. Such measurements must derive from the organization's strategy and provide critical data and information about key processes, outputs and results. The measures or indicators selected should represent the factors that lead to improved customer, operational, and financial performance.
- *Public responsibility and citizenship.* An organization's leadership needs to stress its responsibilities to the public and needs to practise good citizenship. These responsibilities refer to basic expectations of the organization – business ethics and protection of public health, safety and the environment.
- *Focus on results and creating value.* An organization's performance measurements need to focus on key results. Results should be focused on creating and balancing value for all stakeholders. The use of a balanced

composite of leading and lagging performance measures offers an effective means to communicate short- and longer-term priorities, to monitor actual performance and to provide a focus for improving results.

- *Systems perspective.* The core values and the seven Baldrige categories form the building blocks of the system. Successful management of the overall enterprise requires synthesis and alignment. Synthesis means looking at the organization as a whole and focusing on what is important to the whole enterprise. Alignment means concentrating on key organizational linkages among requirements. Thus, alignment means linking key strategies with key processes and aligning resources to improve overall performance and satisfy customers.

The core values and concepts are embodied in seven categories (see Table 3.1):

1   Leadership
    The *Leadership* category examines how your organization's senior leaders address values and performance expectations, as well as a focus on customers and other stakeholders, empowerment, innovation, learning, and organizational directions. Also examined is how your organization addresses its responsibilities to the public and its key communities.
2   Strategic planning
    The *Strategic Planning* category examines your organization's strategy development process, including how your organization develops strategic objectives, action plans, and related human resource plans. Also examined are how plans are deployed and how performance is tracked.
3   Customer and market focus
    The *Customer and Market Focus* category examines how your organization determines requirements, expectations and preferences of customers and markets. Also examined is how your organization builds relationships with customers and determines their satisfaction.
4   Information and analysis
    The *Information and Analysis* category examines your organization's performance measurement system and how your organization analyses performance data and information.
5   Human resource focus
    The *Human Resource Focus* category examines how your organization enables employees to develop and utilize their full potential, aligned with the organization's objectives. Also examined are your organization's efforts to build and maintain a work environment and employee support climate conducive to performance excellence, full participation and personal and organizational growth.
6   Process management
    The *Process Management* category examines the key aspects of your organization's process management, including customer-focused design,

Table 3.1 2000 Criteria for performance excellence – item listing

2000 categories/items		Point values
1.	Leadership	125
	1.1. Organizational leadership	85
	1.2. Public responsibility and citizenship	40
2.	Strategic planning	85
	2.1. Strategy development	40
	2.2. Strategy deployment	45
3.	Customer and market focus	85
	3.1. Customer and market knowledge	40
	3.2. Customer satisfaction and relationships	45
4.	Information and analysis	85
	4.1. Measurement of organizational performance	40
	4.2. Analysis of organizational performance	45
5.	Human resource focus	85
	5.1. Work systems	35
	5.2. Employee education, training, and development	25
	5.3. Employee well-being and satisfaction	25
6.	Process management	85
	6.1. Product and service processes	55
	6.2. Support processes	15
	6.3. Supplier and partnering processes	15
7.	Business results	450
	7.1. Customer-focused results	115
	7.2. Financial and market results	115
	7.3. Human resource results	80
	7.4. Supplier and partner results	25
	7.5. Organizational effectiveness results	115
	Total points	1000

product and service delivery, support and supplier and partnering processes involving all work units.

7   Business results

The *Business Results* category examines your organization's performance and improvement in key business areas – customer satisfaction, product and service performance, human resource results, supplier and partner results, and operational performance. Also examined are performance levels relative to competitors.

The EFQM Excellence Model

The European Quality Award (EQA) was officially launched in 1991 with the aim of enhancing the competitive position of European companies in the world market. The EQA is managed by the EFQM established by fourteen leading European corporations, in September 1988. The purpose of the award is to promote TQM in Europe and all applicants must be able to demonstrate a history of significant commitment to Europe of at least five years.

Like the Baldrige model, the EFQM Excellence Model is a non-prescriptive framework that recognizes there are many approaches to achieving sustainable excellence.

Excellence is defined by the EFQM as an outstanding practice in managing the organization and achieving results, based on a set of eight fundamental concepts which underpin the model. They are described below (EFQM Excellence Model 1999):

- *Results orientation.* Excellence is dependent upon balancing and satisfying the needs of all relevant stakeholders.
- *Customer focus.* The customer is the final arbiter of product and service quality and customer loyalty, retention and market share gain are best optimized through a clear focus on the needs of current and potential customers.
- *Leadership and constancy of purpose.* The behaviour of an organization's leaders create a clarity and a unity of purpose within the organization and an environment in which the organization and its people can excel.
- *Management by processes and facts.* Organizations perform more effectively when all interrelated activities are understood and systematically managed and decisions concerning current operations and planned improvements are made, using reliable information that includes stakeholder perceptions.
- *People development and involvement.* The full potential of an organization's people is best released through shared values and a culture of trust and empowerment, which encourages the involvement of everyone.
- *Continuous learning, innovation and improvement.* Organizational performance is maximized when it is based on the management and sharing of knowledge within a culture of continuous learning, innovation and improvement.
- *Partnership development.* An organization works more effectively when it has mutually beneficial relationships, built on trust, sharing of knowledge and integration, with its partners.
- *Public responsibility.* The long-term interests of the organization and its people are best served by adopting an ethical approach and exceeding the expectations and regulations of the community at large.

The EFQM model (see Figure 1.13) is divided into two parts: Enablers and Results. The Enablers are policies and processes that drive the business and facilitate the transformation of inputs to outputs and outcomes. The Results are the measure of the level of output and outcome attained by the organization. The arrows emphasize the dynamic nature of the model. They show Innovation and Learning, helping to improve Enablers which in turn lead to improved Results.

The full power of the model is derived from the relationship between the enabler criteria and the results criteria. The model is based on the premise that excellent results with respect to performance, customers, people and society are achieved through leadership driving policy and strategy, people, partnerships and resources, and processes.

The model consists of nine elements: five Enablers and four measures of Results. These are further divided into a number of secondary elements. The model's criteria are considered below:

1 Leadership

How leaders develop and facilitate the achievement of the mission and vision, develop values required for long-term success and implement these via appropriate actions and behaviours, and are personally involved in ensuring that the organization's management system is developed and implemented.

2 Policy and strategy

How the organization implements its mission and vision via a clear stakeholder-focused strategy, supported by relevant policies, plans, objectives, targets and processes.

3 People

How the organization manages, develops and releases the knowledge and full potential of its people at an individual, team-based and organization-wide level, and plans these activities in order to support its policy and strategy and the effective operation of its processes.

4 Partnerships and resources

How the organization plans and manages its external partnerships and internal resources in order to support its policy and strategy and the effective operation of its processes.

5 Processes

How the organization designs, manages and improves its processes in order to support its policy and strategy and fully satisfy, and generate increasing value for, its customers and other stakeholders.

6 Customer results

What the organization is achieving in relation to its external customers.

7 People results

What the organization is achieving in relation to its people.

8 Society results

What the organization is achieving in relation to local, national and international society as appropriate.

9 Key performance results

What the organization is achieving in relation to its planned performance.

A comparison of the frameworks: MBNQA versus EFQM Excellence Model

Both the Baldrige Award and the EFQM frameworks attempt to model TQM by identifying its constituent parts. Furthermore, they assume that there is a causal relationship between different constituents of TQM. They are implicitly based on the premise that management leadership and customer/external focus are the two key factors underpinning the efforts to introduce total quality. They suggest that customers play a major role in defining the desired product and service quality levels and that the goal of quality improvement is enhanced by customer satisfaction (Ghobadian and Woo 1996).

The EFQM model and the MBNQA are based on the following management philosophies and principles (Ghobadian and Woo 1996):

1   Everyone in the organization is responsible for quality but it is top management's function to create the necessary environment for driving quality forward.
2   Only top management can influence and alter the system, thus its role (in setting goals and quality policies, establishing targets for the design of systems and procedures, promoting quality awareness, and providing role models by displaying quality behaviour) is crucial to the development of a total quality environment.
3   External focus and customer-oriented quality programmes – it is necessary for a company, managed in a total quality fashion, to benchmark itself against its competitors and have processes and procedures in place to enable it to understand the needs of its customers and manage its customer relationship.
4   High level of participation by employees and teamwork – attainment of consistent quality levels and performance targets require a well motivated and cohesive labour force.
5   Education and training designed to develop the organization's human resources is considered by all of the awards to be one of the pillars of total quality.
6   Emphasis on management by fact rather than by instinct or feel, which requires the design of an information system encompassing a set of measurable and objective indicators relevant to the way the company provides value to customers.
7   A clear understanding of internal processes – self-assessment against fixed and arguably universal criterion is a key emphasis of the awards. This requires the development of a thorough and systematic understanding of all internal processes.
8   Importance of managing supplier relationship and quality.

Structurally, the most important difference in the frameworks is the complete separation of Enablers and Results in the EFQM Excellence Model. Separation of Enablers and Results generally improves the use of TQM frameworks in self-assessment and aids understanding by its specific focus on the 'hows' (Enablers) and Results. However, it also requires the description of matching specific enablers to specific results in different criteria. The particular strength of the EFQM framework is that it explicitly addresses the performance of an organization in meeting the needs of all its stakeholders (Porter and Tanner 1998).

In general, the contents of both models are similar, but some differences exist (Zink *et al.* 1994; Porter and Tanner 1998). The criterion on Leadership of the EFQM Excellence Model appears in the Baldrige with the same name but the EFQM framework considers a wider range of activities. Baldrige also explicitly addresses the area of public responsibility and corporate citizenship (which constitutes by itself a unique criterion in the EFQM Excellence Model). The area 'policy and strategy' can be compared with the MBNQA criterion 'strategic planning'. The questions relating to 'people management' in the EFQM and those relating to 'people results' are to be found in the MBNQA. The comparison of the EFQM subject 'partnerships and resources' with the specific criteria within the MBNQA is difficult. The contents dealt with in the EFQM model in this area are distributed over many criteria within the MBNQA. The criterion 'processes' within the MBNQA is significantly more detailed. While the EFQM structures the criterion according to activities in managing processes, the Baldrige criterion is structured according to the kind of processes. Large differences between the MBNQA and EFQM framework are to be found in the context of the EFQM criterion 'customer results'. Within the EFQM Excellence Model no relevant 'enabler' criterion is defined for the 'results' criterion, but would be addressed by the critical processes. The EFQM results part 'society results' is missing in the Baldrige. Finally, no major differences are found in the criterion 'performance results', since both frameworks distinguish between financial and non-financial results.

Measuring business excellence: pitfalls of the MBNQA and EFQM models

Both the MBNQA and the EFQM excellence models aim to provide the organizations with a means to measure their position against a set of universal criteria, and to identify their strengths and weaknesses in the key areas of business (Ghobadian and Woo 1996) in order to guide them in their path to excellence. But, are they accomplishing this purpose? What are their main strengths? Where do they fail? What could be improved? These are some of the questions that we will address next.

The models we have discussed in this section have a major benefit. They provide companies with a comprehensive framework for assessing their progress towards the new paradigm of management. The use of such models makes a company systematically and regularly review its activities and results. This self-assessment exercise is a big step on the path to continuous improvement and TQM.

Self-assessment measures an organization's progress towards excellence and helps prioritize and target improvements. According to Mangelsdorf (1999), self-assessment is the decisive beginning of the integration of quality management into the business management in many companies, and it paves the way for an integrated management system on the road to BE embracing and harmonizing all the various activities and programs within a company.

Porter and Tanner (1998) state that companies using self-assessment tools:

- experience a greater focus on continuous improvement;
- are able to measure the progress of the organization more effectively;
- experience improved senior management commitment to continuous improvement;
- have increased the awareness levels of TQ throughout the organization;
- have more focus and strategic action planning;
- have improved employee commitment or involvement in continuous improvement;
- have improved operational performance;
- have improved customer satisfaction;
- have improved financial performance.

Furthermore, the use of a model such as the ones proposed by the Malcolm Baldrige and the EFQM programmes is in itself a catalyst for change. The criteria set offers managers a global and adaptable definition of quality, allowing them firmly to grip the issue and implement a quality process (Loomba and Johannessen 1997).

Some would argue that a high score against the awards criteria is not a necessary or a sufficient condition for financial success. Nevertheless, it is important to remember that many internal and external factors influence the financial results and meeting the excellence criteria enhances management's control over internal factors and makes the organization more robust in dealing with pressures brought about by changes in external circumstances.

Moreover, these models have proved to be an important vehicle for sharing experience and good practices among organizations committed to TQM, explaining the increasing number of organizations that use them as a basis for continuous improvement.

However, the ultimate goal of the models we have been discussing is to provide organizations with a practical tool to help them measure where they are on the path to excellence; helping them to understand the gaps; and then stimulating solutions. The question is: are these models achieving this ambitious purpose?

In this particular area we think there is still a long way to go. Both the EFQM and the MBNQA models highlight the important factors for BE and state that there are relationships among them, but they do not make these causal relationships clear by assigning 'true' coefficients/weights to the different criteria, based on statistical evidence. Therefore, the impact of any change on one particular criterion on other components of the model and overall BE is difficult to predict, thus making the prioritization of the improvement efforts ambiguous.

Rather than using suitable statistical methods to determine factor scores, they rely on subjective evaluations. This way, the final BE score is always the outcome of the personal judgements of a particular assessment team, and cannot be easily replicated or generalized. This is an important limitation, particularly when the model is used as a benchmarking tool.

In order to make this last point more clear, let us look at the EFQM model and how it determines the total evaluation score.

The EFQM Excellence Model as an evaluation tool

The EFQM Excellence Model can be used for a number of activities. Examples include self-assessment, third-party assessment, benchmarking and as a basis for applying for the EQA. In order to help with this, the EFQM provides the following two evaluation tools – the Pathfinder Card and the RADAR scoring matrix (The EFQM Excellence Model 1999).

The purpose of Pathfinder is to assist in the identification of improvement opportunities through self-assessment and to help build improvement plans. It is a series of questions designed to be answered quickly and, in the main, it reflects the RADAR logic (see Figure 3.1).

This logic states that an organization needs to:

- Determine the **R**esults it is aiming for as part of its policy and strategy making process. These results cover the performance of the organization, both financially and operationally, and the perceptions of its stakeholders.
- Plan and develop an integrated set of sound **A**pproaches to deliver the required results both now and in the future.
- **D**eploy the approaches in a systematic way to ensure full implementation.
- **A**ssess and **R**eview the approaches followed based on monitoring and analysis of the results achieved and ongoing learning activities. Based

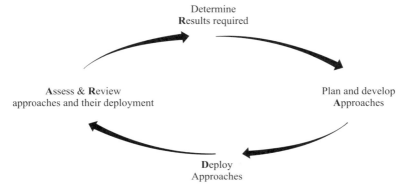

Figure 3.1 The RADAR logic (© EFQM).

on this identify, prioritize, plan and implement improvements where needed.

The RADAR scoring matrix is the evaluation method used to score applications for the EQA. When an organization is graded using the RADAR scoring matrix weights are given to each of the nine criteria to calculate the number of points awarded.

Taking the enabler criteria first, the evaluation is based on three dimensions: Approach, Deployment of the approach, and Assessment and Review.

Approach is concerned with how the requirements of a particular examination item are met. Factors used to evaluate Approach include:

- the appropriateness of the methods, tools and techniques;
- the degree of integration, supporting policy and strategy and linked with other appropriate approaches;
- the uniqueness or innovativeness of the approach;
- the extent to which it is measurable.

Deployment refers to the extent to which the vision, methods and procedures have cascaded vertically and horizontally within the organization. Vertical deployment is a measure of the extent to which the key objectives, such as customer focus, have percolated down from top management to lower levels of the organization and horizontal deployment is a measure of the extent to which functional areas other than operations have embraced the quality philosophy, tools, methods and procedures. It is also recommended to analyse whether it is understood and accepted by all stakeholders and is achieving the planned benefits.

Finally, the Assessment and Review dimension looks at the extent to which the approach embodies effective evaluation/ improvement cycles, provides learning opportunities and is benchmarked with others.

Turning to the results criterion, the evaluation system will take into account, among others, the following aspects:

- the degree of coverage (similar to the deployment dimension of the enabler's criteria);
- the existence of positive trends and/or sustained good performance;
- comparisons with own targets;
- indications that negative trends are understood and re-understood and addressed;
- comparisons have been made with external organizations including 'best-in-class' organizations;
- the organization's ability to sustain its performance.

In the Malcolm Baldrige model the system is very similar and thus will not be described here (for details see NIST 2000).

Final remarks

The MBNQA and the EFQM models became very popular over the last decade and made an important contribution to the diffusion of quality principles and practices. They represent a very important effort for identifying and modelling the quality constructs. They both assume that there is a set of CSFs (with minimal differences), but they do not go as far as it would be desirable in showing the interrelationships among the factors and their contribution to BE.

This is in part due to the lack of validation by suitable data. The factor weights of the different criteria are somehow arbitrary and it is difficult to isolate the contribution of each of them to BE. For example, the EFQM Excellence Model assigns a weight of 10 per cent to the Leadership criterion, what has to be considered excessively low, especially when it is recognized that the leadership needs to be directly involved and drive the TQM programmes and initiatives. Likely, the impact of Leadership is widespread over other criteria, but that makes outputs complex to interpret and improvement measures difficult to prioritize.

We strongly believe that the development of a holistic framework incorporating CSFs and validated by suitable data and appropriated statistical methods would help to overcome some of the problems mentioned above.

Total quality management and business excellence models

In 1982, Thomas Peters and Robert Waterman published their best seller '*In Search of Excellence*' that describes the broad, uplifting, and shared culture of 'excellent' companies which charged-up people for appropriate adaptations. BE is about organizational performance, which means how well organizations do *their jobs* (Drucker 1964). Peter Drucker (1964) believed that the two concepts that underlie organizational performance are efficiency (doing things right) and effectiveness (doing the right things).

The EFQM (1999) uses the term to mean outstanding practice in managing organization and achieving results based on fundamental concepts which include: results orientation, customer focus, leadership and constancy of purpose, processes and facts, involvement of people, continuous improvement and innovation, mutually beneficial partnerships, and public responsibility.

Kanji (1998) defines 'business excellence index (BEI) as a means of measuring stakeholder's (customer's, employer's, and shareholder's) satisfaction simultaneously within an organization in order to obtain a comprehensive evaluation of the organizational performance'. Here the indices can be used to determine how well different areas of the organization, that is, leadership, continuous improvement, and others are performing and their contribution towards BE. The index also allows comparison of BE of different organizations and of the same organization over time. For the construction of the BEI, data are collected through a survey using suitable questionnaires. These questionnaires are written specifically for the organization and ensure that as large a picture as possible is gathered about the organization.

The MBNQA was established in 1987 by the United States Department of Commerce in the hope of producing a strong impact on the quality development of American industry. The Award has three specific purposes: (a) to promote quality awareness, (b) to recognize the quality achievements of American companies and (c) to publicize successful quality strategies (NIST 1991). The MBNQA is based on TQM, and sets standards for excellence that are represented by seven dimensions: (a) leadership, (b) strategic planning, (c) customer and market focus, (d) information and analysis, (e) human resource focus, (f) process management and (g) business results (see Figure 3.1). Applicants are screened on the basis of a written application and inspection by a team of examiners who observe operations and interview employees and managers at all levels.

Hogan (1992) has demonstrated that the MBNQA model can be applied to administrative services of institutions of higher education in America. Hogan found that the model is quite comprehensive and therefore needed only one additional variable, that is, quality of financial management, for it to be used as a self-assessment device. The research indicates that leadership is rated as the most applicable category for the evaluation of quality of administrative services in American institutions. This category is followed by customer satisfaction.

The Deming Prize was established by the Japanese Union of Scientists and Engineers to award companies that demonstrate a successful company-wide quality control programme. The criteria for the award fall under categories of (a) policy, (b) organizational structure, (c) education and dissemination, (d) collection, dissemination, and use of information, (e) analysis, (f) standardization, (g) management system, (h) quality assurance, (i) effects and (j) planning for the future (The Conference Board 1991, cited in Hogan 1992).

Saraph *et al.* (1989) have developed a measurement system of measuring CSFs of quality management based on their survey of 162 quality general managers of twenty-two manufacturing and service organizations in Minneapolis–St Paul area in America. Their conclusion is that there exist eight measures for a quality measurement model: top management leadership, role of quality department, training, product design, supplier quality management, process management, quality data reporting, and employee relations.

Parasuraman *et al.* (1988) proposed, a multiple-item scale model called SERVQUAL for measuring customers' perceptions of service quality. The measurement instrument was derived from a survey of several kinds of businesses in America, that is, a bank, a credit-card company, a firm offering appliance repair and maintenance services, and a long-distance telephone company. An empirical analysis of the data collected from these samples generated five service quality dimensions: tangibles (e.g. physical facilities), reliability, responsiveness, assurance (of service to companies), and empathy (attitude toward customers).

Caruana and Pitt (1997) have reported the results of a survey of marketing directors of more than 130 of the largest service firms in the UK. The purpose of the survey was to investigate the relationship between internal service quality and business performance. Two factors were identified from the study, namely, service reliability and management of expectations. These factors collectively affect a firm's overall performance.

Each study provides dimensions of quality that are different in number and in kind. However, consistent with the research work of Hackman and Wagerman (1995), the variety of models derived from those studies were associated with the same underlying assumptions and concepts. Their seemingly different makeups are due to differences in initial starting models from which they were first developed. Furthermore, the components of the models could not have been exactly alike because they were derived by analysing data from different populations.

Model assessment

The models surveyed were assessed against a group of criteria to determine whether they represent a complete BEM. The criteria are:

1 A model must be based on TQM principles, concepts and assumptions.
2 Measurement instruments used are valid and reliable.
3 The model is valid.
4 The model is generic.
5 The model is flexible to accommodate different types of organization.
6 The measurement of model's quality dimensions are performed simultaneously so that the symmetrical relationships among dimensions are demonstrated.
7 The collective contributions of CSFs to organizational excellence or BE.

The survey of existing models indicates that the dimensions and structure of award models have not been validated. Other measurement models incorporate valid and reliable measurement instruments. It is found that only SERVQUAL, INTQUAL, and KBEM demonstrate causal connections between quality dimensions with organizational performance. However, among these four models only Kanji's Business Excellence Model (KBEM) measures the quality of all key organizational areas simultaneously, demonstrates causal connections among them and shows their collective influence on organizational performance. Thus, KBEM provides a potential solution to the task of finding a representative measurement model for various types of organizations.

Towards measuring business excellence

A prelude to measuring BE is elucidating the measurement of TQM process itself. The performances of TQM quality dimensions are usually measured using performance indicators. Odiorne (1997) says that it is possible to manage things for which their performance indicators can be established. Other things for which there are no indicators can be out of control before realizing it.

Many authors believe that performance measurement is essential to TQM (Zairi 1994a; Lynch and Cross 1995; Dixon *et al.* 1990; Geanuracos and Meiklejohn 1993; Hroned 1993; Sowards 1992; Sink 1991; McCamus 1991). Dixon *et al.* (1990) suggest that unless companies adopt their measurement systems to facilitate the introduction of TQM, implementation will fail to reap the expected benefits.

Zairi (1992) suggests that TQM-based performance measures are required for the following reasons:

1 You cannot manage what you cannot measure;
2 To determine what to pay attention to and improve;
3 To provide a 'scoreboard' for people to monitor their own performance levels;
4 To provide an indication of the cost of poor quality;
5 To give a standard for making comparisons;
6 To comply with business objectives.

Zairi (1992) suggests that traditional performance measurement is disadvantageous to management because it only provides information about the organization's past performance but lacks improvement aspect for day-to-day operation. Zairi adds that organizations have not come out with performance measurement systems for TQM, and this has been attributed to:

1 Failure to operationally define performance;
2 Failure to relate performance to process;
3 Failure to define the boundaries of the process;
4 Misunderstood or misused measures;
5 Failure to distinguish between control and improvement measures;
6 Measuring the wrong things;
7 Misunderstood or misused information by managers;
8 Fear of distorting performance priorities;
9 Fear of exposing poor performance;
10 Perceived reduction in authority.

Generally, there are three approaches to measuring organizational performance, that is, financial, non-financial and mixed measures.

Financial measures

In the past, organizations have been preoccupied with financial measures of organizational performance such as management accounting (Chadwick 1991; Kaplan 1984). Many management accounting techniques had been developed during 1920s to the 1980s and had virtually been the only techniques that were widely practised by organizations during that time. Organizations then had the luxury of being in a favourable economic environment and therefore were not anxious to determine their organizational performance in another way. However, Johnson and Kaplan (1987) have pointed out three weaknesses associated with management accounting:

1   Management accounting information is not up-to-date, not detailed enough, and not focused on critical areas.
2   Management accounting information does not provide accurate costs.
3   Management accounting information causes managers to be concerned with short-term cycle of the profit-and-loss statement that consequently results in decisions associated with making short-term profits rather than long-term economic health of a firm.

Johnson and Kaplan add that because of the procedures and cycle of an organization's financial reporting system, management accounting information is too late, too aggregated, and too distorted for use in managerial planning and decision making. Other criticisms have been hurdled against management accounting that spawned the emergence of other costing techniques such as activity-based costing (Cooper and Kaplan 1998). These too were proven to be inadequate and the need for searching alternative performance measures prevailed. As such, there is a need to develop an appropriate performance measure of TQM process that is not accounting-based.

Non-financial measures

The shortcomings of financial measures have led to process or functional measures. Today, these measures are widely used at departmental levels of organizations where processes take place. The use of non-financial indicators is well accepted in the monitoring and control of process aspects of manufacturing industry (Smith 1990). Many performance measurements of service areas have been adapted from measures used in manufacturing areas. These are, for example, measures of productivity (Gass *et al.* 1987), quality (Graves 1987; Parasuraman *et al.* 1991; Saraph *et al.* 1989), and customer satisfaction (Bergendahl and Wactmeister 1993; Fornell 1994; Kristensen *et al.* 1999).

There has been a varied view on what constitutes a measurement system of organizational processes. Zairi (1994*a*), Hroned (1993) and Bendel *et al.* (1993) believe that process measurements should be derived from internal and customer requirements. According to Sink (1991), process measurement is concerned with five 'quality checkpoints': selection and management of upstream systems; incoming quality assurance; in-process quality management and assurance; outgoing quality assurance; and proactive assurance that an organization is meeting or exceeding customer requirements. Consequently, Sink suggests seven performance criteria of a process: effectiveness, efficiency, quality, productivity, quality of work life, innovation, and profitability/budgetability. Sowards (1992) states that measurement of key result areas, those activities that are critical to the success of an organization, is a basic requirement of quality improvement.

Mixed measures

According to Kaplan and Norton (1992), there is no single measure that can provide a clear performance on the critical areas of the business. Managers would want a balanced presentation of both financial and operational measures. Kaplan and Norton introduced a 'Balanced Scorecard (BSC)' of measures along four dimensions: financial perspective, customer perspective, internal business perspective, and innovation and learning perspective. Ridgeway (1956) says that concentration on a single measure of performance would be dysfunctional because it leads to maximization of that measure to the detriment of overall performance. The notion of a mixed measure of organizational performance is also supported by authors such as Sellenheim (1991), Howell and Soucy (1987*a*,*b*; 1988) and Grady (1991). Grady charges that performance measures need to be balanced, that is, internal measures and external benchmarks, cost and non-cost measures, result measures to assess the degree to which goals are achieved, and process measures to evaluate critical tasks and provide early feedback.

The need for a comprehensive measurement system (encompassing financial and non-financial measures) that is adaptable to changes in internal and external environments of organizations is inevitable. Grady (1991) says that strategies change from time to time, and performance measures must keep pace with these changes. Dixon *et al.* (1990) state that the goal of the measurement system is not only to conform to evolving actions and strategies, but also to nurture it. In other words, the measurement system itself should help the firm adapt to changes in the competitive environment. Eccles (1991) believes that because of the prevailing dissatisfaction with conventional measurement systems coupled with the emergence of new management approaches such as TQM, and rigid quality requirements specified by manufacturers on their suppliers, there is a renewed interest on the subject of performance measurement. Eccles adds that every company will have to redesign, within the next five years, the way they measure their business performance.

Integrating TQM and BE measures

The performance of an organization can be regarded as the interface between TQM and BE. BE is a potent concept in that it is a collective measure of key organizational areas that are symmetrically related. As Kanji (1998*b*) puts it, BEI is the simultaneous measure of stakeholders' satisfaction within an organization in order to obtain a comprehensive evaluation of the organizational performance. Only two models explicitly incorporate the concept of excellence. They are the EFQM Excellence Model (EFQM 1999) and KBEM (Kanji 1998*b*).

The EFQM is a membership-based, non-profit organization, created in 1988 by fourteen leading European businesses, with a mission to be the driving force for sustainable excellence in Europe and a vision of a world in which European organizations excel. The EFQM Excellence Model is a non-prescriptive framework based on nine criteria. Five of these are 'Enablers' and four 'Results'. The Enablers are (a) leadership, (b) people, (c) policy and strategy, (d) partnerships and resources and (e) processes. The 'Enablers' criteria cover what an organization does. The Results are: (a) people results, (b) customer results, (c) society results and (d) key performance areas. The 'Results' criteria cover what an organization achieves. 'Results' are caused by 'Enablers'. The structure of the EFQM model is given in Figure 1.13.

To measure the various criteria in the model, a scorecard named the RADAR-scoring matrix is used whereby weights are given to the nine criteria. Each criterion is broken down into sub-criteria that are scored by the assessors during their visits to organizations where they observe operations and interview managers. The scoring of sub-criteria is based on an anchored rating system where attributes of the enablers and the results are evaluated against a group of descriptions of quality.

Kanji (1998*b*) has proposed a BEM that is capable of measuring an organization's CSFs and BE. The BEM includes a measurement instrument that obtains scores for indicators for each CSF and BE. The scores are then analysed using the partial least squares (PLSs) method to establish whether there exist structural relationships among CSFs and BE in the model. If structural relationships are evident then the strength of causal connections associated with the relationships are determined. Indices are determined for the CSFs and BE that denote organizational performance. The indices can be used to assess the performance of each CSF and BE at any point in time as well as over a certain time period, as well as compare the organization's performance with other similar organizations. An organization will be concerned with CSFs that have low performances so that they can be examined in detail and improved. The indices provide information to monitor organizational performance over time and make comparisons with other organizations.

Kanji's Business Excellence Model

As discussed earlier, KBEM offers a prospect for providing a good measure of the TQM processes in various organizations because it satisfies the modelling criteria.

KBEM is made up of a prime factor, that is, leadership, that directly influences four principles: delight the customer, management by fact, people-based management; and continuous improvement. Each principle, in turn, directly influences two core concepts: internal customer satisfaction and external customer satisfaction; all work is process and measurement; people make quality and teamwork; and continuous improvement cycle and prevention as shown in Figure 1.8. The model culminates in BE, which according to the model structure, is the simultaneous measure of the contributions of prime, principles, and core concepts towards BE (See Figure 2.1).

Leadership

Kanji says that an organization has to be guided through the TQM principles and core concepts by top management leadership in order to achieve BE. Thus, leadership is regarded as the 'prime' in the BEM. Deming's perspective of a leader is one who assumes that workers aim to do the best job they can, and endeavour to help workers reach their full potential (Deming 1982). For lower-level managers, this entails coaching and arranging for training. Top managers must, in turn, help design and implement a strategic vision that grounds a TQM culture, and make sure their own behaviour exhibits the values that support such a culture.

Delight the customer

According to Kanji, delighting the customer means being best at what matters to customers, and this changes over time. A customer might experience various degrees of satisfaction. If the product's performance falls short of expectations, the customer is not satisfied. If performance exceeds expectation, the customer is highly satisfied or delighted (Kotler and Armstrong 1996). An *only* satisfied customer will still find it easy to switch suppliers when a better offer comes along. A study at AT&T shows that 70 per cent of customers who say they are satisfied with a product or service will still be willing to switch to a competitor (Kotler and Armstrong 1996). In contrast, a customer who is highly satisfied is much less ready to switch. Another study shows that 75 per cent of Toyota buyers were highly satisfied and about 75 per cent said that they intended to buy Toyota again. Customer delight creates an emotional affinity for a product or service, not just rational preference, and this creates high customer loyalty. Creating customer loyalty means reduction of customer defection, which will increase profits by way of excluding the costs that would have been incurred on activities needed to attract new customers.

People-based management

According to Kanji, people need to be equipped with the knowledge and skills for the job, and informed about how they are doing so that they become encouraged and responsible with their jobs. People will become committed with their jobs if they are involved and committed to customer satisfaction. The principle of TQM recognizes that systems, standards and technology themselves will not mean quality, therefore the role of people is vital.

Juran derived the term internal customers for organizational employees who form 'customer–supplier' relationships among them. Each upstream customer had specifications that needed to be met by downstream suppliers and all these internal customers were working towards external customer satisfaction. Process analysis will therefore help to satisfy external customers by making the internal organization more effective. This conceptual way of looking at employees and their task dependence is consistent with the notion of machine metaphor by Morgan (1988).

Continuous improvement

Kanji says that total quality is not a quick fix or a short-term goal that is consummated when a target has been met. Total quality is not a programme or a project. It is a management process that recognizes that, no matter how much improvement a company makes, its competitors will continue to improve and its customers expect more from it. Continuous improvement of customer-driven activities and processes is a basic philosophy that underlies customer satisfaction (McNair and Leibfried 1992).

Management by fact

Kanji says that knowing the current performance levels of the products or services in the customers' hands and of all employees is the first stage of being able to improve. If an organization knows where it is starting from, it can measure its improvement. Having the facts necessary to manage business at all levels is a principle of total quality. Giving the facts to people so that decisions are based upon facts rather than 'gut feelings' is essential for continuous improvement.

Dahlgaard *et al.* (1997) state that one of the principles underlying BE is a focus on facts. They add that there are six fundamental principles of BE: continuous improvement, commitment to creativity, customer focus, commitment to continuous learning, empowerment and participation of all staff, and a focus on all facts. The dependence on facts for outstanding practice and achieving results is included in the EFQM's definition of excellence. The General Accounting Office found that one of the common factors leading to performance improvement from TQM was the use of 'fact-based decision-making'. This suggests that TQM systems must be based on a continuous and systematic approach of gathering, evaluation and acting on facts and data.

Internal customer satisfaction

The definition of quality (i.e. 'satisfying agreed customer requirements') equally concerns both internal and external customers. Many writers refer to the customer–supplier chain and the need to get the internal relationships working in order to satisfy the external customer. Whatever is being supplied – information, products or services – to people in the organization depends on their internal customers for quality work. Their requirements are as real as those of external customers – they may be speed, accuracy or measurement. The concept of 'internal customers' is one of the 'big ideas' of TQM. Making the most of it can be time consuming and many of the structured approaches take a long time and can be complicated. However, one successful approach includes taking the 'cost of quality' (see Kristensen *et al.* 1993*b*) to obtain information about the organization's performance and analyse it.

The maximum employee support of TQM efforts has been acknowledged by many TQM writers (Deming 1986; Crosby 1979; Clemmer 1990; Oakland 1993*b*; Kanji 1995; Blackburn and Rosen 1993). Focus on processes and internal customer–supplier relationship and their management has been widely documented by TQM authors, since TQM revolves around effectively managing processes to continually satisfy customers (see, e.g. Kanji 1995; Snee 1993; Oakland 1993*b*; Zairi 1994*a*).

External customer satisfaction

Many companies, when they begin quality improvement processes, become very introspective and concentrate on their own internal problems almost at the expense of their external customers. Other companies, particularly in the service sector, have gone out to their customers to survey what is important to them, and then to measure their own performance against customer targets (Kristensen *et al.* 1993*a*). The idea of asking one's customers to set customer satisfaction goals is a clear sign of an outward-looking company. An understanding of survey and statistical methods is needed for the measurement of customer satisfaction. Other tools that are used in tracking customer satisfaction include customer complaint and suggestion schemes, ghost shopping and lost-customer analysis (Kotler and Armstrong 1996).

All work is process

Business process is another internal focus for continuous improvement. The term process means any relationship, such as billing customers or issuing credit notes, that has an input, steps to follow, and output. A process is a combination of methods, materials, manpower, machinery, etc., which taken together produce a product or service. All processes contain inherent variability and one approach to quality improvement is to progressively reduce variation, first by removing variation due to special causes and then by driving down common cause variation, thus bringing the process under control and then improving its capability. Various statistical methods (e.g. histograms, Pareto analysis, control, charts, scatter diagram) are widely used by quality managers and others for process improvement purposes (Kanji and Asher 1993).

Measurement

Having a measurement of how we are doing is the first stage of being able to improve. Measures can focus internally, that is, on internal customer satisfaction (Kristensen *et al.* 1993*a*), or externally, that is, on meeting external customer requirements. Kristensen *et al.* (1993*a*) when discussing a measurement of customer satisfaction, have used the usual guidelines for questionnaire design, survey and statistical analysis to obtain the customer satisfaction index.

Teamwork

Teamwork can provide an opportunity for people to work together in the pursuit of total quality in ways in which they have not worked together before. People who work on their own, small, discrete, workgroups often have a picture of their organization and the work that is very much compartmentalized. They are often unaware of the work that is done even by people who work very close to them. Under these circumstances, they are usually unaware of the consequences of poor quality in the work they themselves do. If people are brought together in terms of a common goal, quality improvement becomes easier to communicate over departmental or functional walls. In this way, the slow breaking down of barriers acts as a platform for change. Teamwork can be improved by benchmarking, a method which is similar to the statistical understanding of outliers.

People make quality

Deming states that the majority of quality-related problems within an organization are not within the control of the individual employee. As many as 85 per cent of these problems are caused by the way the company is organized and managed. Examples of where the system gets in the way of people trying to do a good job is easy to find, and in all cases simply telling employees to do better will not solve the problem. Exhorting employees to a higher level of performance (e.g. by poster campaigns) can have a counter-productive effect when people see that management fails to tackle the real problem. In these circumstances, motivation alone cannot work. People can only become committed to quality through the practical efforts of managers to remove the barriers to quality improvement.

The continuous improvement cycle

The continuous improvement cycle of establishing customer requirements, meeting those requirements, measuring success and keeping up improvement can be used both internally and externally to fuel the engine of external and continuous improvement. By continually checking customers' requirements, a company can find areas in which improvements can be made. This continual supply of opportunity can be used to keep improvement plans up-to-date and reinforce the idea that the total quality journey is never-ending. In order to practice the continuous improvement cycle, it is necessary to obtain information about customers' requirements continuously by market research. However, market research requires deeper statistical understanding for the proper analysis of the market.

Prevention

The core concept of prevention is central to TQM and one way to move towards continuous improvement. Prevention means causing problems not to happen. The continual process of driving possible failure out of the system can breed a culture of continuous improvement over time. There are two different ways of approaching this. The first is to concentrate on the design of the product itself; the second is to work on the production process. However, the most important aspect of prevention is quality by design, using statistical reasoning.

There are several frequently used tools that help to focus thoughts here. Failure Mode and Effect Analysis (FMEA) is one of the better-known ones. It is associated with both design (design FMEA) and process (process FMEA). The advantage of all these methods is that they provide a structure of thought process for carrying the work through.

Business excellence

BE is a measure of customer's, employer's, and shareholder's (stakeholder's) satisfaction simultaneously within an organization in order to obtain a comprehensive evaluation of the organizational performance (Kanji 1998*b*).

Stakeholders

Stakeholders are the raison d'être of every organization that adopts the TQM philosophy. Stoner *et al.* (1995) define stakeholders as those groups or individuals who are directly or indirectly affected by an organization's pursuit of its goals (e.g. suppliers and customers). Stakeholders can be divided into two groups: internal stakeholders and external stakeholders. Internal stakeholders are those that are strictly part of an organization's environment but for whom an individual manager remains responsible (e.g. employees, shareholders, and board of directors). External stakeholders are those in an organization's external environment who affect the activities of the organization (e.g. unions, suppliers, competitors, customers, and governmental agencies).

Reavil (1998) refers to the stakeholders of higher education as those who pay for or contribute to the organization or benefit from it. There are at least ten stakeholders or stakeholder groups of higher education, namely:

1   Student: The direct beneficiary of the transformation process. A customer in both service and SSM models. The student funds the process, directly or indirectly.
2   Employer: An indirect beneficiary of the process who needs trained staff, and is willing to pay for them.
3   Family and dependants of the students: This puts together the parents of the younger student, and the dependants of the mature student. Both may be contributing, directly or in kind, to the cost of the process.
4   Universities and their employees: Another conglomerate that includes the university as an entity, and those employees for whom it provides a livelihood.
5   The suppliers of the goods and services to universities: The continued viability of the university is important to organizations that regard it as a customer.
6   The secondary-education sector: Supplier of the human input to the university system.
7   Other universities: These are present in the greater system of interest and are essentially competitors to the university. This is particularly valid currently.
8   Commerce and industry: These are the beneficiaries, but indirectly. The activities of the higher-education sector add to the pool of trained staff.
9   The nation, as represented by government: It is generally accepted that education at whatever level is a major benefit to a nation's prosperity.
10 Taxpayers, national and local: If the nation is the general beneficiary of the output of higher education, the taxpayer pays the bill, by either national or local taxes.

Critical success factors for business excellence

Definition of critical success factors

CSFs are those few things that must go well to ensure the success for a manager or an organization. They represent those managerial areas that must be given special and continuous attention to cause high performance (Boynton and Zmud 1984).

Rockart (1982) defined CSFs as those few areas of activity in which favourable results are necessary for a particular manager to reach his or her goals. As for business, Rockart (1979, cited in Leidecker and Bruno 1984) specified that CSFs are the limited number of areas in which results, if they are satisfactory, will ensure successful competitive performance for the organization. They are the few areas where 'things must go right' for the business to flourish. If results in these areas are not adequate, the organization's efforts for the period will be less than defined.

Hofer and Schendel (cited in Leidecker and Bruno 1984) defined CSFs as those variables that management can influence through its decisions that can affect significantly the overall competitive positions of the various firms in an industry. These factors usually vary from industry to industry; however, they are derived from the interaction of two sets of variables, namely, the economical and technological characteristics. They are also conceived from the competitive weapons on which the various firms in the industry have built their strategies.

Jenster (1987) said that CSFs relate to the basic internal and external conditions for the firm's strategy (e.g. customer acceptance, competitive moves), or those competencies and resources (e.g. human, financial) it must attain. Recent research has expanded this notion into a more comprehensive and strategic concept, suggesting that the definition and monitoring of CSFs differ for various strategy types (Jenster 1987).

Ferguson and Dickinson (1982) defined CSFs as factors outside or inside the company that must be identified and reckoned with because they support or threaten the achievement of a company's objectives, or even the existence of the company. They may be positive or negative in their impact on the company.

Development of critical success factors

Daniel (1961, cited in Leidecker and Bruno 1984) first discussed CSFs in an article in the early 1960s. The concept received little attention until a decade later, when Anthony, Dearden, and Vancil (1972, cited in Leidecker and Bruno 1984) utilized the concept in the design of a management control system. The procedure for identifying personnel and organizational factors that can lead to effective and successful performance is called the CSF method (Burello and Zadnik 1986). Burello and Zadnik acknowledged Daniel (1961) as the researcher who pioneered the use of CSF method. The method was to systematically identify the critical information needs of managers. Rockart (1979, cited in Burello and Zadnik 1986) popularized the method when he used it to define the critical areas necessary for successful performance of the information specialist.

Traditionally, CSF method has been applied in business and industrial environments. The areas that have benefited from it are: business process management; planning (Jenster 1987; Schneier *et al.* 1992); IS (Rockart 1982); new product development (Cooper and Kleinschmeidt 1995); library management (Borbely 1981); and new service development (Atuahene-Gima 1996).

Research on critical success factors

Dervitsiotis (1995) introduced the Objective Matrix Model (OMAX) to facilitate the framework for quality assessment and improvement in education. The important tasks of OMAX include:

- Translating strategy objectives to CSFs.
- Determining weights that prioritize strategy objectives.
- Defining appropriate measurement scales for performance related to CSFs, in physical, economic or other units.
- Calculating a performance indicator that combines all weighted values for the individual measurements for the CSFs.

In his research on a business school at University of Pireaus, Greece, the following CSFs were identified:

- An effective policy for the recruitment and admissions of students.
- A solid academic curriculum receptive to innovations that keep it adaptable and current.
- A high calibre of teaching and research staff.
- The necessary facilities for classrooms, library, computer and other laboratories, etc.
- A programme of relevant applied research projects appealing to internal and external customers.
- Job opportunities available to graduates through cooperation programmes with business and industry.
- Available opportunities for cooperation and exchanges with other universities through well-developed networks for teaching staff and students.

Such a selection of CFSs was based on the assumption that the quality of the output (the graduates) depends on the quality of the input (students selected by admission policy) and the quality of the process (curriculum, teaching, research, etc). Each CSF of the institution is assessed based on a string of criteria for quality. Each criterion is weighted and its score was determined say for a particular department. The product of the weight and scores gives the weighted score for that criterion. The overall performance indicator, which is the sum of the weighted scores for all criteria, reflects the policy for a given CSF. According to Dervitsiotis, the OMAX is a versatile approach that can be scaled up to include larger parts or the entire organization. Conversely, it may be scaled down to focus on more detailed processes or smaller organizational units.

At Oregon State University (OSU) the TQM processes were made up of several phases (Coate 1993). One of the phases was the Breakthrough Planning Phase, which was the fourth phase in the OSU TQM model. The highlight of this phase is that the critical processes are identified. OSU believed this step was essential to accomplish the university's mission and laid foundation to TQM processes.

Identification of critical success factors

In integrating TQM into the strategy of the business, Oakland (1993 *a,b*) suggested that the mission already developed is changed into its CSFs to coerce and move it forward. Top managers are responsible for listing the CSFs. In this way they gain some understanding of what the mission or the change requires. As with the CSFs, each process necessary for a given CSF must be identified, and together the processes listed must be sufficient for the CSFs to be accomplished.

CSFs have been instrumental in various organizational processes. The identification of CSFs is a very important step in the application process. The identification of CSFs provides a means by which an organization can assess threats and opportunities in its environment (Leidecker and Bruno 1984). CSFs also provide a set of criteria for an assessment of strengths and weaknesses of the firm.

According to Ferguson and Dickinson (1982), CSFs are particularly significant to the board of directors of companies. They believed that finding a way to identify a successfully functioning board of directors depended on identifying CSFs for the company and dealing with them from the perspective of the 'outside director'. Identification of CSFs can be through evaluation of corporate strategy, environment, resources, operations, and other similar areas. Four such CSFs for the 1980's were: coping with inflation, ensuring the adequacy of financial and managerial resources, finding and keeping competitive position and strategic development. Anthony *et al.* (1976) pointed out that the management control system, besides measuring profitability, identifies certain key variables (also strategic factors, key success factors (KSFs), key result areas and pulse points) that significantly impact profitability. Hofer and Schendel (1979, cited in Leidecker and Bruno 1984) argued that CSFs are obvious, easily identified through a combination of sensitivity and elasticity analysis; they contend that the major problem is in assessing the relative importance.

According to Leidecker and Bruno, while sensitivity and elasticity analyses are useful identification tools, they are not sufficient nor are they the only useful methods for identifying a CSF. The concept of CSFs has been applied at three levels of analysis (firm-specific, industry, and the economic and socio-political environment). Analysis at each level provides a source of potential CSFs. Firm-specific analysis utilizes an internal focus to provide the link to possible factors. Industry-level analysis focuses on certain factors in the basic structure of the industry that significantly have an impact on any company's performance operating in that industry. A third level of analysis goes beyond industry boundaries for the source of CSFs. This school of thought argues that one needs to perpetually scan the environment (economic and socio-political) to provide sources that will be the determinants of a firm's or industry's success.

Identification of CSFs can be an important element in the eventual development of a firm's strategy as well as an integral part of the strategic planning process (Leidecker and Bruno 1984). CSF analysis can aid strategy development process at three specific junctures. The three are: environmental analysis, resource analysis and strategy evaluation. Eight techniques for identifying CSFs are set forth below:

1　Environmental analysis.
2　Analysis of industry structure.
3　Industry business experts.
4　Analysis of competition.
5　Analysis of the dominant firm in the industry.
6　Company assessment.
7　Temporal/intuitive factors.
8　PIMS results.

Rockart (1979, cited in Schneier *et al.* 1992) advocated the following as sources of CSFs:

- the characteristics of the industry;
- an organization's competitive strategy and industry positioning;
- environmental factors;
- temporal factors.

Borbely (1981) suggested some general categories that should first be considered to identify CSFs for the manager of an information centre. They are:

- general environment of the parent organization;
- internal corporate environment;
- information profession;
- information centre.

Applications of critical success factors

As mentioned earlier, traditionally, CSF approach has been applied in business and industry environment. The following are examples of CSF applications.

Business process management

Elzinga *et al.* (1995) observed that many companies are engaged in assessing ways to improve their productivity, product quality, and operations. They found that Business Process Management (BPM) is a new area of such improvements. BPM can be any structured approach used to analyse and continually improve fundamental activities, such as manufacturing, marketing, communications, and other major elements of a company's operation. BPM is a method by which an enterprise's 'Quality' programme (e.g. TQM) is implemented. A part of BPM is the identification of CSFs to enable an enterprise to focus on its vision, mission and goals. The statements of the enterprise's vision, mission and goals are crucial to promulgate and should be made widely known to the enterprise's employees as the guiding principles for the enterprise.

Planning

Jenster (1987) introduced a strategy planning and strategic control process that is tightly integrated with the firm's information system. The method is used for developing, monitoring and integrating critical information into effective strategic management decision support. The CSFs clearly and succinctly communicate critical elements of the strategy to members of the organization. More important, the CSFs direct the attention of key managers to focus on the basic premises of the firm's strategy.

Schneier *et al.* (1992) described how the Performance Measurement and Management (PMM) technique can be used as a tool for strategy execution. This technique describes CSFs as the first step towards strategic execution. These few factors must be executed with excellence to gain and sustain competitive advantage. Once CSFs (or driving forces or core competencies) have been identified, the next step in PMM is to develop performance measures for the CSFs. CSFs indicate to the firm what has to be done to achieve goals. Performance measures determine how well the firm must perform and whether it has been successful.

Many authors suggest that CSFs can be used in an organization's planning function. In addition, they can be used in developing strategic plans, implementing a plan, helping managers achieve high performance, managing resources and monitoring a corporation's activities (Ferguson and Dickinson 1984).

Information systems (I/S)

Rockart (1982) summarized the CSFs of nine companies based on interviews performed on their information system executives. The companies varied from manufacturing, airline, bank, and railroad. He managed to profile the new I/S executive role focusing on three aspects. The aspects are their CSFs, the key techniques and processes they use to manage critical areas and their common individual attributes. The case studies summarized in Rockart's research suggest a generic set of role-related CSFs for I/S executives, namely, service CSFs, communication CSFs, I/S human resources, and repositioning the I/S function.

Yang (1996) conducted a research on information management to identify the key issues confronting managers and developers of information systems for Taiwanese companies. By way of a questionnaire survey and its analysis he derived several key issues that he aggregated into seven higher factors. The key issues were ranked and rated and the rankings were compared with a previous survey and recent surveys in the US. The initial issues for use as input to the questionnaire were identified from the literature.

New product development

Cooper and Kleinschmidt (1995), who studied new product development of firms, focused on five areas: process, organization, strategy, culture, and commitment. The firms were selected from a private list of companies compiled from databases and directories of companies known to be active in new product development in Europe and North America. The study was performed on 161 business units, and questionnaires were directed to corporate executives responsible for new product development effort. The study uncovered key drivers of new product performance at the business unit level. Some of the business units studied boasted superb performance; others had a more mediocre new product track record. By benchmarking against the good and the bad, Cooper and Kleinschmidt were able to obtain much greater insight into the factors and practices that really discriminate between the top and the poorer performers.

Variations of generic critical success factors

From his survey of nine companies on their CSFs, Rockart (1982) found that there is a generic set of CSFs. Even so, Rockart observed that some of the identified model CSFs were absent from individual company lists. This variation suggests that any particular head I/S should not expect to have exactly the same four CSFs that are described in the generic set of I/S CSFs. In this study, the variation in actual CSFs was because of four reasons: the stage of development of the I/S organizations; the recent organization history of the I/S function; the human, organization and makeup of a company; and the perspective of 'world view' that the I/S executive had on the field and on his role in his company.

Hofer and Schendel (1979) said that CSFs vary from industry to industry. The CSFs within any particular industry are derived from the interaction of two sets of variables, namely, the economic and technological characteristics of the industry involved. The competitive weapons on which the firms in the industry have built their strategies are also a source of CSFs.

CSFs vary across industries (Hofer and Schendel 1979; Leidecker and Bruno 1984, cited in Sabherwal and Kirs 1994). For instance, in the 1970s the CSFs of an automobile industry were efficiency of dealer organization, manufacturing cost control and the ability to meet energy standards. During the same time, the process R&D and the ability to assure a steady supply of inputs were considered the CSFs for cement industry.

Critical success factors and their measurements

Schneier *et al.* (1992) said, in the context of the performance measurement management method, that once CSFs (or driving forces or core competencies) have been identified, performance measures for the CSFs can be developed.

Jenster (1987) said that CSFs can be used as the basis for identifying the strategic performance indicators (SPIs) (Jenster 1987). The indicators can be used in measuring short-term progress towards the long-term objectives. They must strive to satisfy six specifications. They should be operational, indicative of desired performance, acceptable to subordinates, reliable, timely and simple.

Leidecker and Bruno (1984) said that the profit impact of an activity or condition is usually the most significant factor for CSFs identification as well as a determination of factor importance. The authors suggested four starting points for profit impact analysis that will assist in the determination of degree of importance of CSFs. They were: major activity of the business, large dollars involved, major profit impact and major changes in performance. In most cases, the type of company or the nature of the industry will determine which CSFs are important. For example, the success of a retail business is greatly influenced by factors such as store location, effectiveness of the merchandizing and inventory control. The wholesaler(s) selling to the same retailer would not expect a CSF to location oriented.

Rockart (1982) said, about his survey on several companies, that for service CSFs, the most important approaches in these companies involve not only techniques for the actual delivery of service but also several service techniques that focus on measuring user perception of service delivery. These measurement devices varied. They include: a daily 'sign-off' inquiry presented to each online terminal user; monthly, quarterly or annual surveys of user opinion through internally generated questionnaires; and in one case, a structured set of interviews administered by an outside consultant organization. According to Rockart, based on the survey results, it appears that there are four CSFs for I/S executives of companies studied: service, communication, I/S human factors, and repositioning the I/S function.

Yang's (1996) study on Taiwanese companies on key issues in information management concluded that there are seven aggregated factors underlying information management for I/S managers and developers in Taiwan. They are:

- strategic planning, organization and communication;
- information regulations and laws;
- information technology (IT) applications;
- software and hardware environments;
- I/S productivity and quality;
- new integrated IT;
- data management.

Udo and Ehie (1996) reported on their study on advanced manufacturing systems (AMS) in several US companies. They concluded that there are four factors affecting the benefits of AMS, namely, triple 'C' (communication, commitment, and coordination) factors, self-interest factors, housekeeping factors and literacy factors. There were ten tangible and fifteen intangible benefits identified based on the literature.

Burello and Zadnik (1986) collected a substantial amount of data from his research on CSFs of local special education administrators in the US. Data analysis revealed that the effective sample of administrators valued the importance of fourteen CSFs with respect to their impact on personal and organizational success more than the random respondents did. The effective respondent group was more intimate and sensitive to power structure and politics of the system and that it combined this awareness with technical knowledge and expertise to influence approval of proposals and ideas that benefited special education. Multiple-district programme respondents felt the CSFs were more difficult with which to achieve success than did the single-district representatives. The analysis revealed little significant differences among CSFs for the respondent variables of setting and size.

Cooper and Kleinschmidt (1995) gauged the following performance measures for their study of business in new product development. They are: success rate, percentage of sales by new product, profitability relative to spending, technical success rating, sales impact, profit impact, meeting sales objectives, meeting profit objectives and profitability *versus* competitors. The factors that drive new product success at the project level are strategic forces, development process factors, market environment factors and organizational factors.

Saberwhal and Kirs (1994) provided the profile of the IT capabilities of academic institutions in the US. The IT capabilities are information retrieval, electronic capabilities, student computing facilities, and computer-aided education. The alignment of CSFs to IT capabilities for different groups of academic institutions provides the performance measure of CSFs for the institutions.

The CSFs in the research on information system development for a flexible manufacturing system (FMS) by Gowan and Mathieu (1996) were:

- Simplification of the production process prior to the design of FMS information system.
- Explicit determination of system interface, data and data format requirements and communication network requirements early in the design process.
- A simple, unambiguous method to communicate the requirements and view of the FMS information system design.
- Subsystem development teams formed, based on a horizontal and vertical decomposition of the information system architecture model. Systems specialists and vendors made subservient to the user(s) and/or user representative(s).
- Funding of information system project by project managers on a conventional basis.
- Bottom-up phased-in integration of the information system with the production system.

Rai *et al.* (1996) identified eight CSFs for strategic alliances in the IT industry from a review of the existing literature: partner congruity, partner evaluation, organizational advocacy, governmental policies, organizational issues, cultural concerns, human resource management (HRM) practices, and partner dominance. According to them, since there are no scales to measure, CSFs existed, a consolidated questionnaire composed of different measurement scales and questions was developed. Respondents were asked to indicate the importance of each item in the questionnaire on a Likert scale.

Korpela and Tuominen (1996) suggested using analytic hierarchy process (AHP) as an approach of assessing the importance of CSFs logistic operations. This can be performed by conducting customer interviews, and the performance of the companies included in the analysis is evaluated with regard to each success factor.

Saraph *et al.* (1989) proposed eight critical factors of quality management through a process that involved identification and synthesis of those critical requirements for quality management that have been prescribed by eminent quality practitioners and academics. The process included an exhaustive literature review. These factors are:

- the role of management leadership and quality policy;
- role of quality department;
- training;
- product/service design;
- supplier quality management;
- process management;

- quality data and reporting;
- employee relations.

The authors developed measures of CSFs of quality management based on generally accepted psychological principles of instrument design. Operational measures of these factors were developed using data collected from 162 general managers and quality managers of 89 divisions of 20 companies. The measures can be used individually or in concert to produce a profile of organization-wide practices. Initial selection of measurement items for each critical factor, pre-testing the instrument, and finalization of the measurement items were used to construct the measurement instrument (questionnaire).

Atuahene-Gima (1996) measured several variables based on a survey instrument developed on the basis of the literature to find out the factors affecting innovation performance in manufacturing and services firms in Malaysia. The author found that for new services the five most important factors impacting the performance of new services are: importance accorded to innovation activity in human resource strategy, management support and teamwork, service innovation advantage/quality, proficiency of market launching activity, marketing synergy and technological synergy.

Powell (1995) developed a TQM measurement scale based on an exhaustive review of the TQM literature, and revised this scale through repeated discussions and site visits with consultants and quality executives. The TQM factors are executive commitment, adopting the philosophy, closer to customers, closer to suppliers, benchmarking, training, open organization, employee empowerment, zero-defect mentality, flexible manufacturing, process improvement and measurement. The TQM performance was represented by financial performance measured subjectively using five questionnaire items.

CSFs were also the basis for identifying the SPIs that Jenster (1987) used in measuring the short-term progress towards the long-term objectives. According to Jenster, strategic performance indicators must strive to satisfy six specifications. They should be operational, indicative of desired performance, acceptable to subordinates, reliable, timely and simple.

This chapter discussed the understanding of BEMs and various pitfalls. In BEMs the leadership plays the vital role and therefore it is important to explain the 'prime', that is, Leadership excellence, in the following chapter.

4 Leadership is prime

Introduction

In Kanji's Business Excellence Model (KBEM) (Kanji 1998*b*) leadership plays the prime role for the creation of excellence in an organization. In this chapter, we investigate why leadership is the prime and how leadership excellence converges from the core values of the organization.

In order to do so, we start by discussing the concept of leadership and reviewing the main theories developed in its study. Then, we identify the fundamental competencies of leaders in a quality organization. Supported by an extensive literature review, we propose a structural equation model for leadership. To illustrate its application, we present a simplified example. Given the criticality of leadership, the emergence of a model that expands the understanding of the leadership construct and its measurement is of the major importance for organizations to pursue Business Excellence (BE). The purpose of this chapter is to make a significant contribution in this regard and open the debate to further discussions and refinements.

The concept of leadership

While leadership has been of interest to society for thousands of years (discussed in Greek and Latin classics, the Old and New Testaments of the Bible, and writings of ancient Chinese philosophers), the scientific study of leadership began in the early part of the twentieth century. Over the last decades, in particular, there has been an extensive research on leadership.

A review of the literature suggests that there are almost as many different definitions of leadership as there are researchers who have attempted to define the concept (Bass 1990, cited in Kakabadse and Kakabadse 1997). It has been defined in terms of individual personality traits, leader behaviours, responses to leader behaviours, interpersonal exchange relationships, interaction patterns, role relationships, follower perceptions, task goals, organizational culture, and nature of work processes (Yukl 1989, cited in Mello 1999).

The origins of the concept appear to be found in folk psychology when it was used to explain social influence on groups (Andrews and Field 1998).

Du Brin (1995, cited in Shriberg *et al.* 1997, p. 4) conducted an exhaustive literature review on the matter and found five representative definitions of the concept:

- Interpersonal influence directed through communication, towards goal achievement
- The influential increment over and above mechanical compliance with directions
- An act that causes others to act or respond in a shared direction
- The art of influencing people by persuasion
- The principal dynamic force that motivates and coordinates the organization in the accomplishment of its objectives.

From the proposed definitions, it may be easily argued that leadership inevitably comprises an influential component.

After this review, Du Brin adopted the view that leadership is the ability to inspire confidence and support among people who are needed to achieve organizational goals.

Northouse (1997: 3) defines leadership as 'a process whereby an individual influences a group of individuals to achieve a common goal' and emphasizes that viewing leadership as a process has the advantage of focusing attention on the transactional and interactive event that occurs between the leader and his/her followers.

If traditionally the study of leadership was clearly focused on the study of the leader, recently there has been growing evidence that leadership does not exist separate to follower perceptions (Andrews and Field 1998).

This reality is reflected in the way Bass (1990, cited in Andrews and Field 1998) sees leadership as 'an interaction between two or more members of a group that often involves a structuring and restructuring of the situations and the perceptions and expectations of the members'.

The way followers regard their leaders will depend upon the leadership prototypes that they will have in mind. Lord (1985, cited in Andrews and Field 1998) presented a model in which leadership perceptions derive from two processes: recognition (identification of traits and behaviours in conformance to existing notions of leadership) and inference (based on particular outcomes).

Leadership vs management

Another debate concerns the distinction between leadership and management, or more particularly, between leaders and managers. There is no ultimate agreement among researchers. For some, the distinction (if exists) is not important at all. According to them, there is a considerable amount of overlap between the two concepts, although for the most the distinction tends to focus on somehow different purposes associated with the roles of managers and leaders.

According to Fayol's perspective, which still holds for many, managers are responsible for: organizing, planning, directing, commanding, and controlling (Shriberg *et al.* 1997: 96). From this standpoint, leadership, essentially concerned with setting direction, is an element of management and, thus, one of the many competencies that a manager should develop.

Bennis and Nannus (1985: 21, cited in Northouse 1997) state that 'management controls, arranges, does things right; leadership unleashes energy, sets the vision, does the right thing'. This view is shared by Kotter (1990) when he states that the overriding function of management is to provide order and consistency to organizations, whereas the primary function of leadership is to produce change and movement. Furthermore, he points out that management and leadership are two distinctive and complementary systems of action.

Traditional leadership approaches

Many leadership theories may be classified into three dominant leadership approaches, namely, traits approach, behavioural approach and situational/contingency approach. Individually, each approach provides valuable insights and has its own limitations. Collectively, the approaches discussed in this section give a multifaceted view of leadership.

Traits approach

Originated in the early 1990s, the traits approach was one of the first attempts to study leadership.

Briefly, the traits perspective sees leadership as a quality which is inherent in particular persons. Therefore, this approach takes a very definitive side on the debate concerning whether leaders are born or can be created.

The theories developed within this approach are sometimes called 'great man' theories because they focused on identifying those innate qualities possessed by great social, political and military leaders (Northouse 1997).

Traits theories were largely developed to try to predict whether an individual would manifest leadership abilities.

Typically, the characteristics of 'great leaders' include (Stogdill 1948, 1974 (cited in Northouse 1997: 14–15); Shriberg *et al.* 1997):

- Intelligence, including judgement and verbal ability
- Alertness
- Insight
- Emotional stability and maturity
- Initiative
- Strong achievement drive and persistence
- Self-confidence
- Sociability
- Originality in problem solving
- Readiness to absorb stress and willingness to tolerate frustration and delay
- Integrity

Table 4.1 Traits approach in brief

Fundamental assumption	There are certain individuals who have innate characteristics that make them leaders, and distinguish them from non-leaders
Main findings	Intelligence, self-confidence, determination, integrity, sociability are the main leadership traits
Measurement instrument	Personality assessment instruments (such as the Leadership Trait Questionnaire and the Minnesota Multi-phase Personality Inventory), which measure individuals' traits and point out areas of strength and weaknesses
Strengths	Intuitively appealing Breadth and depth of studies conducted Highlights the leader component in the leadership process Provides important benchmarks
Criticisms	Failure to identify a definitive person specification for the ideal leader; not conclusive Failure to take situations into account; leadership success is determined only by qualities internal to the leader and assumes that the leadership is environment is not important Methods used in generating the list traits are weak and therefore highly subjective determination of leadership traits Difficulties in measuring traits Ignoring the followers Neglects leadership outcomes, in terms of satisfaction, productivity, etc. Cannot be used for training and development

And the list could be endless. As a matter of fact, this is one of the major drawbacks of the traits approach. It fails to delimit a definitive list of leadership characteristics and the determination of the traits is in itself very subjective. Though much research was done to identify the traits, no clear answer was found with regard to what traits were associated with great leadership.

These criticisms do not mean, however, that the approach is not appealing. It formed the basis of many studies and it provides important benchmarks. Actually, the interest in these theories has enjoyed a resurgence, as the research on charismatic and visionary leadership (also focused on personality characteristics) seems to suggest.

Table 4.1 provides a summary of the main characteristics, strengths and weaknesses associated with the Traits approach.

Behavioural approach

According to this approach, there is a specific set of behaviours which are effective and, once identified, can be taught to others, who may become effective leaders.

The first studies emphasizing the behaviour of the leader (as opposed to the personality characteristics) were conducted at Ohio State University in

the late 1940s, based on the work of Stogdill (1991). Stogdill's research confirmed the idea that leaders' characteristics were indeed an important part
of leadership, but pointed out that situational factors were determinants as
well (Northouse 1997). The findings of Stogdill's surveys indicated that the
traits leaders possess must be relevant to situations in which the leader is
functioning and cannot be viewed in complete isolation.

Ohio State studies led to the understanding of leadership as a set of
behaviours, both task-related (that facilitate goal accomplishment) and
relationship-related (that help subordinates to feel comfortable with each
other, with themselves and with the situation in which they find themselves). These two types of behaviours, were seen as distinct and independent.
Research tended to emphasize that the best form of leadership is high in both
dimensions (Northouse 1997).

Another important contribution to the behavioural approach was given by
the research conducted at the University of Michigan. Two types of leadership behaviours were identified, called as employee orientation (behaviour of
leaders who approach subordinates with a strong human relations emphasis)
and production orientation (behaviour of leaders who stress the technical and
production aspects of a job).

In the 1980s, Blake and Mouton (1984) criticized the view of these types of
behaviours as independent. On the contrary, they argue that these dimensions
are integrally interrelated and when added together are expected to achieve
a certain effect (Northouse 1997). They design a *Managerial Leadership Grid*
based on two factors – concern for production and concern for people –
that can be regarded as similar to the task and relationship behaviours. The
Leadership Grid portrays five major leadership styles.

The model was designed to help managers first identify their current
leadership style and then help them develop the most appropriate style.

The emphasis on followers introduced by the behavioural approach was
expanded during the 1980s through the studies of Bennis, Nannus and Kouzes
and others to include leadership practices of enabling, enlistening, entrusting,
and engaging (Dering 1998).

Table 4.2 presents a brief summary of the research conducted within the
Behavioural approach.

Situational/contingency approach

Research efforts to find a unified understanding of an effective leader style
failed to some extent. The main message of the contingency approach
is that the relationship between leader style and performance is highly
variable. Advocates of this view argue that early leader styles research
failed to reach general conclusions because it failed to take into account
the circumstances within which leadership acts occur (Smith and Peterson
1988).

Table 4.2 Behavioural approach in brief

Fundamental assumption	Effective leadership is related to the way leaders behave
Main findings	A leader's style is composed of primarily two types of behaviours: task and relationship; together they form the core of the leadership process
Measurement instrument	Leadership Description Questionnaire (subordinates are asked to identify the number of times leaders engage in certain type of behaviour) and Leadership Grid Questionnaire
Strengths	Focus of leadership is expanded to include what leaders do and how they act Validation and credibility given by a wide range of studies Heuristic – leaders can assess their actions and determine how they wish to change to improve their leadership style
Criticisms	The association between styles and performance outcomes was not made clear Failure to find a universal style of leadership that could be effective in almost every situation

Situational or contingency approaches focused on the moderating effect that certain situational variables have on the relationship between leader traits and behaviours and outcomes (Mello 1999).

The earliest contingency theory was developed by Fiedler (1967). According to his theory, a leader's effectiveness depends on how well the leader's style fits the context. Within the context of contingency theory, leadership styles (innate) are described as task-motivated or relationship-motivated and situations characterized by assessing three factors (Northouse 1997):

- leader/member relations (degree of confidence, loyalty, and attraction that followers feel for their leader);
- task structure (degree to which the requirements of a task are clearly defined and known, the path to conduct the task has few alternatives, the compliance of the task can be clearly demonstrated and only a limited number of correct solutions to the task exist);
- leader position power (amount of authority a leader has to reward or to punish followers).

Together these three elements determine the 'favourableness' of varied situations; the most favourable being the ones which have good leader/member relations, defined tasks and strong leader position power.

Leader styles were measured using the Least Preferred Co-worker Scale (LPC) which raised many criticisms.

The theory suggests that leaders who are task motivated (low LPC) will be effective in both very favourable and very unfavourable situations; leaders who are relationship motivated (high LPC) will be effective in moderately favourable situations.

Hersey and Blanchard (1993) developed a model stating that leadership is composed of both a directive and supportive dimension, and each has to be applied appropriately in a given situation. They looked at the transactions between leaders and followers in terms of how far the psychological maturity and job experience should be the main factors (prime contingencies) affecting the decisions a leader should make (Georgiades and Macdonell 1998). Situational leadership is based on the assumption that employees' skills and motivation change over time and leaders should change the degree to which they are directive or supportive accordingly. The essence of situational leadership rests on this matching between the leader's style and the needs of subordinates (Northouse 1997).

Directive behaviours assist organizational members in goal achievement through giving directions, establishing goals and methods of evaluation, setting time lines, defining roles and showing how goals are to be achieved. Supportive behaviours, on the other hand, help employees to feel comfortable about themselves, their co-workers and the situation (Northouse 1997).

The appropriateness of each of these behaviours is dependent on the developmental levels of the subordinates, that is, the degree to which they have the competence and commitment necessary to accomplish a given task (Blanchard *et al.* 1985, cited in Northouse 1997). According to the theory, as the level of maturity of the follower increases, the demand for structure facilitation on the part of the leader decreases, as does the need for the leader to provide socio-emotional support.

Leaders need to correctly diagnose where the subordinates are in a given situation and then adapt the leadership style as a result.

Another contingency model was presented by Vroom and Yetton (1973) based on the expectancy theory, exploring the relationship between the leader's style and characteristics of decision problem attributes. The Vroom–Yetton theory describes what leaders should do in certain given circumstances with regard to the level of involvement of followers in making decisions. Following a decision tree that asks about the need for participation, a conclusion can be drawn about how the leader should go about making the decision to be most effective (Horner 1997).

A brief characterization of the situational/contingency approach is given in Table 4.3.

Other models and approaches

Another popular distinction is made between instrumental and charismatic leadership (Graetz 2000; Kets de Vries and Loper 1994; Nadler and Tushman 1990). *Instrumental leadership* is related to organizational design, control and reward, which involves managing environments to create conditions that

Table 4.3 Situational/contingency approach in brief

Fundamental assumption	Different situations demand different kinds of leadership
Main findings	There is no single leadership style effective in all contexts; rather leaders need to adapt their style to subordinates (in Hersey and Blanchard's model) and to the characteristics of each situation, described in terms of leader/member relations, task structure and leader position power (in Fiedler's model)
Measurement instrument	Fieldler's theory uses the LPC to measure the leader style Hersey and Blanchard's model uses questionnaires that describe a set of work-related situations and ask respondents to select their preferred style for each situation from four alternatives
Strengths	Intuitively sensible and appealing Broad scope of application Emergence of a more realistic view of leadership, allowing for the complexity and situational specificity of effectiveness Emphasis on the need for leaders to be flexible (in the case of Hersey and Blanchard's model)
Criticisms	Failure to explain fully why individuals with certain leadership styles are more effective in some situations Difficulties in conceptualizing and operationalizing situational variables LPC does not correlate well with other standard leadership measures and is difficult to complete (it is not intuitive why to measure the own style through the evaluation of another's person style) Bias of the questionnaires that accompany Hersey and Blanchard's model

motivate desired behaviour, while *charismatic leadership* is believed to be crucial for envisaging, empowering, and energizing followers, based on strong interpersonal skills.

Most researchers argue that successful leaders fulfil the two roles. It is the combination of these roles that can be very powerful. However, success in implementing these dual approaches is difficult to achieve.

Studies conducted in the past decade have identified six main behaviours that charismatic leaders tend to exhibit (Rowden 2000):

- Vision and articulation
- Sensitivity to member needs
- Environmental sensitivity
- Unconventional behaviour
- Taking personal risks
- Not maintaining the 'status quo'

Using different organizational metaphors to elicit mental models of leadership, Andrews and Field (1998) conducted a survey that led to the

Table 4.4 Derived models of leadership (Andrews and Field 1998)

Model	Roles
Directive	Make decisions Allocate resources Give direction in completion of a task
Motivational	Motivate through energizing and invigorating Provide support/encouragement
Visionary	Provide a sense of mission Install values and beliefs Assign goals
Boundary spanning	Represent the group to outsiders Exchange information with external parties
Design/maintenance	Planning tasks Provide structure for group Reinforcing procedures

identification of five models: directive, motivational, visionary, boundary spanning and design/maintenance. Table 4.4 summarizes the roles associated with each of those models. In a study across industries and using a relatively wide and diverse sample, they found that the prototype of the directive leader prevails along with a much easier recognition of transactional roles. Nevertheless, the authors call attention to the fact that their research eliminated the context variable which may have contributed to the consistency and simplicity of the model of leader that people report to hold.

Georgiades and Macdonell's (1998) model also puts leadership at the centre of the effective functioning of the organization. The model points to three topics within the leadership task: the establishment of the vision, the alignment of the culture and the specification of management practices.

Recent views and emergent issues on leadership

Organizational complexity and systemic leadership

Emerging organizational models emphasize the need for quality, flexibility, adaptability, speed and experimentation (Graetz 2000).

If we adopt the modern view of organizations as *complex adaptive systems* (Collier and Esteban 2000), with the associated properties of chaos, emergence and generation, the traditional (and somehow static) models of leadership do not provide the necessary answers. Collier and Esteban (2000) argue that 'leadership in these organizations is the systemic capability, diffused throughout the organization and nurtured by the members, of finding organizational direction, of generating and maintaining continual renewal by encouraging, harnessing and directing creative and innovative capabilities, while simultaneously holding in tension the processes of responsiveness to the environment on the one hand, and the maintenance of internal integrity of purpose on the other'. This definition emphasizes the nature of leadership as an ongoing process, rather than focusing on the person of the leader.

Systemic leadership must be regarded as relational and political. People collaborate to realize their shared aspirations, but since values and ideals will always differ, reciprocal interaction will involve 'constructive conflict' (Collier and Esteban 2000). Along similar lines, Rost (1993, cited in Collier and Esteban) defines leadership as 'an influence relationship among leaders and their collaborators who intend real change that reflect their mutual purpose'.

Systemic leadership tends to see each organizational member as a fully responsible autonomous agent with powers of judgement and decision-making. At the same time, each person is assumed to be uniquely responsible for their performance, and therefore held accountable for it.

Closely related to this view is the need to have sound shared values. Leaders must be actively involved in the process of generation and diffusion of organizational values. Systemic leadership puts the sense of belonging to a community at the core of this process, giving organizations a sense of identity.

Organizations most successful in managing the dynamics of loose–tight working relationships tend to combine strong 'personalized' leadership at the top with 'distributed' leadership, that is, the existence of a group of experienced and trusted individuals operating at different levels of the organization (Graetz 2000).

An essential responsibility of leadership in modern organizations is to facilitate communication and information sharing, since this is fundamental to dialogue and questioning, thus enhancing organizational learning.

Collier and Esteban (2000) identified five paradoxes associated with systemic leadership and stated that the management of these tensions keeping both aspects in play is essential to ensure effectiveness:

1 Hierarchy vs participation: leadership is the responsibility of all, and yet it is exercised by one person at any given time.
2 Unity vs diversity: systemic leadership works with unity of purpose, but with a diversity of ideas and interests, so that conflict is inevitable.
3 Asymmetry vs mutuality: the process of systemic leadership relies on the principle of mutuality, on the existence of a level where every member has equal opportunity to exercise influence, enjoys equal regard, and feels able to express ideas and to use initiative. On the other hand, it is also clear that the process is asymmetric in that the weight of influence will be shifting and unequal as different people assume different roles with different responsibilities at different times.
4 Discipline vs creativity: ideas are the lifeblood of generative organizations, but they cannot all be implemented. This has to be managed in a disciplined way which does not discourage or suppress enthusiasm and inventiveness.

5   Creation vs destruction: developing new perspectives means shattering old paradigms and changing old processes and practices. This may well be painful in human terms. It produces anxiety and fear and creates tensions between the participants. Anxieties must be managed so that people feel safe enough to collaborate.

Vision, change and transformational leadership

Leaders need to provide a focal point for the energies, hopes and aspirations of people in the organization. Moreover, they are expected to serve as role models whose behaviours, actions and personal energy demonstrate the desired behaviours expected throughout the organization (Nadler and Tushman 1990).

Organization-wide change demands, therefore, a long-term strategic approach, incorporating both 'hard' (strategy structure, systems and technology) and 'soft' (vision, values, behaviours and attitudes) issues (Graetz 2000). Not surprisingly, the effective management of change is an emergent issue in modern leadership theories placing new challenges for leaders.

The *Transformational Approach* describes how leaders can initiate, develop, and carry out significant changes in organizations. The Transformational Leader Model (introduced by Bass) is concerned with the process of how certain leaders are able to inspire followers to accomplish great things (Northouse 1997).

The transformational leader seeks to influence and motivate his or her collaborators so that they are aligned with the leader's vision. Bass and Avolio (1994, cited in Cardona 2000) specify that transformational leaders try to get their collaborators to emulate them (idealized influence); communicate visions of the future that are attractive for their collaborators (inspirational motivation); stimulate them to be creative, without criticizing their ideas (intellectual stimulation); and provide them with individualized opportunities for learning and development (individualized consideration). Therefore, transformational leaders need to act as strong role models and create a vision that gives meaning and clarifies the organization identity. To some extent, under this model, leaders become 'social architects' (Northouse 1997).

Transformational leadership is often contrasted with Transactional leadership. Transactional leadership was described by Burns (1978, cited in Jung and Avolio 1999) as motivating followers primarily through contingent-reward-based exchanges. Typically, the main focus of transactional leaders is on setting goals, clarifying the link between performance and rewards, and providing constructive feedback to keep followers on task (Bass 1985, cited in Jung and Avolio). The transactional leader, therefore, focuses his or her managerial work on negotiating extrinsic exchanges and on controlling the actions of his or her collaborators so that they follow the leader's will. On the other hand, the transformational leader focuses his or her managerial work on creating an attractive vision (Cardona 2000) and on developing closer relationships with followers based more on trust and commitment than on contractual agreements.

It is possible to identify some similarities with the distinction previously discussed between charismatic and instrumental leadership and it may be stated that the transformational leader tends to be a visionary and charismatic leader. However, according to Bass (cited in Northouse 1997) charisma is necessary but not a sufficient condition for transformational leadership. He argues that transformational leadership motivates followers to exceed expectations by (a) raising followers' level of conscientiousness about the importance and value of specified goals; (b) getting followers to transcend their own self-interest for the sake of the organization; and (c) moving followers to address higher-level needs.

Once again, it is important to notice that both transactional and transformational leadership are necessary and complementary. As a matter of fact, Bass describes transactional and transformational leadership as a continuum.

The Multifactor Leadership Questionnaire (first introduced by Bass in 1985) aims to determine the leader's particular strengths and weaknesses in transformational leadership, by measuring followers' perceptions for a set of factors.

The main drawback of this approach is the failure to define clearly the parameters of transformational leadership.

Looking at leadership from a relational perspective, some researchers add to transactional and transformational leaders another category – the transcendent leadership. The transcendent leaders are described as those who try to develop the transcendent motivation of their followers, that is, the motivation to do things for others, and the motivation to contribute (Cardona 2000). The transcendental leader is concerned with the people themselves and tries to contribute to their personal development.

Leadership within the context of teams

The *exchange theory* initiated by Tribout and Kelley (1959) and Harmons (1961) (cited in Smith and Peterson 1988) – was one of the first attempts to address aspects of leadership within the context of groups. According to this theory, a leader's emergence does not depend simply on the possession of certain traits, but equally on the group's tasks and norms, which will determine those skills and values which will be more rewarding for members. A leader emerges by providing adequate evidence of task competence and conformity to group norms (Smith and Peterson 1988).

With the emergence of teams the question of leadership arises in a context that is different from the one that has traditionally been considered. This is particularly challenging in the case of self-directed teams, which may be defined as 'a group of employees who have day-to-day responsibility for managing themselves and the work they do with a minimum of direct supervision' (Fisher 1993, cited in Horner 1997).

The line between leaders and followers becomes less clear and more flexible, changing the role of leadership as a consequence. The idea of leadership as a person may no longer be appropriate due to the highly collaborative, involved nature of the workforce; looking at leadership as a process may offer a better fit (Horner 1997).

The process of team leadership necessarily places more ownership and responsibility on all team members. Manz and Sims (1989, cited in Horner 1997) have defined a new management style called 'Super Leadership' that seems to be more appropriate in team structures. Instead of one formal leader holding the power, this theory suggests that the locus of control is shifted over time from the leader to the team.

The review of several studies on effective leadership on a team-based organization (Horner 1987) tends to highlight the importance of certain behaviours, such as developing shared knowledge among team members, acting as a mentor, providing information, promoting open communication, providing goals and allocating resources efficiently.

An effective team leader ensures that the team functions as a unit, pulling together the individuals involved, working with a common aim. Research studies tend to indicate that democratic styles of leadership are more likely to produce effective team performance; however, different types of leadership are required at different stages of team development.

Leadership within the context of learning organizations

Peter Senge emphasizes the role of leaders within the context of *learning organizations*. Senge (1990) believes that over the long run superior performance essentially depends on superior learning and stresses that learning must occur at every organizational level as an ongoing process.

As he points out, the 'old model' in which 'the top thinks and the local acts' must give way to integrating thinking and acting at all levels (Senge 1990). Therefore, he highlights the importance of viewing leadership as a creative and collective process, stating that 'leadership in the future will be distributed among diverse individuals and teams who share the responsibility for creating the organization's future' (Peter Senge 1997, cited in Collier and Esteban 2000).

Senge (1990) argues that the traditional view of leaders – as special people who set direction and make the key decisions – is rooted in an individualistic and non-systemic perspective that prevents collective learning from happening.

In contrast, in learning organizations, leaders are expected to be designers (governing ideas, translating ideas into business decisions, and fostering strategic thinking), teachers (or coaches, helping everyone in the organization to gain insightful views of reality), and stewards (serving the people they lead and the mission of the organization). These new roles demand new skills, namely, the ability to build shared vision, to bring to surface and to challenge prevailing mental models and to foster more systemic patterns of thinking.

New management roles and competencies

Bartlett and Goshal (1997) provide an interesting summary of the changes in the management roles at the different levels of the organization.

These new roles necessarily put managers under pressure to acquire and develop new competencies.

McCall (1993, cited in Georgiades and MacDonell 1998) suggested that there are six key requirements for effective leadership:

1   Setting direction (requiring ability to create a vision and ability to design an appropriate organizational structure, put in place adequate reward systems, manage information flows and staffing).
2   Alignment.
3   Values (the long-term ability of the leader to influence others hinges on credibility, integrity and trust).
4   Temperament (a manner of thinking, behaving and reacting that helps an individual operate with relative comfort in a job characterized by making decisions under uncertainty, being at the mercy of uncontrollable forces and being responsible for large numbers of people and resources).
5   Self-awareness (a realistic assessment of his/her own strengths and weaknesses is essential to knowing their own limits and empowering others).
6   Growth (leaders must constantly learn, grow, and change).

Looking at the approaches and concepts presented in the previous sections, we may conclude that the evolution on leadership is strongly associated with the general debates that arise in organizational theory. The emerging issues of each management era have all put new pressures on leaders to develop new competencies and embrace new roles.

However, every theory discussed until now tends to concentrate its efforts on arriving at a definition of an ideal leader (or at least the best leader to a certain situation) without developing any kind of model that could help organizations assess their strengths and weaknesses in terms of leadership. Moreover, traditionally the emphasis is on analysing the leader as an individual rather than the leadership team as a whole, what seems to be much more adequate to contemporary organizations which cannot (and should not) depend on the abilities of a single person. In addition, the questionnaires developed to accompany each theory have (as discussed above) considerable limitations in terms of consistency and reliability of their measurement scales. Comparisons across different organizations and even within the same organization are difficult (if not impossible) to make and links between a particular kind of leadership and organizational performance is problematic to establish. Therefore, it is virtually impossible to identify best practices and learn from others.

In the next section, we present a holistic model which using a Structural Equation Modelling (SEM) approach, simultaneously measures the performance of leaders in key roles and how they contribute to leadership excellence, which in turn is the prime for organizational excellence, as KBEM points out.

Leadership and organizational excellence

Introduction

It is a well-established belief that effective leadership is one of the most crucial factors in the implementation of change and without a positive commitment, any strategy for change is likely to fail.

Leaders in the context of introducing change face two fundamental tasks: first, to develop and articulate exactly what the company is trying to accomplish and, second, to create an environment in which employees can figure out what needs to be done and then do it well (Zairi 1995).

In a recent survey, Prabhu and Robson (2000*a,b*) found that 'world-class' organizations and less successful companies were clearly different in terms of leadership practices (such as the development of a service culture, customer orientation, establishment of human resources strategies, innovation and existence of a quality mindset).

Darling (1999) reports that the analysis of a large number of multinational companies led to the confirmation of the success of the four leadership strategies as follows:

- attention through vision (which is essential to create a focus for the organization);
- meaning through communication (capacity to articulate a compelling image of the future and develop shared meanings and interpretations of reality, facilitating coordinated action);
- trust through positioning (trust provides the foundation which maintains organizational integrity; through establishing and sustaining a position, i.e. a set of actions to implement the vision, the leaders establish trust);
- confidence through respect.

Most researchers (Dale and Cooper 1994; Deming 1986; Oakland 1999; Zairi 1995, 1999) have emphasized the critical role of leadership in the implementation of Total Quality Management (TQM) and numerous examples of role models such as Motorola and Xerox reinforce this conviction.

Deming has addressed both the aspects of behavioural and technical leadership associated with the System of Profound Knowledge in his book *Out of the Crisis*. Combining his previous work on systems and variation with

Table 4.5 Theory of profound knowledge and leadership requirements

Core values of Deming's theory	Leadership requirements
Appreciation for a system	Conscientiousness of the way the organization works as a series of interrelated functions, activities and processes that work together for the aim of the organization
Some knowledge of the theory of variation	Understanding of the concept of variation and its relationship to statistical theory
A theory of knowledge	Familiarity with facts, principles and truths acquired through sight, experience or report and integration
Knowledge of psychology	Understand the diverse ways how people learn and why they behave in a particular way

the areas of knowledge and psychology, the System of Profound Knowledge provides a foundation upon which, his well-known fourteen points rest and simultaneously provide leaders with a road map they may follow to achieve success. In Deming's view, a leader's primary job is to be aware of and how to identify the components of the system, and analyse what the system is delivering at any given moment in the process (Mauro 1999). The four core values of Deming's theory of profound knowledge and associated leadership requirements are shown in Table 4.5.

Leaders are needed to create a quality vision, eliminate/minimize resistance to change, infuse a quality culture, satisfy customers' dynamics demands, and encourage continuous improvement.

Table 4.6 summarizes key leadership competencies to an organization committed to quality and excellence (Dering 1998; Senge 1990; Zairi 1999). Once identified, these competencies can be used to select, develop and reward leaders in quality organizations.

Similarly, a review of the existing excellence model reveals that leadership is essential if an organization is to achieve superior performance. All of them identify some core competencies of leaders in quality organizations.

Easton (1993, cited in Zairi 1994*b*) conducted a study of leadership practices among twenty-two organizations which submitted applications for the Malcolm Baldrige National Quality Award (MBNQA). Some strengths were consistently identified:

- Leaders spend a substantial amount of time reminding people of the importance of customers and improving quality. In addition, a lot of effort is placed in educating people, speaking in public and face-to-face contacts with customers, suppliers and employees.
- Leaders have developed a vision and a set of values to develop a quality culture in their organizations.

Table 4.6 Core competencies of leadership in quality-oriented organizations

Vision and purpose	Creating, and articulating vision, mission, and guiding principles
Ethics and principles	Shaping an organizational culture based on the organizational values that stresses integrity and builds trust; use principles to guide decision-making
Communication	Sharing the vision with all organizational members; encouraging discussion, feedback, and involvement; inspiring confidence in the employees; reinforcing organizational values; establishing empathy
Customer orientation	Directing attention to customer concerns and needs; commitment to serve both external and internal customers; designing systems to respond to their expectations
Organizational change	Creating change; making vision a reality even in the face of resistance or opposition; providing adequate resources for changes to happen
Structures and systems	Establishing organizational policies, structures and practices that are consistent with the TQM vision
Measurement, evaluation and reporting	Establishing systems to measure effectiveness, efficiency and service; creating and maintaining reporting mechanisms
Process improvement	Designing and redesigning processes and systems to improve productivity and responsiveness; organize work in a way that makes interconnectedness between the various roles clear; apply SPC
Team development	Establishing a team-based structure which cuts across all the functions and boundaries; fostering high performance through teams and teamwork
Developing subordinates	Challenging subordinates to learn; setting developmental and career goals; stretching subordinates to full potential
Developing partnerships	Creating a climate of win–win with customers, suppliers and the community, through a strategic approach which will help deliver benefits for all the parties
Innovation and continuous learning	Generating new ideas and stimulating them in others; actively pursuing and encouraging creativity; learn from subordinates, colleagues, suppliers, and customers

- The vision is translated into congruent goals.
- A proper structure supports quality efforts.

On the other hand, the following areas for improvement were identified:

- Senior managers' primary focus is on short-term strategic goals which tend to be financial in nature and their lack of appreciation of quality measures and improvement measures.
- Leaders do not take a process-based approach in their decision-making and their poor utilization of hard facts and information.
- Leaders have a limited and poor understanding of TQM and its potential.

- Leaders set targets in isolation from the process and expect people to perform and deliver the expected results.
- Poor utilization of data relating to customers, suppliers and employees. As such they have very poor understanding of causes of problems and what causes variability in their organizations.
- Although a structure for quality might be present, leaders tend to treat quality as a separate activity.

Business Excellence Models (BEMs) tend to assess leadership in four non-prescriptive areas (Edgeman and Sherer 1999):

- Leadership internal to the organization (particularly as related to TQM, recognition and reward, and resource commitment).
- Involvement with customers, suppliers and other external constituencies.
- Responsibility to society.
- The leadership system.

Leadership Excellence Model

Although, it is in KBEM that the importance of leadership becomes very clear, leadership is not just one more criterion; it is the prime of the model, showing that leadership is responsible for driving the organization in every area towards quality and excellence.

In view of the literature review on leadership in the context of organizations in general, and in the context of organizations committed to organizational excellence in particular, we identified what we believe are the *Critical Success Factors* (CSFs) for Leadership Excellence, namely:

- The existence of strong and shared organizational values (which provide the foundation for the identity of the organization and are reflected in its mission, vision, strategy, and management practices).
- The development and communication of an inspiring vision.
- The definition of a mission that states what the organization stands for.
- The development of a strategy aligned to the mission and vision and ability to create a sustainable competitive advantage over the competitors.
- The establishment of an organizational structure and operational mechanisms that facilitate the implementation of the mission, vision, and strategy.

Leadership Excellence is, thus, the result of an outstanding performance of leaders in all these key areas, which, as the definition of CSFs (see Rockart 1982; Leidecker and Bruno 1984) suggests, have the greatest impact on the competitive success of an organization.

The *Leadership Excellence Index* (LEI) will reflect, in quantitative terms, and through a single and integrated measure, the simultaneous performance of

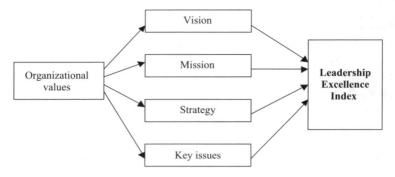

Figure 4.1 Leadership structural equation model.

leaders in the roles of establishing and sharing the values, developing and communicating the vision, defining the mission, selecting and implementing a strategy and managing other operational key issues.

Development of a structural equation model for leadership

The last few sections provided evidence of why leadership is the prime for BE. Here, we present a model that incorporates the leadership CSFs identified and shows how leadership excellence converges from the core values of the organization.

In the leadership model (see Figure 4.1), the organizational values provide the foundation for vision, mission, strategy and other key issues. The way these are developed and implemented will determine the quality of the leadership in an organization, measured by the respective LEI.

The model emphasizes the role of leadership in creating (and communicating) a vision, clarifying the mission and objectives of the organization, defining the corporate strategy to achieve them and dealing with other key issues. As stated earlier, this view is consistent with the recent theories on leadership and strongly based on the literature review.

A major challenge for leaders is therefore to effectively manage the relationships among the organization's vision, mission and strategy and its statement of its values. Next we discuss in some detail the meaning of each of the model's constructs and explore some relationships among them.

Values

Values reflect an individual or collective judgement as to what is valuable or important in life, and provide a yardstick against which personal, organizational and societal behaviour can be evaluated (Kenny 1994).

Values form the culture of an organization and will be reflected in its mission and vision. Values will also influence the courses of action taken to achieve these ends, that is, the organization's strategy.

Some shared values are essential since they

- foster strong feelings of personal effectiveness;
- promote high levels of loyalty to the organization;
- facilitate consensus about key organizational goals;
- encourage ethical behaviour;
- reduce levels of job stress and tension;
- foster pride in the organization;
- foster teamwork.

Furthermore, organizational values are a sign of the type of leaders an organization has and, at the same time, serve as guiding principles that leaders must follow and promote.

In what concerns this, the leader is responsible for:

- Identifying and communicating the core values and principles that guide organizational behaviour and decision making.
- Specifying behaviours that exemplify the company's values or principles and leading by example.
- Ensuring that the reinforcement systems are consistent with organizational values and principles.

The importance of having strong values is not to be underestimated. As Peters and Waterman (1982) found out in their research, the best organizations are those that are 'value driven'. This is exactly our understanding as well, since the values provide the foundation for the vision, mission, strategy and other key components of the leadership role. We believe that leaders have a crucial role in defining and communicating the organizational values, but, at the same time, the organization's values also have an impact on the type of leadership that fits a particular company at a given moment. They generate the patterns of behaviour prevalent in the organization. This suggests that any major change to be introduced in an organization needs to start with considering, and eventually modifying, the existing values. However, it is important to notice that this change is extremely difficult and requires much time and effort. New values cannot simply be imposed.

Probably the most useful idea is that of continual learning in order to be willing to progressively adjust organizational values and align behaviours with the new environmental demands.

Georgiades and Macdonell (1998) propose that an adaptive culture is based upon six core values and beliefs:

- Open and Trusting Relationships (only trust makes people present their points of view and contributions freely; trust demands that promises be kept).
- Commitment to People.

- Participation in Problem Solving Through Teamwork (teamwork enhances efficiency and creativity).
- Commitment to Change and Innovation (to declare that the organization is not dedicated to the status quo and is constantly pressing for improvement and change is the first step in the commitment process).
- Commitment to Individual Autonomy (each individual, provided with and committed to a vision of what the organization could be, should be given freedom and autonomy to act in the best interest of the enterprise).
- Obsessive Commitment to Loyal Customers (gathering systematic feedback and responding constructively to it).

For each of the core values identified, action-oriented behaviours must be articulated. Some of these management practices are addressed in our model in the Key Issues dimension.

Vision

Vision can be defined as a 'mental image of a possible and desirable future state of the organization' (Bennis and Nannus 1997, cited in Lynch and Cross 1995). This painting must be understood and communicated throughout the organization (Thornberry 1997).

Vision relates to some futuristic ideal, to some notion of how things could/should be, and can reflect an inspired state of being for an individual, an organization, or society at large (Kenny 1994).

A vision statement describes what the organization is to become in the future (Thompson 1997) that provides individuals, organizations and societies with a sense of direction and purpose (Kenny 1994). Vision statements should be designed to be vivid, memorable, inspiring, meaningful and brief (Thornberry 1997).

Hamel and Prahalad (1884, cited in Lynch and Cross 1995) have suggested five criteria for judging the appropriateness of a vision statement: foresight, breadth, uniqueness, consensus, and actionability.

The leadership role in creating a compelling vision, translating it into action and sustaining it has been highlighted by many researchers (Bass, cited in Northouse 1997; Bennis and Nannus 1985, cited in Morden 1997; Cardona 2000). It is not enough for leaders to be able to develop a simultaneously inspiring and realistic vision, they need as well to be credible in communicating and implementing it. Leaders can only be considered to be effective once they have shared their vision with all employees.

Credible leaders are seen by their followers as people who can be followed and trusted.

Gabris *et al.* (2000) developed a Leadership Credibility Index consisting of the following variables:

- the Chief Administrative Officer (CAO) communicates his or her vision;
- the CAO communicates the rationale behind his or her vision;

- the CAO shares the vision with others willingly;
- people trust the CAO;
- the CAO delegates authority and power;
- the CAO practises what he or she preaches;
- the CAO follows through on promises;
- the CAO recognizes good performance and rewards it.

As Kenny (1994) points out, visions need values and principles to be implemented and actively pursued. Therefore, the vision reflects the organizational values upon which it is based. On the other hand, the vision provides a link between these values and everyday events (Georgiades and Macdonell 1998).

Mission

The mission reflects the essential purpose of the organization, concerning particularly why it is in existence, the nature of the business(es) it is in, and the customers it seeks to serve and satisfy (Thompson 1997).

The purpose of the mission is to communicate to all the stakeholders inside and outside the organization what the company stands for (Lynch 2000).

Mission and vision are sometimes presented as very similar terms. However, as Georgiades and Macdonell (1998) state, the organization's mission is a statement of its purpose not its direction or sense of destiny.

Ackoff (1986, cited in Thompson 1997) suggests that a good mission statement has five characteristics:

- It contains a formulation of objectives and enables progress towards them to be measured.
- It differentiates the company from its competitors.
- It defines the business(es) that the company wants to be in.
- it is relevant to all stakeholders.
- it is exciting and inspiring.

The mission summarizes the reasoning and values that lie behind it (Lynch 2000) and the leader needs to generate, trust, enthusiasm and commitment among organizational members for the chosen purpose. Therefore, the mission is tightly linked to the organizational values as well. It incorporates the company's philosophy.

Strategy

Strategies are means to pursue the purpose and overall objectives of the organization (Lynch 2000). Strategy and organizational values need to be aligned.

It is leadership's responsibility to create a strategy that will cause the organization to succeed. The strategy has to derive from the environmental analysis of the organization's business and its own resources and potentialities. A winning strategy is expected to anticipate, guide change and create commitment in the organization's members.

Key issues (management practices)

Management practices are linked to the core values and are essentially the action-oriented behaviours that bring to life the organization's values (Georgiades and Macdonell 1998).

It is not enough to conceive and communicate a vision; nor it is sufficient to state the purpose of the organization and then conceive a strategy accordingly. Leaders have to accomplish several day-to-day activities and establish mechanisms that put into operational terms what was stated in the mission, envisioned in the vision and what is necessary to carry out the organization's strategy.

As suggested by Georgiades and Macdonell (1998), managerial practices are both transformational and transactional. The transformational roles of the leaders are adequately covered in our model in the constructs previously discussed. Thus, in the Key Issues dimension, we are primarily concerned with the transactional roles of leaders.

The specification and modelling by senior management of management practices is the fulcrum of organizational transformation (Georgiades and Macdonell 1998). Once a new management practice is introduced, it is essential to change the performance and reward systems accordingly. Feedback is also crucial in monitoring the impact of the changes.

The management practices cannot be regarded in isolation. They support the implementation of the organizational values. Table 4.7 provides an example of possible management practices associated with key organizational values of an adaptive culture (Georgiades and Macdonell 1998).

Additionally, the starting point for the specification of these practices is the vision statement and the strategic programme which is aligned with the vision.

Moreover, leaders need to look beyond their own organizational boundaries, developing partnerships with customers, suppliers and the community. Effective leadership will be based on creating a win–win climate through, perhaps, working with fewer suppliers but on a strategic approach which will help deliver benefits for each party (Zairi 1995).

Networking is absolutely essential in modern competitiveness. Through networking, benchmarking activities can take place, to compare practices, methods and performance, to learn new ways of performing essential tasks.

Leadership measurement instrument

Measurement is essential in order to have a clear indication of the effectiveness of the leadership and to ensure that the deployment of best practices is in place.

Table 4.7 Organizational values and supporting practices

Organizational values	Management practices
Open and trusting relationships	A manager keeps promises and commitments (builds a reputation for standing by the commitments that have been made; ensures consistency between plans and actions)
	A manager shares key information with subordinates
	A manager is honest; never dissembles (is consistent and dependable; behaves in a way he/she would expect from others; sets organizational interests above self-interest)
	A manager builds supportive relationships with peers, subordinates and bosses
Commitment to people	A manager is concerned with welfare and well-being of subordinates (does not compromise on issues of health and safety; listens to problems when there is need to talk through)
	A manager encourages frank and open discussions about subordinates' performance (prepares for appraisals, asks questions and listens to answers; follows up on agreed corrective actions)
	A manager agrees on clear performance objectives (negotiates targets rather than imposing them; accepts the possible impact that external factors might have on performance; is prepared to accept his/her own share of blame for missed targets)
	A manager demands honest, accurate performance (encourages subordinates to seek reasons for success or failure; quantifies performance in a way as objectively as possible; consults widely for personal feedback to use)
	A manager gives guidance, counselling and training to improve subordinates' performance (makes self-accessible to people who need guidance and support; regularly reviews training plans)
Participation in problem-solving through teamwork	A manager helps the team to understand their role in the wider organization
	A manager encourages the team to define team goals
	A manager encourages the team members to define individual roles and responsibilities
	A manager encourages frank and open discussion about the way the team works
	A manager encourages the team to become involved in problem solving
Commitment to change and innovation	A manager constantly responds to customer feedback
	A manager encourages subordinates to try out new ideas (rewards and praises attempts to try new ideas; is willing to allow time and put resources to try new things)
	A manager encourages benchmarking
	A manager constantly tries learning new things and gets training
Commitment to individual autonomy	A manager gives authority to act and make decisions without upward reference (expects individuals to monitor their own timekeeping; praises individual initiatives)
	A manager encourages others to act in ways that promote the best interests of the business
Obsessive commitment to loyal customers	A manager meets and talks regularly with customers
	A manager constantly seeks customer feedback
	A manager encourages staff to be involved with customers

The assumption that leadership comprises a set of behaviours that can actually be observed, measured and developed is critical in the development of an SEM. Such a model includes a set of latent variables, each of them translated into a set of manifest variables, which correspond to an item in the questionnaire.

As discussed above, our leadership excellence model includes six main constructs (organizational values, vision, mission, strategy, key issues and leadership excellence), which cannot be directly measured. Rather, a set of manifest variables (indicators) must be associated with each of these constructs and then measured through the development and administration of an appropriated questionnaire.

With the aim of developing such a measurement instrument, a comprehensive and extensive literature review (from the questionnaires used within the various traditional leadership approaches to the recent assessment frameworks created for the purpose of BEMs) was conducted. This ensures the content validity of the instrument.

A preliminary version of the leadership excellence questionnaire is in Appendix B, where each of the questions is answered on a one-to-ten scale, from 'very little' to 'very much'.

An illustrative example

In order to illustrate, in simple terms, the way the leadership structural equation model works and how it can be used to measure LEI, a typical service sector company (X) was utilized. Data were used to determine the indices of the CSFs of the model and the final LEI score. Figure 4.2 shows the BEM with values of the structural parameters.

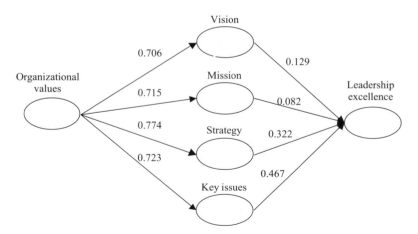

Figure 4.2 Structural parameters for company 'X'.

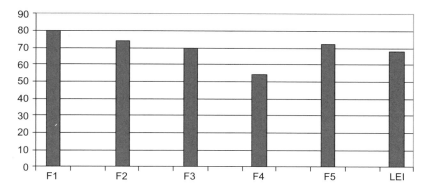

Figure 4.3 Indices of Critical Success Factors (CSFs) and leadership excellence for company 'X'.

Notes: F1. Organizational values; F2. Vision; F3. Mission; F4. Strategy; F5. Key Issues; LEI. Leadership Excellence Index.

The structural parameters (or path coefficients) are computed using Partial Least Squares (PLSs) and show the strength of the relationship between independent and dependent variables of the model. All the structural parameters have positive values, indicating that the causal connections in the model have a symmetrical relationship. The results show that organizational values (prime) have a strong causal connection with the four CSFs. Moreover, it is important to keep in mind that the indices are all related because the values of the path coefficients from which they are derived, are computed by simultaneous equations.

Figure 4.3 shows the indices of CSFs and leadership excellence for Company 'X'. If we agree that an excellence index of 75 or more is regarded as excellent (Kanji 2000*b*), the final LEI of 67.6 for the given company must be considered as reasonably good.

The values of CSFs for leadership excellence in Figure 4.3 can help top management make decisions concerning improvement plans and resources allocation. CSFs with low index scores are natural candidates for improvement. Knowing the relationship between CSFs and leadership index is useful to determine which CSFs more strongly need to be improved, and by how much, in order to increase leadership excellence.

The Excellence Seeker's Approach (see Kanji 2000*a*) involves the use of an optimization algorithm for determining which indices to increase and by how much to achieve a given target level of excellence. Since organizations usually face some constraints, the algorithm allows the introduction of upper limits of improvement for one (or more) CSFs.

In our example, let us assume that the company fixed upper limits for CSFs at 85 per cent and a target level of leadership excellence equally at 85 points. The required performance levels for every CSFs are shown in Table 4.8.

Table 4.8 Revised indices of CSFs and leadership excellence

Critical success factor and leadership excellence	Upper limit	Original index LEI = 68	Target leadership excellence index percentages		
			75	80	85
Organizational values	85	80	83*	85	85
Vision	85	74	74	74	74
Mission	85	69	69	69	69
Strategy	85	55	55	69*	84*
Key issues	85	72	85*	85	85

*New index for higher target level.

Table 4.9 Reliability of empirical measurements for company 'X'

Critical success factors and leadership excellence	Reliability – α
Organizational values	0.772
Vision	0.724
Mission	0.771
Strategy	0.758
Key issues	0.899
Leadership excellence	0.968

The current measurement instrument that we used was already to some extent redefined by means of an iterative procedure that removes a small number of manifest variables that do not fully explain the respective construct. The final reliability coefficients of measurement scales are presented in Table 4.9. The Cronbach coefficient (α) was calculated. The results suggest the reliability of most scales. The cases of organizational values, strategy and leadership excellence are particularly satisfactory. Further refinements are possible, based on future empirical tests of the model.

Still, the positive parameter values together with the relatively high reliability values for latent variables support the presence of the proposed model.

Conclusions

Leadership has, for a long time, been a topic that attracts the attention of both academics and practitioners. In spite of the extensive literature in this matter, there is almost a complete absence of models to explain how leadership works.

From an exhaustive literature review, we identified a set of CSFs that we believe may be applied in many different settings. Based on these requirements of effective leadership we proposed a structural equation model describing the relationships among six constructs. Each construct was then operationalized using multiple questionnaire items. Using data from a typical service sector company, we determined the path coefficients, correlations and reliability measures for the overall system, based on PLS estimations. This sound and robust methodology leads to leadership measures that are innovative and helps the identification of leadership areas that need to be addressed more carefully if the overall excellence index is to be increased.

Based on the research findings, it is possible to draw several conclusions about the company's performance on the five keys areas of the Leadership Excellence Model.

- Overall, the leadership performance of this company is relatively good, since all its CSFs, with the exception of strategy, are near 70 per cent or above.
- The score in the prime of this model – organizational values – is particularly high, showing that leaders are playing an important role in the development and communication of sharing meanings and interpretations of reality.
- It seems to also have in place a compelling and challenging vision that has been effectively communicated throughout the organization.
- However, the strategy is pushing down the LEI score. It may well happen that strategy is also not adequately aligned with the vision and organizational values. Leaders may also fail to anticipate and guide change. Monitoring resources and performance and using feedback mechanisms is essential to achieve improvement in this area.

Rather than seeing this model as a completely separate tool, we recommend it to be used in integration with the generic KBEM, in which leadership is the prime. In the following chapter we provide the details of measuring KBEM using BEI.

5 Measuring business excellence

Introduction

> Total Quality Management (TQM) is the culture of an organization committed to customer satisfaction through continuous improvement. This culture varies both from one country to another and between different industries, but has certain essential principles which can be implemented to secure greater market share, increased profits and reduced costs (Kanji 1997).

The above statement emphasizes that creating a quality culture within an organization is increasingly recognized as one of the primary conditions for the successful implementation of TQM. It requires uncovering current underlying culture and examining the appropriateness of the objectives in order to adopt TQM. To close the gap between the old and the required new culture one must also explore the quality improvement process for achieving business excellence through customer satisfaction.

In discussing the pyramid principles of TQM, Kanji (1996) suggested that to achieve customer satisfaction the organization had to improve continuously in all aspects of its operation. This can only be achieved through leadership by making decisions on objective evidence of what was actually happening and involving all employees in quality improvement activities leading ultimately to Business Excellence (BE).

Before it is possible to embark on a successful move towards TQM or BE, it is first necessary to have in place a culture that wants to produce quality goods and services. If the workforce is not attuned to this type of thinking then the working environment resistance to change will be stronger.

In general, the quality culture that exists in an organization would have been built upon over the years that the organization has been in existence. The many failures and successes that the workforce had endured, the attitudes of the founder, and possible subsequent Managing Directors, all go together to produce a given culture. For TQM, it is necessary to have a culture that is ready and open to change. Therefore, one of the prime aims of TQM is that the processes and products will be continually improved. Continuous improvement can also mean, especially at an early stage, a continuous change. Therefore, if employees are not open to change, then the chances for success with TQM become less and less.

One of the ways in which continuous improvement takes place in an organization is to encourage workers to indicate how a process or product can be improved. It is therefore necessary to create the environment in which this can happen (Atkinson 1990).

Cultures differ from organization to organization, and the nature of their activities can make a huge difference to the culture that exists. For example, a company that has a high turnover rate of staff is likely to have a culture that does not encourage people to remain. If the aim of a company is to develop long-term relationships with its employees then it needs to create a culture which makes people want to stay with the company, makes them feel wanted and makes them feel that they have a future (Atkinson 1990).

Many organizations focus their efforts on customer retention because the strategy is less costly to implement. It has been found that loyal customers are those that are highly satisfied with an organization's products and services. Therefore, if repeat business is wanted, in today's economy it must be essential, then we need to develop a culture where, to complain about poor service is almost the norm. After all, a company can only do something about a problem if it is told about it by its customers. As one successful entrepreneur in the US puts it, 'A customer who complains is my best friend' (Stew Leonard, President of Stew Leonards Dairy Store).

For many organizations, creating a quality culture strategy is a daunting task. It would seem at first glance that the larger company has the most difficult task to spread the quality culture throughout the organization. Nevertheless, some of the major companies have made that possible. The reason for this is that these companies may have practised good quality principles for a number of years. However, to achieve BE it is necessary for the organization to work at all times to preserve the quality culture and improve upon it in order to develop total quality culture over a long period of time for the benefit of all the employees and to achieve BE.

Characteristics of quality culture

Like countries, business organizations also have their own cultures. It is the totality of the norms, beliefs and values that control the behaviour of individuals and groups within any given organization that can be described as organizational quality culture. However, many organizations are not even aware of their own culture or its distinct characteristics.

They become aware of it when they have to communicate with managers from other organizations with different cultures. Sometimes, individuals realize their own culture when mergers and acquisitions take place and a great deal of cultural adjustment is thrust on them.

We also know that traditional and long-established organizations have their own quality cultures which have evolved over the long period of their existence. These cultures are influenced by the culture of the country and the nature of the business of the organization. There is always a question of how fast an organization should attempt to modify its quality culture. The wise thing is to change as fast as practicable but certainly not as slow as the organization may find comfortable and cosy. That can run the risk of the boiled-frog phenomenon. If you put a frog in water and warm up the water gradually, the frog will be so comfortable as the water warms up that it will not realize when the water becomes too hot and it is boiled to death. That is what a cosy quality culture can do to an organization.

Many managers these days pay proper attention to their organizational quality culture because they view culture as an asset (Egan 1994). Some people have also suggested that organizations with adaptive quality cultures, geared to satisfy the changing demands of customers, employees and shareholders, can outperform organizations without such a culture. Companies with sound quality culture can increase their sales three times more than the organization without such a culture. Therefore, a successful company needs more than just sound business strategy; it needs a quality culture to support the strategy.

It is our understanding that sometimes organizations reflect the personality and character of the founder member's norms and beliefs. This can be seen easily by considering Henry Ford, who is known for his immeasurable impact on the shape of his organization's quality culture; other examples include Walt Disney at Disney Productions, David Packard at Hewlett-Packard, etc. However, according to Schein (1985), when the founder moves on, the quality cultures they have embedded do not lose their momentum. The process and people in the company have become the carriers of the culture, and the quality culture continues in the organization.

In general, quality culture has certain characteristics which can be described as follows:

- A quality culture which is lively and progressive can be found to be constantly evolving and helping to change the business.
- A progressive quality culture within a business readily evaluates and responds to stimuli.
- Like religious or political groups, business organizations also have the extreme quality culture, that is, culture tries to preserve what is considered to be the true original set of beliefs.
- Large social migration sometimes creates hybrid quality cultures by the multinational companies.
- Changes in quality culture of an organization occur when a leader provides stimulation with ideas that challenge tradition, for example, Henry Ford, David Packard and Walt Disney.
- Behind all successful business organizations there have been leaders who revived and changed the quality culture of their organizations.

- In most cases quality cultural changes are based on retaining and developing what is good in an existing quality culture and adding to it new TQM principles that will stimulate organizational progress and create BE.

The new elements which will stimulate quality culture and create business excellence are the basic principles of TQM. They include

- delighting the customer;
- continuous improvement;
- management by fact;
- people-based management;
- leadership.

Further details of these TQM principles are given in Kanji (1996).

Business Excellence Index

The Business Excellence Index (BEI) is a means of measuring customers', employer's and shareholders' ('stakeholder's') satisfaction simultaneously within an organization in order to obtain a comprehensive evaluation of the organizational performance (Kanji 1998*b*).

Here, the index can be used in a similar manner to measure how well different areas of the organization are performing. It has been constructed in such a way so as to allow a direct comparison across each area while at the same time being able to compare the same business in different geographical areas. The index also allows a particular business to be measured over time.

For the construction of BEI, the data are collected through a survey using suitable questionnaires. These questionnaires are written specifically for the organization and ensure that as large a picture as possible is gathered about that organization.

The index monitors a number of different areas which are all combined into the final calculations to present a single number between one and 100. It is this single number that represents a particular business score which makes our comparison of BE so easy.

In the measurement of BE process a number of different quality dimensions of business are measured and each is analysed to produce the index total.

In this section, quality dimensions that are used in the BEI measurement process provide a model (see Figure 5.1) combining prime, principles and the core concepts from Kanji's (1998*b*) original model. They are:

- Leadership (prime)
- Delight the customer (principle)

- Internal customer satisfaction (core concept)
- External customer satisfaction (core concept)
- Management by fact (principle)
- All work is process (core concept)
- Measurement (core concept)
- People-based management (principle)
- Teamwork (core concept)
- People make quality (core concept)
- Continuous improvement (principles)
- Continuous improvement cycle (core concept)
- Prevention (core concept)
- Business Excellence

Results for each of the above quality dimensions can also be reported separately. Figure 5.1 shows Kanji's original model and how each quality dimension is linked together for the calculation of the BEI. The data for the application of the generic model and the condensed model can be obtained by using a survey method with high-quality statistical rigour. As a matter of fact, the index can be produced by using a sophisticated and extremely robust statistical method called latent variable Partial Least Squares (PLSs) method.

For the requirements of the BEI as a suitable measurement, it is necessary for the model to deliver meaningful results in terms of causal (cause–effect-oriented) relationship and a structural approach (meaning that the analysis shall be model based). The model to be used shall emerge from theory specifying the BE process, where a pre-defined structure is essential in order

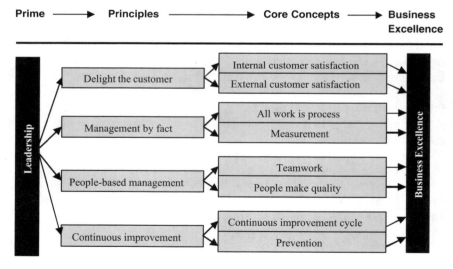

Figure 5.1 Kanji's Business Excellence Index (KBEI).

to be able to analyse interaction and to derive any cause–effect relationships. Further, the BE process is based on the conclusions that merely samples of customers will be assessed, and the employed model is to be seen only as a simplification of the true relationship. Thus, in order to be able to make precision estimates, a probabilistic model rather than a deterministic model has been adopted in this chapter.

It is also concluded that a simultaneous system approach rather than a partial model approach is required for this analysis in order to estimate the entire model at once. Hence, we have adopted a structural model based on a probabilistic approach using simultaneous equation estimation techniques for the measurement of BE. To achieve BE, many organizations have adopted the Business Scorecard approach for process improvement. The section below shows some commonality between the Business Scorecard approach and BE methodology. Further details of Kanji's Business Scorecard (KBS) can be found in a later chapter.

Kanji's Business Scorecard

For many companies, to remain a leader in a dynamic and unpredictable marketplace it is necessary to achieve BE in four key areas of enterprise. They need to:

1 maximize stakeholder value;
2 achieve process excellence;
3 improve organizational learning;
4 delight the stakeholder.

They also need to ensure that their achievements in these areas feed off each other to form a cycle of continuous improvement, so that:

- delighting the customers helps generate revenue and satisfactory returns for the investor;
- increased revenue helps fund investments in processes and learning;
- better process and learning help people to delight the stakeholders and create BE.

Stakeholders are those groups or individuals who are directly or indirectly affected by an organization's pursuit of its goals. Stakeholders are of two types – internal and external stakeholders. Internal stakeholders, such as board of directors and shareholders, form part of the organization to which an individual manager remains responsible. They are distinguishable from external stakeholders such as customers, competitors, media, financial institutions and labour union that affect an organization's activities from the outside.

One of the responsibilities of the board of directors is to protect shareholders' interests. The performance of shareholders' equity, that is, shareholder value, is influenced by BE. An organization that achieves BE creates a large net-worth that therefore increases shareholder's equity. The measure of BE then provides a yardstick by which an investor judges an organization's equity performance. Therefore, it is of fundamental importance for business managers to create shareholder value. The shareholder value-oriented companies therefore focus on long-term cash generation by balancing future growth, risk and return. These business endeavours can be achieved only if every manager is capable of making the right decisions. It is therefore necessary for an organization's leader to improve the quality of decision-making.

Clearly, the focus on shareholder value therefore improves the quality of decision-making and enables all stakeholders to share in the resulting enhancement in share price. The quality of the decision-making process follows the path shown in Figure 5.2.

In order to achieve BE (i.e. stakeholder value) it is necessary to give equal weight to all four areas of enterprise rather than concentrating exclusively on the financial perspective. Each area also defines a number of key corporate objectives and assigns an agreed set of measurement criteria to each factor, so that everybody in the organization can see at a glance how the big picture is shaping up and how changes in one area are affecting achievement in another. A Business Scorecard to categorize the above activities is given in Table 5.1.

Figure 5.2 The path of quality decision-making.

Hence, to achieve BE companies must demonstrate that they excel across various performance areas (see Table 5.1), each of which is properly covered by agreed measurement criteria. Figure 5.3 provides a diagrammatic approach of a Business Scorecard for an organization.

In general, the Business Scorecard approach does not prescribe which performance areas should be used or how they should be measured. These should

Table 5.1 Business Scorecard

Business scorecard category	Stakeholder value	Process excellence	Organizational learning	Delighting stakeholder
Critical success factors criteria	Business excellence	All work is process Measurement	Leadership Teamwork People make quality Continuous improvement Prevention	External customer satisfaction Internal customer satisfaction

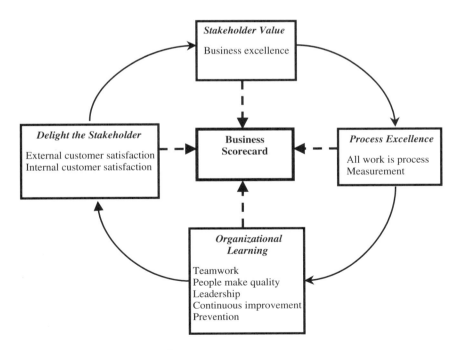

Figure 5.3 Business Scorecard.

be unique to each company and to each individual level of management and can be developed with proper consultation using the generic TQM model. Over time, the Business Scorecard will translate into individual company and departmental scorecards, which in turn will influence every organizational role and every individual's job description and performance criteria. However, from our study it is clear that for a company to achieve BE it is necessary for it to adopt a TQM process and the Critical Success Factors (CSFs) (see Kanji and Tambi 1999) which provide the Business Excellence Model (BEM).

Business Excellence Model

For a BEM, it is necessary to obtain a suitable general TQM model for organizations that incorporate CSFs and can be validated using suitable statistical techniques on relevant data. The CSFs of TQM can be derived from a survey using a suitable generic TQM model reported in the literature. The researcher had conducted an extensive search for a TQM model that satisfies certain criteria suitable for use by various organizations.

The selection criteria used in this chapter provide the scope of the model, that is, general or special-purpose, emphasis on TQM principles, inclusion of CSFs and model validation. Examples of models that were examined are Deming, Baldridge, European, Australian, Japanese, Pyramid (Kanji 1996) and other models. From the examination of these models, Kanji's (1996) Modified Pyramid model was selected for the research. The Pyramid model is a generic model that is made up of four principles and eight core concepts as shown in Figure 5.4.

In this chapter a structural model has been used specifically for determining the BEI where fourteen or ten interrelated latent variables are introduced. Its format is the result of the specific questions and problems addressed and requirements specified for BEI. It is based on well-established theories and approaches on BE criteria and draws on a number of currently used quality dimensions.

Here, a set of manifest (measurable) variables is associated with each of the latent variables and the structure is called the BE analytical model, where the entire model is necessary for determining the BEI. The main difference between the original model (fourteen latent variables, Figure 5.1) and the condensed model (ten latent variables, Figure 5.10) is that the core concepts for each of the individual principles are combined to obtain the measurable variables, that is, instead of eight core concepts, there are now only four concepts.

Although the term CSFs has not been used in the Pyramid model (Figure 5.4), nevertheless it is said that an organization system must be guided through the TQM principles and core concepts by top management leadership in order to achieve BE (Kanji 1998*a*). In addition, the understanding given in this chapter on the model components indicates that the components synthesize those critical requirements for quality management prescribed by eminent quality practitioners such as Juran, Deming, Crosby, Garvin,

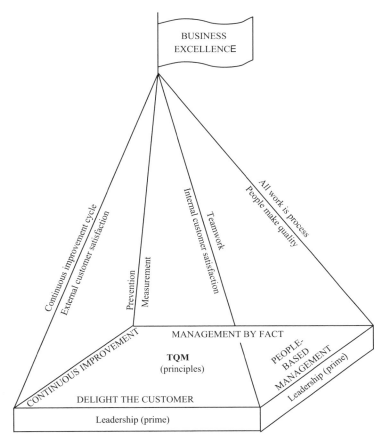

Figure 5.4 Kanji's (1996) modified pyramid model.

Feigenbaum, Ishikawa and Taguchi. In recent surveys (Kanji and Yui 1997; Kanji and Tambi 1999), results indicate the prime, principle and core concepts of Figure 5.1 as the CSFs. Moreover, most of the models in use (e.g. Deming, European, Baldridge and Japanese) are indicative or non-prescriptive models, whereas Kanji's Business Excellence Model (KBEM) (Figure 5.1) is an improvement or prescriptive model.

For the measurement of BE, the main objective is to develop a suitable latent variable structural model that shows relationship between variables, other intervening variables and ultimately BE. A measurement scale must be developed so that the model can be used to profile organization-wide quality practices. On the basis of survey results (see Kanji and Tambi 1999), it is found that for many organizations the barriers of TQM predominantly originate from organizational members. Also, there are unique reasons for implementing TQM and a set of CSFs exists which influences organizational performance. In general, the CSFs differ in terms of degree of importance and in that organizational culture influences the TQM implementation process. The benefit from this study is that it draws organizational decision-makers' attention to key areas that need effective management, which in reality provides the organization with a continuous improvement and BE priority.

The author believes that the systematic approach of determining CSFs for overall organizational quality management has never been proposed in previous research works. The model, the author advocates, would show the interrelationship among the factors and their contributions towards BE. This has been achieved by constructing, testing and reviewing a latent variable structural model by using a statistical method known as causal analysis. In addition, a measurement instrument has been designed and validated to provide a profile of organization-wide quality management in terms of the CSFs and BE.

Critical success factors

CSFs are the few key areas of the organization, if properly managed, that will improve the organization's competitiveness and BE. Based on previous research works, the CSFs can be categorized based on their degree of importance. Williams and Ramprasad (1996) had suggested a taxonomy of CSFs whereby the factors are grouped into four classes that indicate their degree of importance.

In our case, the measurement of BEI will involve determining weightings of CSFs. A latent variable structural model of CSFs will be constructed and the strength of causal connections among the latent variables will be analysed. The latent variables will be measured by their manifest variables, which in turn will be represented by measurement items in a questionnaire.

Latent variable structural model

The latent variable structural model is used to represent the causal relationships among latent variables (CSFs and BE). The proposed model that is based on KBEM is given in Figure 5.5. The purpose of this work is to estimate the strengths of the causal connections among the latent variables and to test the goodness-of-fit of the structural model. To estimate the strength of these causal connections, it is necessary to operationalize each of the latent variables in terms of manifest variables (measurement items). The manifest variables are measured using measurement items and serve as indicators of the latent variable.

A latent variable structural model is expressed in a system of simultaneous equations known as structural equations for the original model (Figure 5.1).

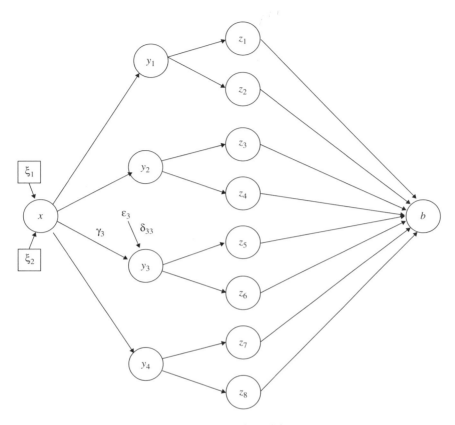

Figure 5.5 Proposed latent variable structural model.

The components of a structural equation are the latent variables, structural parameters and a disturbance term (see Figure 5.5). The estimates for the structural parameter component can be determined by using computer programs such as *LISREL, SAS, PLS* and *AMOS.* The structural equations generate hypothetical variance/covariance matrix of manifest variables. The degree to which a structural equation model reflects reality is given by the degree to which the hypothetical variance/covariance matrix is similar to, or has a good fit with, the empirical variance/covariance matrix for the same manifest variables. The chi-square for goodness-of-fit statistic is used to evaluate whether manifest variables are related to their respective latent variables. It is also used to test whether the structure among the latent variables is consistent with the data. This new model will provide a deeper understanding and greater theoretical knowledge about the implementation of TQM in various organizations and the measurement of BE.

Measurement items

From an extensive literature survey on organizational requirements for effective quality management, suitable measurement items will be developed for the latent variable. The items define the meaning and scope for each factor. To establish content validity, the items for each factor and BE will be critically reviewed by quality practitioners. Following that, the measurement items will be revised if required and the remaining items pre-tested. To enable Quality Directors to indicate the degree of extent of practice of each item by their organization, a ten-point interval rating scale will be developed. For each latent variable, the actual level of practice can be represented by the average of the measurement item ratings for that factor. A vector of the average of fourteen factors for the original model (Figure 5.1) can be used as a profile of an organization's BE.

A latent variable structural model is a graphical model that specifies the presumed structure of causal connections among latent and manifest variables. It indicates the functional relations that relate effects to causes and specifies the form(s) of the functional equations that are to be used to represent functional relations. A latent variable is a hypothetical or theoretical construct, that is an unobserved variable presumed to exist within a structural model but for which direct measurements are not available. It is not possible to estimate the strengths of causal relationships with latent variables alone because the latent variables are not measurable. To estimate the strengths of these causal relations, it is necessary to operationalize each of the latent variables in terms of manifest variables that are believed to be caused by a latent variable. In this sense, each latent variable has the role of a common factor, and the manifest variables serve as manifest indicators of the common factor. The empirical content of each manifest variable is reflected directly by assigning observable events to values on the measurement scale of the variable.

Figure 5.6 shows the KBEM illustrated as a latent variable structural model. A notation by Bentler and Bonnet (1980) is used in the model to distinguish between manifest and latent variables. There are several notations that are used in the model. Altogether there are fourteen latent variables, that is, the ξ's and the η's. The variable that denotes leadership is referred to as an exogenous latent variable. This variable acts as a cause but whose occurrence is not to be explained by the model. The other latent variables, η_i', are endogenous variables, which are dependent variables (i.e. effects) whose occurrence is explained by the structural model. It can be seen from Figure 5.6 that the starting point of the model is the exogenous variable, leadership, that has an effect on four endogenous variables, delight the customer (η_1), management by fact (η_2), people-based management (η_3), and continuous improvement cycle (η_4). Each endogenous latent variable causes two other endogenous variables, namely, internal customers satisfaction (η_5), external customer satisfaction (η_6), all work is process (η_7), measurement (η_8) teamwork (η_9), people make quality (η_{10}), continuous improvement cycle (η_{11})

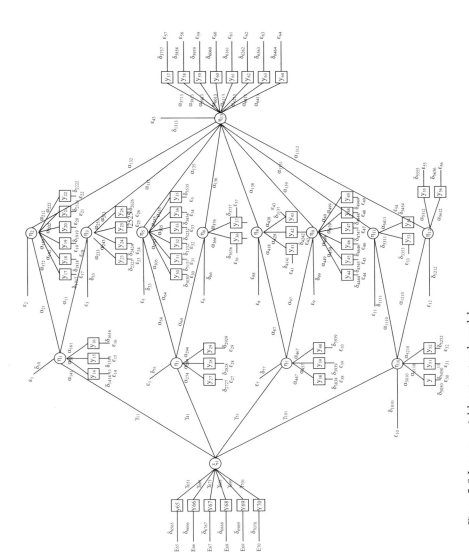

Figure 5.6 Latent variables structural model.

and prevention (η_{12}), respectively. Finally the variables $\eta_5-\eta_{12}$ cause η_{13}, that is, BE. Each latent variable is a cause of its constituent manifest indicator variables, y's. In structural models, all manifest variables are treated as endogenous variables.

The straight single-headed arrows show the direction of causation. Associated with each straight arrow is a structural parameter, that is, γ_{ji}, α_{ji}, δ_{ji}. The structural parameter associated with an arrow from an exogenous variable to an endogenous variable is designated by the Greek letter γ_{ji}, the subscript j indicating the number of endogenous variable, and the subscript i, indicating the number of exogenous variable. The structural parameter associated with an arrow from one endogenous variable to another endogenous variable is indicated by α_{ji}, with the subscript j indicating the number of the endogenous variable, that is, the effect variable and the subscript i indicating the number of endogenous variable, that is, the causal variable. The structural parameter associated with an arrow from a disturbance variable to an endogenous variable is designated by γ_{ji}, with subscripts. All structural parameters assume values that reflect the strengths of causal relationships. Specifically, each structural parameter reflects the amount of change in an effect (endogenous variable) that results from a unit of change in a cause (exogenous variable or preceding endogenous variable) with all other causes of that effect held constant. A key objective of representing the BEM as a latent variable structural model is to do a confirmatory analysis to estimate the values of the structural parameters. The ε_i's associated with each endogenous variable are the 'disturbance terms'. Disturbance terms involve variation in an endogenous variable that is not to be attributed to the causes of that variable included explicitly, in a structural model. For example, for the endogenous variable η_{13}, variable ε_{13} accounts for all variations in η_{13} that cannot be attributed to η_1, η_2, ..., and η_{12}. In the structural model, the sources of variation include (a) random shocks and/or unmeasured or omitted causes, (b) random measurement errors in the effect and the causes, where the primary concern is error in one or more of the causes, and (c) non-random measurement, such as bias in scales of measurement and method variance. The inclusion of the disturbance variable in the BEM makes it a probabilistic model.

Functional relations

The causal relations in the model can be expressed as functional relations, that is, a function of an effect on one or more causes. The functional relations are asymmetric because their causal directions are unidirectional. It can be observed from the structural model that there are four types of functional relations:

- Relation between an exothermic latent variable and endothermic latent variable;

- Relation between an exothermic latent variable and manifest indicator variables;
- Relation between an endothermic latent variable to one or more endothermic variable(s);
- Relation between a latent endothermic variable with manifest indicator variables.

In structural models, functional relations are analysed by using structural equations.

Structural equations

The four types of functional relations described in the previous section can be expressed as a system of equations known as functional equations. For the BEM, there are thirteen endogenous latent variables and fifty-seven manifest variables, which means that altogether there would be seventy equations in the system of functional equations.

Empirical support for functional equations

The confirmatory analysis using manifest variables may proceed only if the manifest variables are reasonably accurate representations of the constructs. The objective of such an analysis is to check whether a structural model can be confirmed. Confirmation implies that a structural model, and functional equations representing the model, are useful for making causal inferences to explain how variables occur (excluding purely exogenous variables). Non-confirmation implies that the structural model (functional relations and equations) are not useful in this respect.

The functional relations and equations in a linear structural model may be used to derive a set of predictions regarding the observed correlations (or variance/covariances) among the manifest variables. A structural model is confirmed if the predictions regarding correlations (variances/covariances) among manifest variables are consistent with the observed (i.e. empirically derived) correlations (variances/covariances) among manifest variables. Non-confirmation is implied if predictions and observed correlations (variances/covariances) are inconsistent.

Confirmation of predictions implies support for the structural model represented by the functional relations as equations. Non-confirmation of predictions implies that one or more components of structural model (functional relations and equations) is (are) false, in which case it is concluded that the structural model proposed originally is invalid. Predictions regarding correlations (variances/covariances) among manifest variables and confirmation/non-confirmation of these predictions can be addressed empirically by testing predictions regarding the magnitudes of estimates of structural parameters.

Solutions and estimates of structural parameters   The PLS method is used to solve for structural parameters in the structural equations. The parameters of a latent variable structural model can take the form of a fixed type parameter or non-fixed type. A structural parameter corresponding to a missing arrow is regarded as fixed and equal to zero. All arrows pointing from a disturbance to any other variable have parameters fixed at zero. In structural models with latent variables, we make the assumption that the distribution of the manifest variables is a function of their variance/covariance matrix. By making this assumption, it is possible to determine the non-fixed parameters of the model. The estimated and fixed structural parameters of a structural equation model determine a hypothetical variance/covariance (correlation) matrix for the manifest variables (Yo) under the assumption that the model is valid.

The structural parameters y and a computed are actually unstandardised regression coefficients of the structural equations. In the PLS method, the structural parameters of structured equation linking latent variables and manifest variables are called structural weights. A number of computer programs are available for computing the estimates of the parameters of structural equation models such as *LISREL*, *COSAN*, and *SAS.PLS*. The *SAS.PLS* program is chosen and is explained in the following section.

PLS.SAS computer programs

Model configuration

The 'direction' of the latent variables, whether inward or outward, as specified in the model, is given to the program. The terms 'inward' and 'outward' describe the outer relations in the model configuration. A latent variable is pointing inward if it is entering the model structure or outward if it is leaving the structure. In this case, only the final variable, that is, business excellence, is the outward variable, while others are inward variables. The outer relation coefficients are estimated by an iterative schedule.

The matrix COV

This is the correlation matrix of all observable variables in the model. The program calculates the matrix from raw data that are entered in EXCEL format and imported to *SAS* where it is converted into *SAS* data set.

Vector N

This vector gives the number of indicators for each latent variable in the order as they appear in COV.

Vector IR

This vector indicates what variables are involved as dependent and independent variables in each inner relation.

Vector IRN

This vector determines how many variables there are in each inner relation.

Vector IO

This vector indicates whether the outer indicators go in (1 is assigned) or out (0 is assigned) for each variable in the inner relations.

Size

This is the sample size of input data.

Maxnoit

This is the maximum number of iterations for the PLS procedure, MAXNOIT is given as 100 for all data set.

Criterio

This is the converge criterion which is given a value of 0.000001. Iteration stops when all coefficient estimates converge within CRITERIO.

Program Output

PLS.SAS generates several types of outputs:

1   Outer coefficients (γ, a)
2   Inner coefficients (γ, a)
3   Correlation matrix (r_{ji})
4   Standard deviation (SD)
5   t coefficients
6   Pearson correlation coefficient square (inner r^2)
7   Pearson correlation coefficient (inner r)
8   Cronbach coefficient (α)

Outer coefficients (structural weights)

The outer coefficients are the unstandardized structural weights of manifest indicator variables. Structural weights must have values significantly different from zero for a confirmation or non-confirmation of a model. Specifically, each structural weight reflects the amount of change in an effect (endogenous variable) that results from a unit of change in a cause (exogenous variable or endogenous variable), with all other causes of that effect held constant.

Inner coefficients (structural parameters of latent variables)

Structural parameters are the coefficients of functional equations linking latent variables. Structural parameters must have values significantly different from zero for confirmation or non-confirmation of the model. These values reflect the strengths of causal relationships. Specifically, each structural parameter reflects the amount of change in an effect (endogenous variable) that results from a unit of change in a cause (exogenous variable or preceding endogenic variable), with all other causes of that effect held constant.

Correlation matrix γ_{ij}

This is the Pearson correlation, r, matrix among all exogenous and endogenous variables in the model. Values in the matrix corresponding to latent variables that have cause and effect relationship provide additional indication of strength of their relationship.

Standard deviation

The standard deviation is the standard error of sample estimate of a structural parameter associated with a causal connection. It provides information on the spread of the parameter estimate from the mean.

Coefficients

The t coefficient of a structural parameter is the confidence interval around the estimate of the structural parameter. By using the standard error of the parameter, if the confidence intervals constructed around the structural parameter differ significantly from zero, then it can be concluded that there exists a causal connection between the variables in question.

Coefficient of determination r^2

The coefficient of determination r^2 represents the proportion of regression sum of squares corresponding to latent variables. The regression model explains the proportion of the total variation due to the cause-variable and the proportion due to randomness and other variables.

Pearson correlation coefficient r

Pearson correlation coefficient r is the correlation of latent variables that have causal connections. The closer this value is to ± 1, the stronger is the relationship between the variables in both directions.

Cronbach coefficient α

Cronbach α value provides indication of internal consistency of latent variables, which serve as common factors, that are being empirically reflected by manifest variables. It is computed using the variance of individual questionnaire items and covariance between items:

$$\alpha = \frac{k}{k-1}\left(1 - \frac{\sum \sigma_i^2}{\sum \sigma_i^2 + 2\sum\sum \sigma_{ij}^2}\right)$$

where k = the number of parts (items) in the scale, σ_i^2 = variance of item i, and σ_{ij} = covariance of the items.

According to Nunnaly, in early stages of research, coefficient α should have a value exceeding 0.7 for the latent variable to be a reliable measure. For a value lower than standard and the number of items are sufficiently large, the customary approach is to determine manifest variables that could improve a value if they are deleted from the model.

Significant testing of prediction regarding parameters associated with causes

Stated simply, inclusion of a variable on a cause in a functional equation indicates that the structural parameter associated with that variable is hypothesized to be different from zero. The predictions that estimates of structural parameters associated with causes in functional equations should be significantly different from zero can be verified by employing the conventional significant tests for unstandardized regression weights. If all estimated structural parameters for a particular functional equation are significant, then all predictions are confirmed with regard to our first test of confirmation. If all predictions in all equations are confirmed, the structural model is regarded as being consistent with data.

Output of business excellence model

The outputs of BEM are as follows:

- Indices of TQM, CSFs and BEI according to organization, department, division, units and collaborative activities:
  - all organization
  - category of organization
  - industrial organization

- comparisons of indices among organization, department, etc.
- evaluate sensitivity of organizations CSF indices based on model's structural parameters.

These outputs can be interpreted by TQM experts for continuous quality improvement of institutions.

An example

In order to investigate how this structured model can be used to measure the BEI, an example is provided in this section. A typical example of the BEI for a group of companies (i.e. overall, manufacturing and individual companies) is given in Figure 5.7, where overall indicates both service and manufacturing industry. Figure 5.8 provides indices of BE and CSFs for manufacturing organizations. Figure 5.8 provides indices for manufacturing company 'A' (for confidential reasons the name of the company is not mentioned), about their BEI and CSFs. In reality, the data were collected from managers of fourty-one European organizations. Measurement and calculation of BE were obtained using previously described statistical methods in order to provide the managers with a quality health check of their organization.

The present example shows how the measurement of BE can be used by Quality Directors for monitoring quality-related performance of their organization. These measurements can help the decision-makers to identify those areas of quality management where improvement should be made. Comparisons between different organizations could also be made to help prioritize quality improvement efforts. Organizations scoring highly on most of the

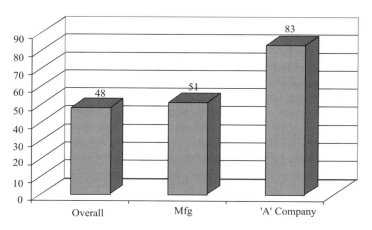

Figure 5.7 Business Excellence Index (BEI).

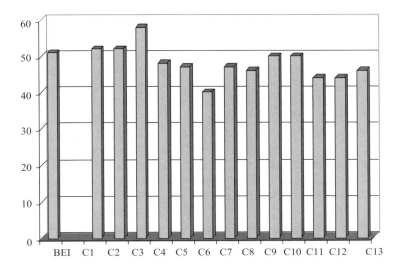

Figure 5.8 CSFs for manufacturing company.

Notes: C1. Leadership; C2. Delight the customers; C3. Customer satisfaction; C4. Internal customers are real; C5. Management by fact; C6. All work is process; C7. Measurement; C8. People based management; C9. Teamwork; C10. People make quality; C11. Continuous improvement; C12. Continuous improvement cycle; C13. Prevention; BEI. Business Excellence Index.

CSFs and BEI (see Figure 5.9, company 'A') may consider applying for national and international quality awards.

Condensed model of business excellence

The original generic model of BE and TQM given in Figures 5.1 and 5.5, respectively, would provide operational measures of the CSFs that can be used individually or in concert to produce a profile of organization-wide quality practices and BE. Such measures could be used by decision-makers to assess the status of quality management in the organization in order to direct improvements in the quality area. Since the model would be able to assess an organization's quality characteristics and attributes, therefore award-giving, an organization could use these for their selection process. For practical reason, it is sometimes necessary to combine the core concepts of the original model of Figure 5.1 to give a condensed model given in Figures 5.10 and 5.11.

This section provides a guideline of how the condensed model or the special-purpose model should be used for assessment of quality management status. It also describes what individual CSFs and the overall BE mean. Here the scores of the individual CSFs would be based on measurement items and the BEI will be based on a vector of averages of ratings of the CSFs.

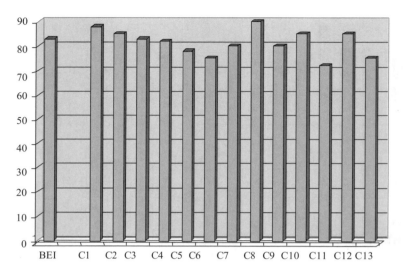

Figure 5.9 BEI of 'A' and indices of CSFs.

Notes: C1. Leadership; C2. Delight the customers; C3. Customer satisfaction; C4. Internal customers are real; C4. Management by fact; C6. All work is process; C7. Measurement;
C8. People-based management; C9. Teamwork; C10. People make quality; C11. Continuous improvement; C12. Continuous improvement cycle; C13. Prevention; BEI. Business
Excellence Index.

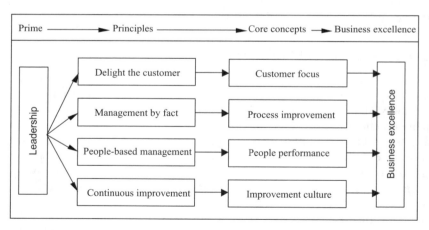

Figure 5.10 Condensed business excellence model (Kanji 1998*b*).

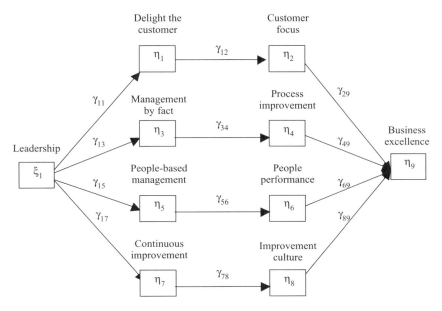

Figure 5.11 Kanji's Business Excellence Model.

An example (condensed model)

In order to investigate how this structured model can be used to measure the BEI, an example is provided in this section. In 1998, the author carried out a survey on European service and manufacturing organizations by collecting data via questionnaires from the managers of those organizations. The data from the survey were used to determine the indices of CSFs and BEI. Data analysis is performed on the entire data as well as being carried out separately for manufacturing organizations and for a selected manufacturing company, that is, company 'A'. Figures 5.12, 5.13 and 5.14 show the BE structural model with values of structural parameters for all organizations, manufacturing organizations and company 'A', respectively. The reliability values of empirical measurements in each case are given in Tables 5.2, 5.3 and 5.4, respectively.

The structural parameters show the strength of the relationship between independent and dependent variables of the model. All the structural parameters have positive values, indicating that the causal connections in the model have a symmetrical relationship. The results show that leadership (prime) has a strong causal connection with the first four CSFs that in turn affects other factors and ultimately BE. The variation in the parameter values for all organizations, manufacturing organizations and company 'A' reflects industry and

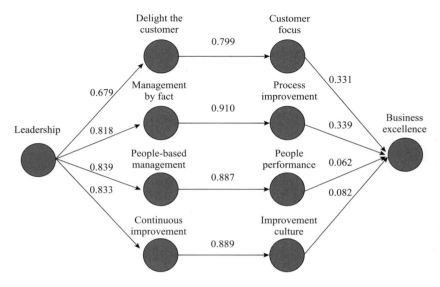

Figure 5.12 Structural parameters for all organizations.

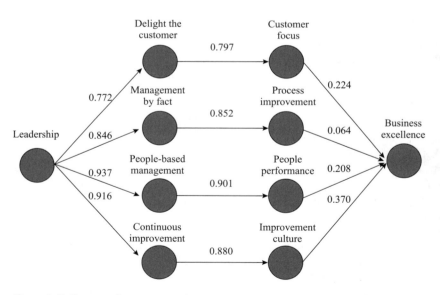

Figure 5.13 Structural parameters for manufacturing organizations.

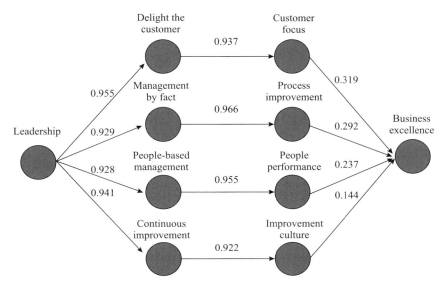

Figure 5.14 Structural parameters for company 'A'.

Table 5.2 Reliability of empirical measurements for all organizations

Critical success factors and business excellence	Reliability – α
Leadership	0.846
Delight the customer	0.737
Customer focus	0.803
Management by fact	0.876
Process improvement	0.805
People-based management	0.701
People performance	0.722
Continuous improvement	0.717
Improvement culture	0.829
Business excellence	0.893

firm-level effects. However, the positive parameter values coupled with high reliability values for latent variables support the presence of the proposed generic CSFs. The parameters for the last four variables that are connected to BE have relatively small values. This shows that the performance of the last four latent variables each collectively contributes to BE. Measurement and calculation of BE was obtained using previously described statistical methods in order to provide the managers with a quality health check of their organization.

Table 5.3 Reliability of empirical measurements for manufacturing organizations

Critical success factors and business excellence	Reliability – α
Leadership	0.887
Delight the customer	0.817
Customer focus	0.705
Management by fact	0.747
Process improvement	0.888
People-based management	0.778
People performance	0.812
Continuous improvement	0.912
Improvement culture	0.913
Business excellence	0.916

Table 5.4 Reliability of empirical measurements for company 'A'

Critical success factors and business excellence	Reliability – α
Leadership	0.885
Delight the customer	0.828
Customer focus	0.838
Management by fact	0.812
Process improvement	0.927
People-based management	0.905
People performance	0.907
Continuous improvement	0.858
Improvement culture	0.855
Business excellence	0.980

Figure 5.15 charts BEI for all organizations, manufacturing organizations and company 'A', respectively. As a guide, organizations with a BEI of 75 or more are regarded as excellent organizations. The BEI for the manufacturing company 'A' of 71 is higher than overall and manufacturing BEIs. Thus, company 'A' is a reasonably good manufacturing company with a BEI that exceeds industry average. The indices of other organizations could be determined in the same manner. A breakdown of indices for the three samples is given in Figures 5.16–5.18.

Two observations can be made about the indices. First, a high value of BEI corresponds to high values of CSF indices. Second, the BEI is influenced by the structural weights and the scores of manifest variables (not shown) that are linked to it as specified by the BEI mathematical formula. Knowing the relationship between CSFs and BEI is useful for examining the strength of each CSF to determine which one needs to be improved by how much, and in

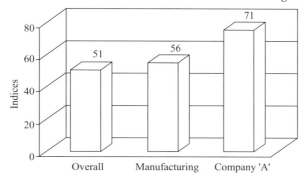

Figure 5.15 CSFs and BE indices for all organizations, manufacturing organizations and company 'A'.

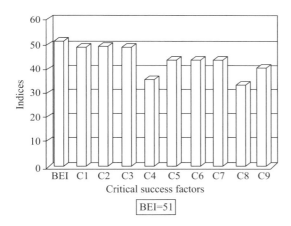

Figure 5.16 Indices of CSFs and BEI for all organizations.

Notes: C1. Leadership (49); C2. Delight the customer (49); C3. Customer focus (49); C4. Management by fact (38); C5. Process improvement (44); C6. People-based management (44); C7. People performance (44); C8. Continuous improvement (35); C9. Improvement culture (41); BEI. Business Excellence Index (51).

what ways in order to improve BE. Since the weights indicate the strength of relationship between variables, they could be used to determine the amount of improvement needed in CSFs to improve BE.

Here, the BEI was measured using the *SAS.PLS* method, which generated a weight for each question. The latent-variable scores were calculated by using a mathematical expression derived by Fornell (1994) using the weight (w);

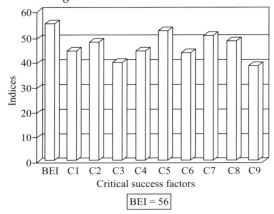

Figure 5.17 Indices of CSFs and BEI for manufacturing organizations.

Notes: C1. Leadership (44); C2. Delight the customer (49); C3. Customer focus (41); C4. Management by fact (44); C5. Process improvement (53); C6. People-based management (44); C7. People performance (52); C8. Continuous improvement (49); C9. Improvement culture (44); BEI. Business Excellence Index (56).

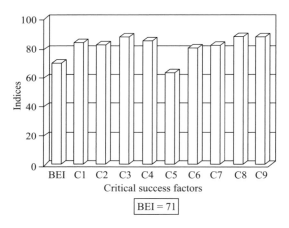

Figure 5.18 Indices of CSFs for BEI for company 'A'.

Notes: C1. Leadership (84); C2. Delight the customer (83); C3. Customer focus (89); C4. Management by fact (86); C5. Process improvement (64); C6. People-based management (81); C7. People performance (85); C8. Continuous improvement (89); C9. Improvement culture (89); BEI. Business Excellence Index (71).

and the arithmetic mean (x) for each question:

$$BEI = \left[\frac{\sum_{i=1}^{n} w_i x_i - \sum_{i=1}^{n} w_i}{9 \sum_{i=1}^{n} w_i} \right] \times 100$$

where n is the number of manifest variables for each latent variable.

The present example shows how the measurement of BE could be used by Quality Directors for internal assessment of the quality-related performance of their organizations. These measurements can help the decision-makers to identify those areas of quality management where improvement should be made. Comparisons between different organizations could also be made to help prioritize quality improvement efforts. Organizations scoring high on most of the CSFs and BEI may consider applying for national and international quality awards. Here, 'delight the customer' index provides a measurement of the external customer satisfaction index.

In conclusion, the model for estimating the BEI consists of a system of equations describing relations among fourteen constructs (see Figure 5.2) or a condensed model describing ten constructs. Each construct is operational using multiple questionnaire items and the entire system is estimated using PLS. This modelling methodology offers a number of advantages over the other BE measures calculated by most organizations. First, the use of multiple questionnaire items for each construct increases the provision of the estimate of BE. Second, the individual questionnaire items are measured on a ten-point scale in order to enhance reliability. Third, the BEI measure is constructed by weighting the individual items, that is, leadership, customer delight, process improvement, people performance, continuous improvement, etc., such that the resulting index has a maximum correlation with stakeholder value.

Sequence for obtaining Kanji's Business Excellence Model

KBEM uses a Structural Equation Modelling (SEM) approach. A few books and articles present the concepts associated with structural equation models and discuss the steps in applying this relatively complex statistical approach.

Given below is a brief explanation on the issues of SEM and steps for the measurement of KBEM index.

- *Latent variables* correspond to concepts and cannot be measured directly. They are operationalizations of constructs in a structural equation model. In KBEM case, the prime, principles and core concepts are all latent variables. Since they cannot be directly observed, they must be represented by manifest variables.
- *Manifest variables* are, therefore, observed values for specific items or questions which are used as indicators of latent variables. In KBEM, a set of manifest variables were identified to adequately cover the domain of each construct. The manifest variables correspond to the questionnaire items.
- Sometimes the set of manifest variables that represent one particular latent variable is referred to as a *measurement scale*. Measurement scales must obey certain conditions. Apart from adequately representing the domain of the concept (validity), scales are expected to be unidimensional (representing a single construct), and statistically reliable (stable and consistent for which, in KBEM approach, Cronbach's coefficient α

is calculated). This is obviously different from the simple notion of *scale* as the range of values a variable can assume. In KBEM questionnaire each item is answered in a one-to-ten scale.

- The weights in structural equation models are usually designated as *path coefficients* and represent the strength of the relationships among different variables. In a structural equation model, both inner and outer coefficients are estimated.
- *Inner coefficients* reflect the strength of causal relationships among variables. They are the coefficients of the equations linking latent variables and each inner coefficient represents the amount of change in an effect variable that results from a unit of change in a cause variable. The coefficients in KBEM are expected to be all positive, showing that all CSFs contribute to BE and reinforce each other.
- *Outer coefficients* correspond to the weights of the manifest variables. The higher they are, the more relevant they are in explaining the correspondent manifest variables.
- *Indices* are the scores obtained for each manifest variable, based upon the correspondent manifest variables and the path coefficients in the model.

The steps for the measurement of index in KBEM require the following sequence:

1   Develop the theoretically based model: any structural equation model must have a strong theoretical foundation. Relevant constructs are identified, logical causal connections proposed and the specification error considered. In KBEM the CSFs were carefully identified and are consistent with the thinking of the most prominent quality management researchers.

2   Construct a path diagram which depicts in a diagram a series of causal connections that represent the predictive relationships among constructs that correspond to the usual way KBEM is pictured in the papers, as a series of interrelated constructs.

3   Convert the path diagram into a set of structural and measurement models. At this stage, the model is specified through a series of equations that defines: (1) the structural equations linking constructs; (2) the measurement model specifying which variables measure which constructs; and (3) a set of matrices indicating any hypothesized constructs among constructs or variables. Before applying any software or making any calculations in the KBEM, the set of indicators (manifest variables) for each latent variable is decided. That means that by then the questionnaire made up of the selected indicators for each construct of KBEM is ready.

4   Administer the questionnaire and obtain the measurement items from results of the questionnaire.

5   Estimate the proposed model, running the equations on a computer to get estimates for the path coefficients and the factor indices. SEM uses the

variance–covariance or the correlation matrix as its input data. Once the input data type is selected, it is necessary to decide how the model will be estimated. In KBEM case, the correlation matrix is used and the estimates calculated according to PLS. The software used is the *SAS* or a special program developed for the MatLab package, that is, *KW management software*. The estimates for all coefficients are calculated simultaneously.

6 The results for the model estimation must be carefully analysed. Sometimes it is necessary to identify/correct offending estimates. Since KBEM is a theoretical model with sound theoretical justifications, these situations seldom occur.

7 Assess goodness-of-fit. Besides evaluating overall model fit, it is necessary to analyse whether or not the measurement of each construct fits the requirements of unidimensionality and reliability. Briefly, Cronbach's α is used as a reliability measure, while outer coefficients and r^2 must be analysed to assess the power of explanation of each measurement scale and of the structural model as a whole.

8 Interpret and eventually refine the model.

Conclusions

One of the benefits of the present method of BE is that it is applicable to both manufacturing and service industries and allows organizations to compare themselves against the different organizations with whom they are competing. This is of particular benefit to organizations which are not doing as well as they might, as it will give them an incentive to do something about their failings. Besides being able to compare organizations within the same sector, since the index is a single number, it is possible for them to compare across industries, and how well they are doing against the national index (when calculated).

Organizations can use the data from the index to assess the contribution by the leadership, identify potential barriers to entry within markets, predict return on investments and pinpoint areas in which customers are not being satisfied.

Conducting regular BE surveys would provide the organization with straightforward and consistent information at a realistic cost. Since the BEI survey allows you the flexibility to include additional questions to those needed for the index construction, new developments can be evaluated and other hypotheses tested.

A typical programme would consist of half-yearly or yearly surveys. For the first survey the report will include a detailed analysis of all the relevant questions. Subsequent survey reports need only contain a level of detail that would be agreed at the outset. If some changes in the index score (up or down) were reported, an additional analysis could be commissioned to pinpoint the likely causes. From an initial agreement to proceed with an index construction project, whether it be a one-off or a five-year programme, the first stage would be to design an appropriate package for the organization. This would involve the identification of customers, deciding on the method of collection of data, the form of index questions and additional questions to be added and detail of reporting. It will be necessary to select an appropriate sample of customers.

As well as comparing individuals against other organizations, the data will also be open for in-depth analysis. For example, it will be possible to look at the scores for individual components, allowing you to see which areas of BE are being dealt with more satisfactorily than others. The BEI will also allow the organizations to compare different areas of its business both directly and over time, as shown in Figure 5.8.

In conclusion, the model for estimating the BEI consists of a system of equations describing relations among fourteen constructs (see Figure 5.6). Each construct is operational using multiple questionnaire items and the entire system is estimated using PLS. This modelling methodology offers a number of advantages over the other BE measures calculated by most organizations.

First, the use of multiple questionnaire items for each construct increases the provision of the estimate of BE. Second, the individual questionnaire items are measured on a ten-point scale in order to enhance reliability. Third, the BE measure is constructed by weighting the individual items, that is, leadership, customer satisfaction, teamwork, prevention, etc., such that the resulting index has a maximum correlation with stakeholders' value.

Although the model does not include stakeholders' value, that is, profitability, it is straightforward to estimate the economic consequences of quality initiatives. In particular, BE exhibits a positive relation with customer satisfaction, that is, customer retention and greater market share which increases the present value of the customer asset.

In the following chapter, KBS has been developed to complement KBEM by focusing on measurement of the organization performance using other stakeholders.

6 Kanji's Business Scorecard

Introduction

The Balanced Scorecard (BSC) was first devised by Kaplan and Norton (1992) as a measurement framework that was expected to overcome some of the deficiencies of traditional performance systems. It gives a holistic view of the organization by simultaneously looking at four important perspectives (financial, customer, internal processes, innovation and learning). Apart from being a measurement framework, the BSC achieved recognition as a strategic management system.

The new approach to performance measurement suggested in the BSC is consistent with the initiatives under way in many companies: cross-functional integration, continuous improvement, customer–supplier partnerships, and team rather than individual accountability. In this sense, it fits well into the quality management philosophy, embracing some of the Business Excellence (BE) principles of Kanji's Business Excellence Model (KBEM).

Nevertheless, the BSC, as presented by Kaplan and Norton, is not without limitations. The causality links suggested among the four perspectives are particularly problematic and ambiguous. Additionally, it fails to explicitly recognize the contributions of important stakeholders, such as employees and suppliers.

Taking into account the potentialities and limitations of the traditional BSC, we propose the development of a new framework integrating the elements of the KBEM (Kanji 1998*b*) and taking advantage of the strengths of its sound methodological support. The BSC may be improved by integrating the Total Quality Management (TQM) principles and Critical Success Factors (CSFs) that constitute KBEM.

The Kanji's Business Scorecard (KBS) we present in this chapter is not a conceptual model only, it is also a measurement model. Furthermore, Kanji's approach has the potential to give a deeper understanding of how achievements in the different areas feed each other to form a cycle of continuous improvement.

Finally, the implementation of KBS can help organizations to develop, cascade and implement a strategy for BE.

Review of literature on the Balanced Scorecard

Origins and principles

Today managers compete in such a competitive and complex environment that establishing accurate goals and understanding how they can be achieved is vital.

In this context, it is a truism to say that effective management depends on the effective measurement of performance and results. Executives understand that their organization's measurement system strongly affects the behaviour of managers and employees (Kaplan and Norton 1992). It is therefore desirable that the system is linked to the espoused strategy of the organization in order to have the maximum impact.

Traditional financial measures do not match entirely with the competencies and skills companies need to face today's business environment. Recognition is given to the view that purely financial evaluation of performance is not enough in an environment where non-financial assets, business relationships and organization's capabilities increasingly determine the prospects for success (Kaplan and Norton 1996).

Accounting figures do not emphasize the elements which will lead to good or poor future financial results. The problem may even be aggravated if the company is in a situation in which it feels forced to pursue short-term financial results rather than the organization's long-term goals (Kaplan 1984; Johnson and Kaplan 1987). The Economic Value Added, for instance, has emerged as an important measure, but while it has the benefit of making managers more aware of the cost of capital, profit captures performance with a time lag and can thus be improved by actions that can hurt future profitability (such as decreasing investment in customers, R&D or employees) (Epstein and Manzoni 1998).

The protection of short-term financial performance is a main driver behind the search for a more complete set of performance measures. Broader performance measurement systems are increasingly seen as a device for delivering long-term strategic objectives (Butler *et al.* 1997).

On realizing the shortcomings of financial measures (and management accounting in particular), operational measures began to take a more important role in the measurement of business performance.

As Kaplan and Norton (1992) argue, no single measure can provide a clear performance target or focus attention on the critical areas of the business. The complexity of managing an organization today requires that managers be able to view performance in several areas simultaneously. Managers need a real-time balanced presentation of both financial and operational measures. In reality, many organizations have for a long time already been using measurement systems incorporating financial and non-financial measures, but the BSC goes beyond that by driving measures from the organization's mission and strategy (Kaplan and Norton 1996).

Kaplan and Norton devised a 'balanced scorecard' – a set of measures that gives managers a fast but comprehensive view of the business. The BSC includes financial measures that tell the results of actions already taken. And it complements the financial measures with operational measures on customer satisfaction, internal processes, and the organization's innovation and improvement activities – operational measures that are the drivers of future financial performance. Therefore, it enables companies to track financial results while simultaneously monitoring progress in building the capabilities and acquiring the intangible assets they would need for future growth.

The BSC has an antecedent on the idea of *Tableau de Bord*, which became popular in France in the beginning of the twentieth century (Epstein and Manzoni 1998). Similarly, the Tableau de Bord advocates that operational measures provide important information on the impact of decisions. Essentially, the development of the Tableau de Bord involves translating the vision and mission into a set of objectives, from which each unit identifies its Key Success Factors (KSFs), which are translated into a series of quantitative Key Performance Indicators (KPIs). Actual performance should then be periodically compared to some yardstick chosen on the basis of both past performance and benchmarking (Epstein and Manzoni 1998). Reality shows, however, that the Tableau de Bord tends to fall short of the BSC, in that it overemphasizes financial measures, does not achieve the same level of synthesis, tends to disseminate existing performance indicators rather than starting from vision and strategy, and measures are often only gathered internally inside the firm rather than externally from customers.

According to Kaplan and Norton (1996), the BSC must retain a strong emphasis on financial outcomes, which ultimately are the result of the causal paths established in the scorecard. Thus, financial results are obtained by successful implementation of strategic initiatives in key business process perspectives (Mooraj *et al.* 1998).

Many have criticized financial measures because of their inadequacies, their backward-looking focus and inability to reflect contemporary value-creating activities. Financial indicators are typically considered to be 'lagging indicators of performance', because they record the effect of decisions not when decisions are made, but rather as the financial impact of these decisions materializes, which can be long after the decision was made (Epstein and Manzoni 1998). Some critics go much further. They argue that financial measures do not improve customer satisfaction, quality, cycle time and employee motivation. In that view, financial performance is the result of operational actions, and financial success should be the logical consequence of doing the fundamentals well. Kaplan and Norton (1992) recognize, however, that financial measures are necessary both because a well-designed financial control system can actually enhance general improvements in every aspect of the business and because improved performance is expected to be reflected in better financial measures. As stated by Kaplan and Norton (1992), 'the hard truth is that if improved performance fails to be reflected in the bottom line, executives should re-examine the assumptions of their strategy and mission'.

'Old' performance measures overlook the importance of the firm's relationship with its environment, in particular with its customers. Hence, the need is apparent for a set of performance criteria more overly oriented towards the firm's end-markets (Butler *et al.* 1997).

The BSC allows managers to look at the business from four important perspectives, thus constituting a holistic view of the organization.

It provides answers to four basic questions (Kaplan and Norton 1992):

- How do customers see us? (customer perspective)
- What must we excel at? (internal perspective)
- Can we continue to improve and create value? (innovation and learning perspective)
- How do we look to shareholders? (financial perspective)

The BSC defines and assesses the CSFs considered necessary to fulfil the corporate goals to ensure future success (Hepworth 1998). The identification of these key performance measures constitutes a prerequisite to developing the scorecard.

Besides working at the corporate management level, the BSC concept can also be applied to measure, evaluate and guide activities that take place in specific functional areas of a business.

The Balanced Scorecard: contributions, strengths and weaknesses

The BSC is distinct from other strategic measurement systems in that it contains outcome measures and the performance drivers of outcomes, linked together in cause-and-effect relationships (Kaplan and Norton 1996). One of the reasons the BSC is such a powerful tool is precisely that it stresses the linkages for achieving outstanding performance in related measures, rather than concentrating on isolated measures. As some people suggest, 'the added value of the balanced scorecard is in the drawing together of all the key business areas and identifying the linkages that deliver success'. Thus, the scorecard helps to fight sub-optimization by forcing managers to consider all key measures that collectively are critical for the success of the organization and highlighting the need to analyse trade-offs (Letza 1996; Tsang 1998).

The assumption that there is a cause-and-effect relationship is essential because it allows measurements in non-financial areas to be used to predict future financial performance (Nørreklit 2000). The measurement system should then make the relationships among objectives (and measures) in the various perspectives explicit so that they can be managed and validated.

The BSC claims to identify cause-and-effect relationships between the different elements of an organization. Nørreklit (2000), however, considers that these relationships are problematic. The causality between quality and financial results, for instance, has not been proved on an empirical basis and some studies even reject it. In addition, according to Nørreklit (2000) if a cause-and-effect relationship requires a time lag between cause and effect, then it is problematic that the time dimension is not part of the scorecard. From a neo-classical perspective, adds the same author, the relationship between customer satisfaction and financial results is a logical one and not a cause-and-effect relationship. Profits are conditioned by customer satisfaction and they are not its cause.

Nørreklit (2000) concludes that there is no causal relationship between measures from the four perspectives. Instead, the arguments indicate that the perspectives are interdependent. The influence between measures is not unidirectional in the sense that learning and growth are the drivers of internal business processes, which are the drivers of customer satisfaction, which in turn is the driver of financial results. The reasoning is circular. So instead of a cause-and-effect relationship, the relationship between the areas is more likely to be one of interdependence.

There are indeed indications that Kaplan and Norton want to refer to finality and not to causality. In one of Kaplan and Norton's figures, the arrows point in both directions (1996*a*), indicating assumed finality. Altogether, the power of the instrument to make statements and to serve the purposes of management control will be greatly reduced (Nørreklit 2000).

The understanding of some companies (like an information technology (IT) company in Asia) is, however, different. The IT company defines a chain of causes and effects where learning and growth indicators enable the company to achieve the internal business process indicators that will enable the company to achieve customer indicators and lead, in turn, to the achievement of financial indicators.

Probably, the main benefit of the BSC is its ability to translate an organization's vision and strategy into tangible objectives and measures. The BSC uses indicators to communicate a strategy and to measure the success of its implementation. To translate the corporate goals into operational terms, the company's balanced scorecard should be deployed to each business unit.

Kaplan and Norton (1996: 292) emphasize that 'the process of developing the balance scorecard gives an organization, usually for the first time, a clear picture of the future and a path to for getting there'.

As stated by Mooraj *et al.* (1998), 'by evaluating the relevant factors of each segment of the BSC which may have an impact on a financial aim, the appropriate measures can be identified and the alignment of actions to the strategic goal is facilitated'. Used correctly it can empower an organization by operationalizing the strategy discussion, and then by assigning the accountability for well-defined results (Gering and Rosmarin 2000).

As recognized by Mintzberg (1994) among many others, strategy implementation is the cause of many problems. Kaplan and Norton (1996) identify four specific barriers for effective strategic implementation and explain how the BSC can contribute to overcome some of these problems:

- Vision and strategies that are not actionable. (Where disagreement exists about how to translate the mission and vision statements into actions, the consequence is fragmentation and sub-optimization of efforts. The process of building a scorecard clarifies the strategic objectives and identifies the few critical drivers for strategic success. The process creates consensus and teamwork among organizational members.)
- Strategies that are not linked to departmental, team, and individual goals. (The communication and goal setting process of the BSC dramatically improve the alignment of all organizational participants to the strategy.)
- Strategies that are not linked to long- and short-term resource allocation. (Many organizations have separate processes for long-term strategic planning and for short-term budgeting. The consequence is that discretionary funding and capital allocations are often unrelated to strategic priorities. By integrating both time horizons the BSC avoids this deficiency.)
- Feedback that is tactical not strategic. (Most management systems provide feedback only about short-term, operational performance; little or no time is spent in examining indicators of strategy implementation and success. Without feedback, organizations have no way to test and learn about their strategy. The BSC provides indications of how the strategy is being implemented and whether it is working.)

As Kaplan and Norton (1996: 147) argue, 'companies that can translate their strategy into their measurement system are far better able to execute their strategy because they can communicate their objectives and targets. This communication focuses managers and employees on the critical drivers, enabling them to align investments, initiatives and actions with accomplishing strategic goals'.

The communicational role of the BSC is particularly important in a business context where organizations cannot determine all the local actions required to implement a strategy. The long-term vision and strategy, embodied in the BSC, gives employees a strong indication of how they can contribute to the success of the organization and encourages them to suggest ways by which the vision and strategy can be achieved. By communicating the strategy and by linking it to personal goals, the scorecard creates a shared understanding and commitment among all organizational participants (Kaplan and Norton 1996).

Therefore, the BSC is more than a performance measurement system. It is commonly adopted as a strategic management system to (Kaplan and

Norton 1992, 1996; McClintock 2000):

- Describe the organization's vision of the future and create shared understanding;
- Clarify and update corporate strategy;
- Communicate strategic objectives throughout the organization (it establishes a communication system that bridges the gap between goals set by high-level executives and the frontline workers whose performance is ultimately responsible for reaching these goals);
- Align customer needs and business objectives;
- Work as a holistic model of the strategy allowing all employees to see how they contribute to organizational success, and contributing to align departmental and personal goals to corporate strategy;
- Focus on efforts to change, by identifying opportunities for initiatives in the areas that are lagging behind;
- Link strategic objectives to targets and budgets (financial and physical resources must be aligned to the strategy; long-run capital budgets, strategic initiatives and annual expenses must all be directed to achieving targets for the objectives and measure of the scorecard);
- Build a reward system that is geared for achieving targets (alignment and accountability will be enhanced when individual contributions to achieving scorecard objectives are linked to recognition, promotion and compensation programmes);
- Align strategic and operational reviews;
- Obtain feedback on the effectiveness of the strategy policy deployment and implementation to track progress over time and facilitate strategic review.

Kaplan and Norton (1996) also claim that the BSC addresses another deficiency of traditional management systems, by linking a company's long-terms strategy with its short-term actions. It is a useful tool to translate the vision and strategy into actions at local level. In Kaplan and Norton's (1996: 47) words, 'the scorecard should tell the story of the strategy, starting with the long-run financial objectives, and then linking them to the sequence of actions that must be taken with financial processes, customer internal processes, and finally employees and systems to deliver the desired long-run economic performance'. The main message is that in short and medium term the ultimate financial objectives can be reached by adequate customer service and effective business process only. However, in order to sustain success in the long term, the organization must also realize its objectives as concerning the learning and growth perspective (Lengyel 2000).

Each of the four areas define a number of corporate objectives and assigns an agreed set of measurement criteria to each factor, so that everyone in an organization gets an overall view of the business and easily understands interdependencies.

The aim is to present management with a concise summary of the CSF of a business, and to facilitate the alignment of business operations with the overall strategy (Mooraj *et al.* 1998). This brings a significant benefit of developing a BSC: it is a learning exercise in which firms improve the knowledge of their activities and processes.

In today's turbulent context, organizations need double-loop learning. The double-loop learning occurs when managers question their assumptions and reflect on whether the theory under which they are operating is consistent with current evidence, observations and experience (Kaplan and Norton 1996). The BSC constitutes an effective learning process, since it integrates: (1) a shared strategic framework that communicates the strategy and allows each participant to see how to contribute to the achievement of the overall strategy; (2) a feedback process that collects performance data about the strategy and allows the hypothesis about interrelationships among strategic objectives and initiatives to be tested; and (3) a team problem-solving process that analyses and learns from the performance data and then adapts the strategy to emerging conditions and issues (Kaplan and Norton 1996).

A good BSC should have a mix of outcome measures (lag indicators) and performance drivers (lead indicators) (Nørreklit 2000).

To be effective, the model has to be rooted in the management and the organization. Such rooting requires the scorecard to fit the concepts and relationships which the management uses when the company formulates its strategy and vision (Nørreklit 2000). Additionally, the unique culture and existing company philosophy have to be incorporated in the scorecard for it to be acceptable to managers (Letza 1996).

In sum, the BSC has strengths and weaknesses.

Strengths of the BSC approach

- Puts together, in a single report, many of the seemingly disparate elements of a company's competitive agenda.
- Ability to translate an organization's vision and strategy into tangible objectives and measures.
- Holistic approach to performance measures.
- Focus on a limited number of critical measures (avoiding information overload).
- Flexibility and adaptability to fit each organization in particular.
- By forcing managers to consider all the important operational measures together, gives a sense of interdependency among different organizational areas.
- Strong focus on customer and market.
- Forces managers to develop a clear and shared view of what they are trying to achieve and what the critical levers and means to reach those

objectives are (Epstein and Manzoni 1998), helping to focus everyone's attention towards the future.

- Easy to use.

Weaknesses of the BSC approach

- A conceptual model only (not easy to convert into a measurement model).
- Interactions between criteria are not clearly shown.
- Causal relationships are problematic (more like interdependence).
- Not a comprehensive system approach, focus is only on customers, forgetting other important stakeholders.
- Only focus on results.

Other weaknesses:

- It fails to highlight employee and supplier contributions (see Nørreklit 2000).
- It does not identify the role of the community in defining the environment within which the company works.
- It focuses primarily (and almost exclusively) on top-down performance measurement.

Nørreklit (2000) adds that:

- It does not monitor the competition (the emphasis on the customer perspective implicitly ignores the broader market perspective) or techno-logical developments, which means that the focus of the model is static rather than dynamic.
- The control model is highly top-down, making it difficult for the required interactive control and double-loop learning.
- Due to its top-down strategy, the balanced scorecard will primarily create external commitment (based on manager's orders and rewards). If the external commitment is too high, then it motivates employees to focus their attention on what is measured.

Epstein and Manzoni (1998) state that Kaplan and Norton's four perspectives are presented as an organizing framework rather than a constraining straightjacket. From their study of two companies, they suggest a few potential additional perspectives for the BSC, including the impact of the firm on society (firm's impact on employment, local communities and environment) and the firm's economic, political and social environment (environment contingencies that can have a major impact on the firm's performance), while calling attention to the need for keeping the number of boxes rather small in order to preserve the conciseness and clarity of the BSC presentation.

Some Balanced Scorecard applications

Organizations initially adopt the BSC for a variety of reasons: clarifying and gaining consensus on strategy, focusing organizational change initiatives, developing leadership capabilities, and gaining coordination among different organizational segments.

Like every other major change, the development and adoption of the BSC requires the full engagement and commitment of the leadership at the top.

The process of building and implementing a BSC must be customized. As Kaplan and Norton (1996) state, 'the balanced scorecard is not a template that can be applied to a business in general or even industry wide. Different market situations, product strategies and competitive environments require different scorecards. Business units devise customised scorecards to fit their mission, strategy and culture'. Therefore, the specific content of the four 'boxes' of the BSC must be adapted to the circumstances of each organization.

The BSC needs to be more than a collection of critical successful indicators on KSFs. The multiple measures on a properly constructed BSC should consist of a linked series of objectives and measures that are both consistent and mutually reinforcing (Kaplan and Norton 1996).

The selection of the indicators to be included in the BSC should follow a conscious and deductive process starting from the objectives the firm is trying to pursue and the critical means that will get it there (Epstein and Manzoni 1998). The set of indicators needs to reflect and operationalize the organization's mission and strategy to be effective. This development and selection process of the right performance indicators is complex. The indicators must be *controllable*[1] (i.e. target achievement should not be overly influenced by events or decisions that are out of managers' control), but they should also be reasonably *complete*[2] (i.e. they should not fail to capture important dimensions of performance) (Epstein and Manzoni 1998).

Moreover, introducing a BSC inevitably brings some change and resistance. Changes affecting the availability of performance-related information can be particularly threatening, as they have the potential of modifying the balance of power within the organization (Epstein and Mazoni 1998).

Another associated issue relates to the need to link the BSC with company's goals and rewards. One of the major problems of many performance measurement systems is that they fail to reward the behaviours they hope to obtain from their employees (Kerr 1975, cited in Epstein and Mazoni 1998). In order to prevent this from happening, it is important to achieve a high degree of consistency between the goals the companies are pursuing and the basis upon which they reward people.

Once the BSC is developed and implemented, it must also evolve over time, as the company's environment, capabilities and/or strategy change (Epstein and Mazoni 1998).

The scorecard has been applied by many companies. It is estimated that, at the end of the year 2000, 40 per cent of the Fortune 2000 companies use it. Examples of users include in the USA, Rockwater, Intel, Apple Computers,

American Express, and the US Department of Transportantion; in the UK, BP Chemicals, Miliken, the NatWest Group, Abbey National and Leeds Permanent Building Society. There are also commercial packages to help companies create their BSC, such as software programs that enable business performance indices to be created by extracting data from computer-based Information Systems (I/S) (McKendrick 1997, cited in Martinsons *et al.* 1999).

Companies implementing the BSC have realized significant benefits and performance improvement, confirming to some extent the advantages suggested in the previous section.

Once carefully considered, the problems associated with the implementation of the BSC, Kaplan and Norton are optimistic in terms of the time required to start feeling the benefits. They consider sixteen weeks as a typical time period to design, develop and roll out a BSC. Positive results are expected then to appear in six months, with more dramatic improvements taking a full year.

IT company measurement of balanced scorecard

Goals	*Measures*
Financial perspective	Return on investment Revenue growth Profitability Cash flow Operating expense Account receivable
Customer perspective	Market share Customer satisfaction Delivery time Customer retention and loyalty (number of existing customers; percentage growth of business with existing customers) Customer acquisition Responsiveness (time)
Internal business process perspective	Productivity Quality of operation
Learning and growth perspective	Employee competency and capability Empowerment Employee satisfaction Access to strategic information IT use Employee retention Employee morale Employee training and development

Banks' measurement of balanced scorecard

Strategic objectives	Strategic measurements	
	Core outcomes (Lag)	Performance drivers (Lead)
Financial		
F1 Meet shareholder expectations	Return on equity	
F2 Improve operating performance	Combined ratio	
F3 Achieve profitable growth	Business mix	
F4 Reduce shareholder risk	Catastrophic losses	
Customer		
C1 Improve agency performance	Acquisition/Retention (vs plan)	Agency performance (vs plan)
C2 Satisfy target policyholders	Acquisition/Retention (by segment)	Policyholder satisfaction survey
Internal		
I1 Develop target markets	Business mix (by segment)	Business development (vs plan)
I2 Underwrite profitably	Loss ratio	Underwriting quality audit
I3 Align claims with business	Claims frequency Claims severity	Claims quality audit
I4 Improve productivity	Expense ratio	Headcount movement Managed spending movement
Learning		
L1. Upgrade staff competencies	Staff productivity	Staff development (vs plan)
L2. Access to strategic information		Strategic I/T availability (vs plan)

I/S measurement and evaluation

Martinsons *et al.* (1999) suggest that traditional methods (such as ROI, NPV, payback period) fail to evaluate the investments in IT and I/S, since they do not capture the value of intangible benefits. Therefore, they argue that the BSC is a more appropriate tool to measure and evaluate IT and I/S. In their paper they detail how the BSC can serve as a decision support tool for I/S managers. In this sense, they suggest the following perspectives for a balanced

I/S scorecard: user orientation, business value, internal process, and future readiness. The modifications introduced aim to reflect the view of the I/S department as an internal service supplier and the fact that I/S projects are commonly carried out for the benefit of both end-users and the organization as a whole.

Environmental performance

A more innovative application of the BSC is reported by Johnson (1998). The author shows the benefits of using the BSC approach in the selection of a balanced set of environmental performance indicators (EPIs). In this case, Johnson (1998) suggests the consideration of the following four perspectives: (1) learning, innovation, growth, and people; (2) internal business processes; (3) customers and external stakeholders; and (4) finances. The main concern is to embrace a wider understanding of external stakeholders to include government, regulators, environmental organizations and facility neighbours, among others.

Total Quality Management, Business Excellence and the Balanced Scorecard

The new approach to performance measurement suggested in the BSC is consistent with BE and TQM initiatives under way in many companies: cross-functional integration, continuous improvement, customer–supplier partnerships, and team rather than individual accountability. In addition, corporate efforts to decentralized decision making through empowerment, improved efficiency and competitiveness, increased cooperation and execution of strategy are consistent with the BSC approach (Walker 1996).

As stated by Butler *et al.* (1997), traditional measurement systems have a control bias, that is, they specify the particular actions they want employees to take and then measure to see whether or not the employees have taken these actions – they try to control behaviour. The BSC, on the other hand, assumes that people will adopt whatever action is necessary to arrive at the agreed goals. In this sense, the BSC follows McGregor's 'Theory Y', which assumes that the employee, if directly involved in the goal-setting process, can be relied upon for self-control (Lee *et al.* 2000).

Furthermore, as Martinsons *et al.* (1999) emphasize, the evolution of the BSC concept during the 1990s reflects assumptions and theories that underlie business process re-engineering, as advocated by quality management. Process-based metrics are seen as a key element in a strategic management system that drives performance improvement and enables the top management team to make well-informed decisions. In addition, the BSC encourages having multiple measurements for cross-functional and integrated business processes, which constitutes a significant improvement over traditional performance measurement systems (Kaplan and Norton 1996).

Customer satisfaction is at the core of any quality definition. The BSC, in turn, provides organizations with a customer-based planning method that is consistent with the quality concept adopted.

The novelties introduced in the year 2000 revision of the ISO standards, in particular the idea that the documented process management system has to cover all business processes of the value-chain including the analysis of customer requirements, the monitoring of customer satisfaction and the cycle of revision and learning (Lengyel 2000) represents a clear evolution tendency in the direction of the adoption of a BSC by companies that follow the ISO 2000 standards. Lengyel (2000) highlights that this integration is widely justified:

- A significant part of the measurement analysis subsystem of the quality management system can be made up of BSC process measurement indicators;
- The source of the customer-related indicators could also be the BSC measurement system;
- The strategic goals of the BSC are an important input for the continuous improvement of quality system.

BE requires continuous improvement. A similar message is provided by the learning and growing perspective, which allows the infrastructure to enable ambitious objectives in the other three perspectives to be achieved. Kaplan and Norton (1996: 126) state that 'objectives in the learning and growth perspective are the drivers for achieving excellent outcomes in the first three scorecard perspectives'. Moreover, the enablers for learning and growth, identified by Kaplan and Norton, come mainly from sources such as employees, systems and organizational alignment, which is in accordance with crucial TQM principles such as people training and development, consistency of purpose and the systemic view of organizations.

A few attempts have been made to compare the BSC with BEMs. One of them is presented by Lengyel (2000). He found that the BSC covers most criteria of the EFQM Excellence Model. In many cases, the content of each BSC perspective tends to be widespread by several BEMs criteria. In Lengyel's (2000) view, the BSC has one main advantage over the EFQM model: it connects strategic and operative planning not only by determining the objectives, but also by defining the way to achieve them. On the other hand, the EFQM model is a more uniform and standard system making comparisons across organizations easier. The author argues that integration between the two approaches can be beneficial and that some companies (such as the British Post Office and the Hungarian Telecommunications Company) apply both of them with positive results.

The Vocational Training Council (VTC) of Hong Kong has conducted an interesting exercise of integration between the BSC and other strategy and quality management approaches. The result was a strategy formulation framework described in some detail in Lee *et al.* (2000). Briefly, the first step is to build a SWOT matrix to identify the CSFs of the situation and then build the BSC with the definition of the different perspectives for success and excellence performance. The next step is to make use of the Quality Function Deployment (QFD) methodology with the BSC attributes defined as the 'whats' and the Malcolm Baldrige National Quality Award (MBNQA) criteria as the 'hows'. A holistic strategy formulation framework is proposed to allow institutions to develop and implement their education strategic plan (Lee *et al.* 2000).

In the SWOT analysis it is important to assess the organization's strengths and weaknesses from the point of view of both its internal and external customers. As Lee *et al.* (2000) suggest, a main advantage of the SWOT analysis lies in the concern with matching specific internal and external factors. By first conducting a SWOT analysis, the organization will develop 'a set of strategies that make sense and that can be used as a stepping stone toward the actual implementation of the balanced scorecard' (Lee *et al.* 2000).

The application of QFD, as an engineering method and a planning process, can help organizations to properly define the methods, systems and resources needed to put in place the selected strategies and to achieve the desired results. Using the BSC categories as the 'whats' and the MBNQA criteria as the 'hows', the consequent QFD helps to identify the critical criteria and success implementation factors (Lee *et al.* 2000).

As QM advocates, measurement is the foundation of an effective management strategy (Brown 1994). However, only if the data thus gathered is used to make better decisions and to drive improvement efforts, is the measurement system a real value to the organization. That is also the idea behind the principle 'management by fact' in KBEM.

Selecting the vital few metrics on which to collect data is difficult. The Baldrige award criteria recommend a balanced set of metrics that should include data on customer satisfaction, employee satisfaction, financial performance, organizational performance, product/service quality, supplier performance, and safety/environmental/public responsibility.

By combining the financial, customer, internal process and innovation, and organizational learning perspectives, the BSC helps managers understand, at least implicitly, many interrelationships.

The application of the BSC should be unique to an organization and each level in the organization. In this sense, the BSC, like most BEMs, is not a prescriptive approach.

Kanji's Business Excellence Model and the Business Scorecard

The BSC may be improved by integrating TQM principles and CSFs that constitute KBEM. Kanji's model, on the other hand, may be described using the BSC configuration.

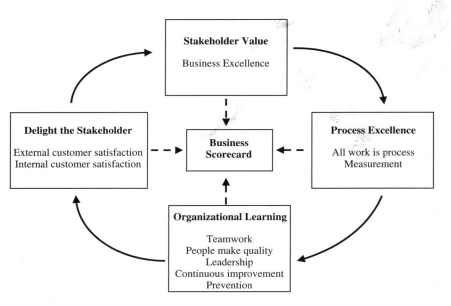

Figure 6.1 Comparative Business Scorecard (Kanji 2000).

As a matter of fact, it is possible to compare the four areas identified by Kaplan and Norton (1992) with the ones proposed by Kanji (1998*b*) (see Figure 6.1). Kanji argues that to achieve BE companies need to:

1   maximize stakeholders value;
2   achieve process excellence;
3   improve organizational learning;
4   delight the stakeholder.

Business excellence CSFs, along with the organization's values, will be used as the basis for the definition of the scorecard measures (see Figure 6.2).

Next, further comparisons between these two approaches are discussed in greater detail and, using an example, some insights are given on how a BSC could be developed.

Customer perspective vs delight the stakeholders

The BSC demands that managers translate their general mission statement on customer service into specific measures that reflect the factors that really matter to customers (Kaplan and Norton 1992).

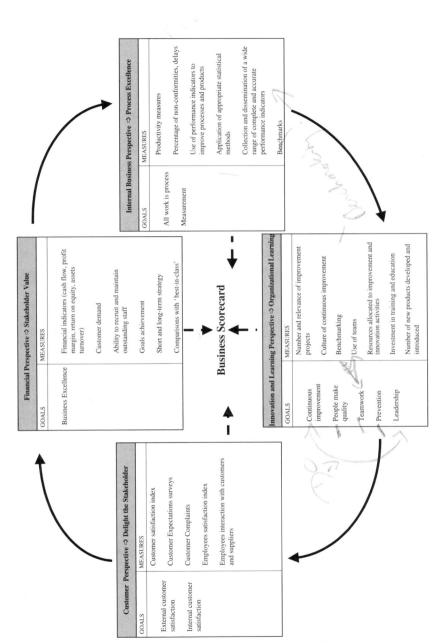

Figure 6.2 Performance measurement in Kanji's Business Scorecard.

Table 6.1 Delight the stakeholders perspective

Goals	Measures
Customer identification	Customer expectation surveys
Customer satisfaction	Customer satisfaction index
Preferred airline	Frequent-flyer membership

The quality philosophy also has the customer as its main focus. To delight the customer, an organization needs to assess its customers' expectations and be able to meet (and even to exceed) them. A close relationship with customers will facilitate information sharing and increase loyalty.

In the case of an airline company (see Table 6.1), apart from measuring the customer satisfaction index and conducting regular surveys, it may be meaningful to use other measures such as frequent-flyer membership.

However, Kanji's view goes a step further by considering that not only customers should be considered, but also that it is essential for an organization to take into account the needs and expectations of all its stakeholders, that is, all those groups or individuals who are directly or indirectly affected by an organization's pursuit of its goals (investors, community, employees, suppliers, etc.).

Internal business perspective vs process excellence

Customer-based measures are important, but they must be translated into measures of what the company must do internally to meet its customers' expectations. Managers need to focus on those critical internal operations that enable them to satisfy customer needs (Kaplan and Norton 1992).

It is therefore important to think of an organization as an interrelated net of processes or, put in Kanji's terms, organizations need to recognize that all work is process.

Companies should decide what processes and competencies they must excel at and specify measures for each. In the airline's example, key processes are: sales and reservations, passenger handling, ground handling, and flight services.

Process excellence (see Table 6.2) implies that an organization has developed a good information system that allows the identification of the root causes of problems when they arise. In that sense, measurement is essential. Moreover, employees need to feel responsible for the management of the processes in which they are involved and have the expertise to solve problems that may arise.

Innovation and learning perspective vs organizational learning

The targets for success keep changing. Intense global competition requires that companies make continual improvements to their existing products and

Table 6.2 Process excellence perspective

Goals	Measures
Responsive sales and reservations	Average rings before a telephone reservation or a sales call is answered
	Regular employee appraisals in terms of ticketing and sales competence
Effective check-in operations	Average passengers queuing time at check-in for a flight
Effective baggage and ramp handling	Percentage of on-time departures
	Level of mishandled baggage
	Average flight turnaround time
Quality in-flight service	Regular employee appraisals in terms of customer care, communication with passengers, responsiveness and courtesy
An effective quality chain	Staff surveys aimed at internal supplier/customer relationships
Efficient and effective working systems and staff rostering	Various employee productivity measures

Table 6.3 Organizational learning perspective

Goals	Measures
Continuous employee development	Investment made in employee training and education
	Staff appraisals measuring increase in key competences
New markets development	Number of new routes and destinations
New product development	Number of new customer product packages developed
New partnership development	Number of new strategic alliance agreements entered with suppliers, competitors and corporate customers

have the ability to introduce entirely new products with expanded capabilities (Kaplan and Norton 1992) (see Table 6.3).

Customers' needs are continuously changing. Organizations need to be proactive and must invest in improvements and innovations, both related to products and processes. In this sense, training and education at all levels of the organization are essential.

Principles like teamwork, continuous improvement and prevention fit well in this philosophy. Moreover, leadership has a crucial role in implementing a culture of continuous improvement and innovation.

Table 6.4 Stakeholder value perspective

Goals	Measures
Survival	Cash flow
	Relative decrease in cost of capital
	Aircraft financing
	Average daily aircraft utilization
Optimization of	Available seat kilometres and revenue passenger kilometres
revenue	Yield
Profitability	Profit margin
	Return on equity
	Return on share capital

Financial perspective vs stakeholder value

Financial performance measures indicate whether the company's strategy, implementation and execution are contributing to bottom line improvement. Typical financial goals have to do with profitability, growth and shareholder value (Kaplan and Norton 1992) (see Table 6.4).

Similarly, the traditional perspective of the BSC is somehow restricted by focusing exclusively on shareholders. All stakeholders (not just the shareholders) are to be considered if BE is to be achieved.

Kanji (2000) further explains, 'An organization that achieves business excellence creates a large net-worth and therefore increases shareholder's equity. The measurement of BE then provides a yardstick by which an investor judges an organization's equity performance'.

The shareholder value must be understood in a long-term perspective, balancing cash generation, future growth, risk and return.

Developing Kanji's Business Scorecard

In the previous section, we have highlighted how the adoption of TQM principles contributes to the enrichment of the traditional scorecard. However, it is possible to go a step further and build a framework with enhanced measurement abilities and increased managerial potentialities.

As Kanji (1998) emphasizes, in order to achieve BE it is necessary to give simultaneous attention to areas that comprise the scorecard. Furthermore, the author reinforces that achievements in each of the four areas need to feed each other to form a cycle of continuous improvement, so that:

- Delighting the stakeholders helps generate revenues and satisfactory returns to the investor;
- Increased revenues help to find investments in processes and learning;
- Better process and learning help people to delight the stakeholders and create BE.

Thus, critical for the development of any scorecard is the cause and effect relationship. As mentioned earlier, traditional approaches do not specify how each area interacts with others. Structural Equation Modelling (SEM) provides a clear mathematical framework for the determination of interrelationships. KBS therefore is better seen as suggested in Figure 6.3.

Similarly to Kaplan and Norton's (1992) strategic foundation of the BSC, we also believe that the KBS measurement model should be based upon the organizational values, which in turn are translated into its vision, mission and strategy (see Kanji and Sá 2001, *Measuring Leadership Excellence*). Organizational values are the prime for process excellence, organizational learning and stakeholders' delight. Effective management of these CSFs will lead not only to good financial results, as suggested by Kaplan and Norton (1992), but also to a higher Business Scorecard Index (BSI), meaning that the organization is providing good value for all stakeholders and has a strong quality reputation, which is a more embracing and long-term-oriented concept.

As mentioned earlier, a good system of measures and indicators needs to be developed to help organizations to monitor performance and pursue excellence.

Each block in Figure 6.3 corresponds to a latent variable in the structural equation model. Since latent variables (constructs) cannot be directly observed and measured, a set of manifest variables (indicators) was developed. It is important to adequately cover the construct domain while keeping the number of indicators as small as possible. The resulting questionnaire (see Appendix A) reflects the balance between these two conflicting demands.

KBS aims to complement KBEM by focusing on measuring how the organization is performing from the outside perspective. As a matter of fact, while KBEM is mainly an internal assessment framework, where data are collected from the organization's leaders and employees, KBS is mainly directed towards an external assessment of the organization from the point of view of its other important stakeholders. Organizations intending to apply the KBS should then consider who their fundamental stakeholders are and establish a way of collecting feedback from them. One possible way is to periodically administer the questionnaire to a panel of stakeholders.

Figure 6.3 Kanji's Business Scorecard.

In the next section, we will illustrate the application of the KBS and how it can be used to measure BSI.

Illustrative example

A typical service sector company (X) was utilized to illustrate the way KBS works. Data were used to determine the indices of the CSFs of the model and the final BSI. Figure 6.4 shows the business excellence model with values of the structural parameters.

Based on Partial Least Square (PLS) estimations, path coefficients, correlations and reliability measures for the overall system were computed.

The structural parameters (or path coefficients) are indications of the strength of the relationship between independent and dependent variables of the model. Figure 6.4 shows that all coefficients are positive and significant, strongly supporting the holistic and synergic nature of the model. The results show that organizational values (prime) are strongly associated with the three other critical dimensions.

With the purpose of assessing the reliability of the scales used to measure the latent variables in the KBS model, the Cronbach coefficient (α) was calculated. Table 6.5 displays the results.

Figure 6.5 shows the indices for each of the model variables, as well as the resulting BSI achieved by Company 'X'.

It is possible to notice that the organization is not doing very well in several dimensions. Organizational values and process excellence scores (around 50 per cent) are particularly worrying. Several reasons may be behind this relatively poor performance. Behind the organizational value index, it may well be the case that the company either does not have strong values and a strategy aligned to them or it is not communicating them properly to its

Figure 6.4 Structural parameters for company 'X'.

Table 6.5 Reliability of empirical measurements for company 'X'

Critical success factors and business scorecard index	Reliability – α
Organizational values	0.764
Process excellence	0.848
Organizational learning	0.914
Delight the stakeholders	0.833
Business scorecard index	0.958

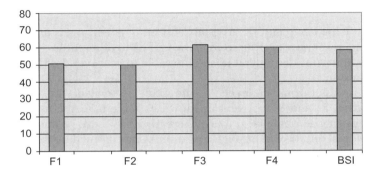

Figure 6.5 Indices of CSFs and BEI for company 'X'.

Notes: F1. Organizational values; F2. Process excellence; F3. Organizational learning; F4. Delight the stakeholders; BSI. Business Scorecard Index.

stakeholders. Additionally, the organization is hardly delivering what people expect, possibly due to a lack of measurement in key processes. Yet, the organization's willingness to learn and improve, along with its ability to respond to changes in its environment, are contributing to a reasonable stakeholders' delight score and pushing up the BSI. However, the final index of 58.7 clearly indicates that there is lots of room for improvement.

CSFs with low index scores are obviously natural candidates for improvement, however it is important to notice that some of them may have a stronger correlation with the final BSI, as suggested by the different path coefficients. One possible way of more precisely assessing where to concentrate efforts to make real improvement happen in the most economical and efficient way is using the Excellence Seeker's Approach (see Kanji 2000*a*). The Excellence Seeker's Approach involves the use of an optimization algorithm for determining which indices to increase and by how much to achieve a given target level of excellence. Since organizations usually face some constraints, the algorithm allows the introduction of upper limits of improvement for one (or more) CSFs.

Table 6.6 Revised indices of CSFs and Business Scorecard Index

Critical success factor and leadership excellence	Upper limit	Original index BSI = 59	Target business scorecard index			
			65	75	85	92
Organizational values	85	51	51	67*	85*	85
Process excellence	85	50	50	50	50	85*
Organizational learning	85	62	62	62	83*	85*
Delight the stakeholders	85	60	73*	85*	85	85

*New index for highest target level.

Table 6.6 helps Company 'X' to establish improvement plans and effectively allocate resources in order to increase its BSI to different levels, while at the same time considering that it is not feasible to go beyond 85 per cent in any dimension.

The required performance levels for the CSFs associated with BSI are, respectively 65, 75 and 85 per cent as shown in Table 6.6. A considerable improvement can be obtained only by increasing the score of the 'delight the stakeholders' dimension, through measures such as providing them with better and more reliable information and carefully listening to their needs. In order to achieve an index of 75, the organization also has to improve the way it communicates what it stands for and develop consistent strategies. By getting all factors to their upper limit, the organization can potentially achieve a BEI of 92 points.

Conclusions

The need to develop simple, comprehensive and relevant measures was behind the development of new performance instruments. Among them, the BSC achieved considerable popularity, particularly due to its potential to be simultaneously used as a tool for strategy development and implementation.

Despite this considerable success, the BSC does not fully explain the factors that lead to superior performance and the way they relate with each other. This can be done only by building a framework that incorporates the CSFs and uses a mathematical model to describe the embedded relationships.

It is our belief that these performance drivers are to be found in the TQM philosophy and can be successfully integrated in an innovative measurement model. Using the four perspectives proposed by Kaplan and Norton (1992) as a starting point and by enlarging their understanding, KBS suggests that organizational values, process excellence, organizational learning and 'delight the stakeholders' are the fundamental dimensions to be managed and monitored. In order to analyse the relationships existing among them, the SEM approach seems to be the most powerful and reliable methodology.

Therefore, the latent variables of the KBS model were operationalized using multiple questionnaire items.

Overall, the empirical results obtained in the example presented (in particular the positive path coefficients and the high reliability scores) tend to confirm the validity of the structural model and its value in assisting organizations on their road to excellence.

For company 'X' some initial comments and recommendations can be made:

- The final BEI is reasonable (around 60 per cent), but some performance areas such as organizational values (51 per cent) and performance excellence (50 per cent) are barely adequate.
- The fact that the score of the prime of the model – organizational values – is low is particularly worrying, suggesting that further efforts need to be done in communicating what the organization stands for, creating a sense of community and showing that the strategy is actually putting these values into motion.
- The relatively poor process excellence indicates that the organization has a large rate of non-conformities, delays and wastage. Better measurement and analysis of key processes and benchmarking may help to raise the score.
- These negative effects are carried, to some extent, by the organization's inability to learn. The organization has a culture of continuous improvement and an ability to interpret changes in the environment that contribute to a good index in delighting the stakeholders.
- By using this continuous improvement and learning attitude as a competitive advantage and by concentrating efforts in the weakest areas of the BSC, the company can considerably improve its performance.

Despite the possibility of using KBS as a completely separate approach, it may be beneficial to apply it in conjunction with the generic KBEM. As mentioned earlier, they are complementary in the sense that the former focuses mainly on internal stakeholders while the latter takes the measurements from a more external perspective. Additionally, their simultaneous use encourages organizations to question whether their internal measurements are right and allows cross-validation of both models. Combination of KBEM and KBS can provide Kanji's performance measurement (see web page www.gopal-kanji.com).

Notes

1 A performance indicator is controllable to the extent that it is only influenced by elements under the unit's control. Controllability is important because it is often said that in order to maximize motivation and minimize perceptions of unfairness, 'people should only be evaluated based on what they control'. Controllability is

also important from a learning point of view; uncontrollable dimensions pollute the information contained in the indicator by making it difficult to distinguish the impact of one's efforts from the effect of 'external' factors.

2 A measure is complete when it captures 'the whole truth' about the unit's performance (Epstein and Manzoni 1998).

7 Excellence in business excellence models

A comparison of EFQM and KBEM methodologies

Introduction

In business, the need to establish corrective action is paramount for achieving higher Business Excellence Index (BEI). This chapter discusses Business Excellence (BE) methodology using European Formation for Quality Management (EFQM) Excellence Model and Kanji's Business Excellence Model (KBEM).

The evolution of the excellence model and its use has acted as an effective lever for the development of Total Quality Management (TQM) and BE within organizations. This development has not just been about the greater visibility of TQM that has been created but has also, by the use of the model, created a deeper appreciation of the nature of TQM.

The Deming Prize, a pioneer among the excellence models, was launched in Japan in 1951. Malcolm Baldrige's Award, which was established in the United States of America in 1987, puts more emphasis on customer satisfaction and service than the Deming Prize. The EFQM and Kanji's Excellence Model are a natural follow-up in this evolution of the excellence model and are discussed in the following sections.

The EFQM Excellence Model

The EFQM Excellence Model is a non-prescriptive framework that recognizes that there are many approaches to achieving sustainable excellence. Within this non-prescriptive approach there are some fundamental concepts which underpin the EFQM model. These are results orientation, customer focus, leadership and constancy of purpose, management by processes and facts, people development and involvement, continuous learning, innovation and improvement, partnership development, and public responsibility (EFQM website 2000).

EFQM defines excellence as an outstanding practice in managing the organization and achieving results based on those eight fundamental concepts.

The EFQM Excellence Model is a non-prescriptive framework based on nine criteria. Five of these are 'Enablers' and four 'Results'. The 'Enablers' criteria cover what an organization does. The 'Results' criteria cover what an organization achieves. 'Results' are caused by 'Enablers' (EFQM website 2000). The 'Enablers' are: leadership, policy and strategy, people, partnership and resources, processes. The 'Results' are: customer results, people results, society results, key performance results.

The model is based on the premise that 'Excellent results with respect to Performance, Customers, People and Society are achieved through Leadership Driving Policy and Strategy, People, Partnerships and Resources and Processes'. The EFQM model is presented in diagrammatic form (Figure 1.13). The arrows emphasize the dynamic nature of the model. They show innovation and learning helping to improve enablers that in turn lead to improved results (EFQM website 2000).

The model's nine boxes represent the criteria against which to asses an organization's progress towards excellence. Each of the nine criteria has a definition, which explains the high-level meaning of that criterion. To develop the high-level meaning further, each criterion is supported by a number of sub-criteria. Sub-criteria pose a number of questions that should be considered in the course of an assessment. Finally, below each sub-criterion are lists of possible areas to address. The areas to address are not mandatory nor are they exhaustive lists but are intended to further exemplify the meaning of the sub-criterion (EFQM website 2000).

At the heart of the model lies the logic known as RADAR, which consists of four elements: **R**esults, **A**pproach, **D**eployment, **A**ssessment and **R**eview. This logic states that an organization needs to:

- Determine the **R**esults it is aiming for as part of its policy- and strategy-making process. These results cover the performance of the organization, both financially and operationally, and the perceptions of its stakeholders.
- Plan and develop an integrated set of sound **A**pproaches to deliver the required results both now and in the future.
- **D**eploy the approaches in a systematic way to ensure full implementation.
- **A**ssess and **R**eview the approaches followed based on monitoring and analysis of the results achieved and ongoing learning activities. Based on this, identify, prioritize, plan and implement improvements where needed.

When using the model within an organization, for example, for the purposes of self-assessment, the **A**pproach, **D**eployment, **A**ssessment and **R**eview elements of the RADAR logic should be addressed for each Enabler sub-criterion and the **R**esults element should be addressed for each Results sub-criterion (EFQM website 2000).

Kanji's Business Excellence Model

TQM is about continuous performance improvement. To improve performance, people need to know what to do and how to do it, have the right tools to do it, be able to measure performance and to receive feedback on current levels of achievement (Kanji 1998).

Kanji defines BEI as a means of measuring customer's, employer's and shareholder's (stakeholders) satisfaction simultaneously within an organization in order to obtain a comprehensive evaluation of the organizational performance. Here, the index can be used to measure how well different areas of the organization are performing. It has been constructed in such a way so as to allow direct comparison across each of these, while at the same time being able to compare the same business in different geographical areas. The index also allows a particular business to be measured over time. For the construction of the BEI, the data are collected through a survey using suitable questionnaires. These questionnaires are written specifically for the organization and ensure that as large a picture as possible is gathered about that organization (Kanji 1998).

KBEM is made up of a prime factor, that is, leadership, that directly influences four principles: delight the customer, management by fact, people-based management, and continuous improvement. Each principle, in turn, directly influences two core concepts, internal customer satisfaction and external customer satisfaction, all work is process and measurement, people make quality and teamwork, and continuous improvement cycle and prevention. The model culminates in BE, which according to the model structure, is the simultaneous measure of the contributions of prime, principles, and core concepts towards BE (Kanji 2000). KBEM is shown in Figure 5.1.

KBEM shows arrows that link up TQM CSFs throughout the model's structure. The direction of arrows shows the direction of causal connections. In this model, leadership is the prime that establishes an institution's set of principles that are divided into two core concepts, each as shown in the diagram. If the organization sees the TQM process through its principles and core concepts, then it will achieve BE.

According to KBEM, there is a clear link from leadership to BE. Here, the organization has to be guided through the TQM principles and core concepts by top management leadership in order to achieve BE (Kanji 1998*b*).

Brief comparison between EFQM and KBEM

The EFQM and KBEM have some similarities. Both models offer a rigorous approach to organizational improvement, offer an approach to the measurement of progress through periodic self-assessment, suggest an assessment based on facts not perceptions, focus on leadership, customer-orientedness, emphasize on people development, education, training, teamwork and on processes.

Some differences exist between these two models. The context of customer in the EFQM model is only external while KBEM explicitly mentions internal customers beside external customers. KBEM also places more emphasis on delighting customers rather than satisfying them. Continuous improvement is explicitly mentioned in KBEM. The public/society responsibility, partnership and resources development, which are not TQM principles that exist in the EFQM model, are absent in KBEM.

EFQM gives the maximum weight to customer satisfaction. This is followed by business results, processes, leadership, people management, people satisfaction, resources, policy and strategy and impact on society, in order of importance. KBEM, on the other hand, involves the organization in determining the weighting of CSFs.

Kanji and Tambi (1999*a*) said that the key difference between the approaches used in EFQM and KBEM is that the former does not utilize suitable statistical methods to determine factor weights, factor scores and total evaluation score. It also does not show structural relationships among factors and how the factor scores contribute to BE. An example is given in the work of Dahlgaard *et al.* (1987) on factor scores of European Quality Award (EQA) participants in 1992. Their study shows that the average score of each quality criterion of companies has no relation with its degree of importance. They also say that traditionally, all the factors associated with Enablers and Results are not analysed simultaneously. The factor weights are given arbitrarily and the value given to leadership is unrealistically low from a TQM point of view, that is, 10 per cent. This is because TQM views leadership as the most important agent of change and therefore is the prime factor in terms of criticality. In addition, the element of continuous improvement is missing in this model.

Excellence in EFQM Excellence Model

The EFQM model is aimed at providing the organizations with a means to measure their position against a set of universal criteria, and to identify their strengths and weaknesses in the key areas of business. The model provides a company with a comprehensive framework for assessing its progress towards the new paradigm of management. One of the benefits of the model is that it makes the company systematically and regularly review its activities and results.

The EFQM model gives a clear separation between Enablers, which drive the business and facilitate the transformation of input to outputs and outcomes, and Results, which are the measure of the level of outputs and outcomes attained by the organization. The model also shows that innovation and learning help to improve Enablers that in turn lead to improved results. The model emphasizes some criteria, such as leadership, management by fact, people development, education, training, teamwork, process and also managing supplier–partner relationship.

The EFQM model has a broader coverage of Results that includes people, customer, society and performance. The model also puts the necessity of the organization to benchmark against its competitors and best-in-class organization. Porter and Tanner (1998) said that one of the strengths of the EFQM model is that it explicitly addresses the performance of an organization in meeting the needs of all its stakeholders.

The EFQM model is a relationship model which links together nine criteria, against which organizations assess and measure their own excellence and target continuous improvement. The criteria are divided into two areas, Enablers and Results. The model is also unique, in that it explicitly recognizes the impact on society of managerial actions (McAdam and Welsh 2000).

Porter and Tanner (1996) argue that one major weakness of the EFQM excellence framework is that the implementation of action plans is the responsibility of the line manager. In comparison with the corrective action plans featured by ISO 9000, for example, the implementation and review process of self-assessment is less structured. Porter and Tanner (1996) also suggest that in some cases, for example, where there is a well-developed tradition of self-assessment within the organization, it is necessary to develop a hybrid framework that overcomes limitations of individual frameworks such as the EFQM Excellence Model. Similarly, in relation to business results, Porter and Tanner (1996) suggest that this criteria should be extended to include the quality results of products and services, the quality results of business and support services and the quality results of suppliers.

McAdam and Welsh (2000), after conducting a survey at higher education institutions in Northern Ireland, conclude that, the EFQM model is used in quite different ways and for quite different purposes. Within a single organization the rationale of use may change over time. For example, one organization could use the model as a planning tool, another organization might simply work slowly through a change generated by self-assessment, and a third might use it as a means of changing the culture that pervades the organization. However, critics like Seddon (1998) point out that there is the danger that using the model can simply be a matter of going through the motions and that managers become preoccupied with 'doing things right' rather than doing the right things, and in the process fail to challenge the very assumptions they have been using to run the organization in the first place.

McAdam and O'Neil (1999) criticized the EFQM model by using TQM framework as below:

- EFQM model does not formulate strategy, nor does it properly evaluate strategy, rather it evaluates the process of forming strategy.
- There is a lack of a predictive element that would help identify new customers and markets, reflecting the lack of strategic integration referred to already.
- The model is an audit tool of what is already happening. It does not indicate best or preferred practice in an organizational context.
- The model does not show how business processes can be identified or improved.

In summary, the EFQM model has merit as a business audit approach but should not be viewed as synonymous with TQM.

Kanji, in interview with Emerald, said that one of the problems with Business Excellence Models (BEMs) such as EFQM, Baldrige and the Japanese model is that they do not measure BE as such. This is partly because not everything in these models has a quality dimension. Because they are designed by business people interested in gaining quality awards, such models are based on many other criteria. Large companies, the major contributors to these models, establish the criteria which they think are important for their companies. Their goal is not to promote BE *per se*. Another criticism that is often made is that, while there has been an increase in the number of award points needed, this does not lead to improvement in the quality of the operations assessed and therefore has no bearing on improvement of the quality of the organization as a whole.

As mentioned before, the EFQM gives maximum weight to customer satisfaction followed by business results, processes, leadership, people management, people satisfaction, resources, policy and strategy and impact on society, in order of importance. However, the EFQM model is not showing the interrelationship among the CSFs and their contribution to BE. It is in part due to the lack of validation by suitable data. The factor weights of the different criteria are somehow arbitrary and it is difficult to isolate the contribution of each of them to BE (Kanji 2000*b*).

The EFQM model highlights the important factors for BE and states that there are relationships among them, but they do not make these causal relationships clear by assigning true coefficients/weights to the different criteria, based on statistical evidence. Therefore, the impact of any change of one particular criterion on other components of the model and overall BE is difficult to predict, making the prioritization of the improvement efforts ambiguous. Rather than using suitable statistical methods to determine factor scores, the EFQM model relies on subjective evaluations. Thus, the final BE score is always the outcome of the personal judgements of a particular assessment team, and cannot be easily replicated or generalized (Kanji 2000*a*).

For example, suppose company 'A' wants to perform self-assessment based on the EFQM Excellence Model, the first thing that should be done is getting commitment from the top management to support the self-assessment process. The next step is to set up the assessor team, then train them regarding the EFQM Excellence Model and how to perform the assessment. After the training, the assessor team should gather the necessary data to perform the assessment in accordance with the EFQM Excellence Model as described below.

Concerning Enablers, every criterion is subdivided into a number of sub-criteria (four to six), all of them having the same weighting. To every single sub-criterion, some examples are to make the content more tangible. The Result criteria are only subdivided into two sub-criteria (Zink and Schmidt 1998).

In addition to this first structural level both groups are subdivided again:

1   Concerning the 'Enablers' it is distinguished between 'approach' (in the sense of concept) and 'deployment'.
2   Concerning the 'Results' it is distinguished between 'results' and 'scope' (in the sense of completeness).

In the assessment, 'approach' and 'deployment' or 'results' and 'scope' are evaluated to the same extent, which means one will have to take the average. However, it may sometimes be necessary to make distinctions between approach and deployment in order to consider that developing a concept is relatively easy whereas a consequent realization of the concept is much more difficult. In all of the assessment dimensions, the idea of continuous improvement can be found (Zink and Schmidt 1998).

For the 'Enablers' one has to prove:

1   the adequacy of methods, instruments and techniques used;
2   the extent to which the concept is systematic and preventive;
3   the use of review cycles;
4   the realization of improvements resulting from the review cycles;
5   the extent to which the concept is integrated into daily work.

Assessing Deployment means checking how adequately and effectively the approach was used:

1   vertically through all relevant levels;
2   horizontally to all areas and activities;
3   in all relevant processes;
4   concerning all relevant products and services.

Assessing the Results includes the following factors:

1   existing positive trends;
2   comparing them with own targets;
3   comparing them with the performance of competitors and 'best-in-class' organizations;
4   details proving that the results are caused by the approach;
5   the ability of the organization to maintain its leading position.

The scope of the results can be described by:

1   the extent to which all relevant areas of the company are covered;
2   the extent to which the parameters chosen to measure results are shown;
3   the extent to which the relevance of the results shown can be understood (Zink and Schmidt 1998).

The assessor should point out the strengths, opportunities for improvement, and evidence of each criterion. Then the assessor team member gives the score for the criterion individually. The individual score is then shared with the team and the final score is made based on consensus. After that, the action plan for improvement is developed and agreed. The regular review should be performed to review the progress against the action plans.

By using this method, the evaluation result will tend to be subjective. If there is a dominant person within the assessor group, then it is possible that his/her opinion of score will overwhelm the rest of the assessor group. To reduce this subjectivity, the training of the assessor is very important. The more experienced assessor is expected to give the more objective evaluation. However, the subjectivity factor still cannot be eliminated.

The other problem that exists is the difficulty in prioritizing the action plans, since there is a lack of causal relationship between each CSF to BE. For example, after performing self-assessment company 'A' finds that the scores of 'leadership', 'policy and strategy', 'people', 'people result' and 'customer result' are low, the company then develops action plans for improvement. Since all these criteria are affecting each other, it will be difficult for company 'A' to prioritize the improvement effort. It makes it difficult to decide which action should be performed first.

Excellence in KBEM

KBEM measures the quality of all key organizational areas simultaneously, demonstrates causal connections among them and shows their collective influence on organizational performance. Thus, KBEM provides a potential solution to the task of finding a representative measurement model for the various types of organizations (Kanji 2000).

Kanji's Business Excellence Index (KBEI) includes a measurement instrument that is validated to obtain scores for indicators for each CSF and BE. The indices can be used to determine how well different areas of the organization are performing and their contribution toward BE. Organizations will be concerned with CSFs that have low performance so that they can be examined in detail and improved. This model also allows the comparison of BE of different organizations and the same organization over time.

In KBEI, the measurement involves determining weighting of CSFs. These measures can be used by decision-makers to assess the status of Quality Management (QM) in the organization for a direct improvement in the quality area. Kanji (1998) said that most of the models in use (e.g. Deming, European, Baldrige, Japanese) are indicative models, whereas KBEM is an improvement model.

KBEM describes what individual CSFs and the overall BE mean. Here, the scores of the individual CSFs will be based on measurement items and the BEI will be based on a vector of averages of ratings of the CSFs (Kanji 1998).

According to Kanji and Tambi (1999*a*), KBEM offers users several advantages over other QM models. These are the BEM advantages:

- covers all TQM factors that influence BE;
- statistically shows structural relationships among TQM factors;
- performs simultaneous computation of mathematical equations of factor relationships to obtain factor indices and BEI;
- gives estimates of strength of relationships among factors and between factors and their respective indicator measurements;
- compensates for elements of bias in measurements by incorporating a measure of disturbance (error);
- provides goodness-of-fit of the model for the data;
- generates a robust estimate of parameters and provides a good measure of quality which has statistical validity;
- outputs can be easily interpreted.

Suppose company 'A' uses the KBEI to perform self-assessment; first, the management should determine the CSFs that affect the company's performance. The KBEI questionnaire should then be developed to consist of CSFs and cover fourteen index elements originally developed by Kanji. The individual questionnaire items are measured on a ten-point scale in order to enhance reliability.

The survey/evaluation is then conducted and the survey result is analysed to identify the strengths and areas for improvement, the score for individual elements and the score for BE. The BE measure is constructed by weighting the individual items so that the resulting index has a maximum correlation with stakeholders' value.

Using this method, the company will be able to prioritize action plans easily. The CSFs that have a low score are the priority for improvement to achieve BE.

Conclusions

In Kanji's model, leadership provides the base in the model that controls the behaviour of every principle and core concept. Without good leadership, and management being committed to the process, the chances of success are slim. The challenge of leadership is to unite the whole company behind common aims and objectives, and to steer the organization through future change.

Kanji's emphasis on leaderships' crucial role in promoting and supporting a culture where quality improvement activities could enhance the performance of the organization is even clearer than the EFQM Excellence Model. This can be observed in Kanji's symbolic quality pyramid, where leadership is the base of the pyramid, and every other principle and core concept is built upon that leadership base. The pyramid's top is BE.

Kanji's excellence model is capable of measuring an organization's CSFs and BE. The model includes a measurement instrument that obtains scores for indicators of each CSF, as well as BE. CSFs are the few key areas of the organization, which if properly managed, will improve the organization's BE. The CSFs can be categorized based on their degree of importance.

In Kanji's model, the measurement will involve determining weightings of CSFs. A latent-variable structural model of CSFs should be constructed, and the strength of causal connections among the latent variables should be analysed. The latent variables are measured by their apparent variables, which in turn will be represented by measurement items in a questionnaire.

The scores are then analysed using the Partial Least Squares (PLS) method to establish whether structural relationships exist among CSFs and BE in the model. The causal connections among the latent variables show the goodness-of-fit of the structural model.

For implementing Kanji's excellence model in an organization, a suitable measurement item has to be developed, based on the survey of that organization, to identify the organization's requirements for effective QM. These items define the meaning and scope of each critical factor. To establish the validity of the content, the items for each factor and BE should be critically reviewed by the organization's management team. By using a ten-point interval rating scale for items of each factor, the final score for that factor will be generated. The final score for that factor is the mean value of all the items within that factor. So, for each latent variable/factor, the actual level of practice can be represented by the average of the measurement item ratings for that factor. A vector of the average of fourteen factors (leadership + four principles + eight core concepts + BE) can be used as a profile of the organization's BE.

The advantage of using Kanji's excellence model to measure BE lies within the model's accuracy in relating the BEI with its correlation to all the success factors. By using the PLS method you can easily see if the obtained index for BE is valid or not. You can directly observe whether some score of some factor differs from the rest and how it influences the final BEI. The possibility of using this mathematical modelling, to confirm the model's credibility and measuring the BEI with its correlation to all the success factors, is the greatest strength of Kanji's model compared to any other BEM.

The obtained BEI is the simultaneous measure of stakeholders' satisfaction within an organization, in order to obtain a comprehensive evaluation of the organization's performance.

The model will provide operational measures of the CSFs that can be used within the organization to produce an overreaching profile of the organization's BE. The management could use such a measure to initiate direct improvements within the organization.

Kanji's excellence model can be used both in manufacturing and service industries and can make it possible to compare different organizations.

Because the index of each factor is a single number, it is possible for the organizations to be compared across industries, in general, as well as how well they are doing in a specific factor, compared to others.

The possibility of designing a survey, which fits your specific organization, provides you with a great deal of flexibility to include additional questions to make the model better fit your organization. This will open the door for continuous improvement of the excellence model due to the fact that the Kanji's excellence model provides shaping and design, which allows the extension or adjustment of the survey which will not cause problems for comparing the results over time and can be replicated and generalized. This was an apparent limitation with the EFQM Excellence Model.

The main concern of EFQM Excellence Model is similar to that of any scoring mechanism. If you are scoring your organization, or any other, it is difficult to ignore the fact that the score you give will affect the perception of others about how good that organization is. Even more important is the question of your personal opinion, how unprejudiced the scores are and whether your organization is as good, or not, as similar organizations in business or competition.

Of course, the importance of this issue can be reduced if the questions within the model of scoring are very clear and have no place for misunderstanding or prejudice. Scoring is against a set of universal criteria. These criteria can be made as distinct as possible to reduce this source of error, but a certain amount of uncertainty will remain. So the final BE score will always be the outcome of the personal judgement of a particular assessment team, and cannot be easily replicated or generalized. This is a limitation when a model is used as a benchmarking tool.

The EFQM Excellence Model highlights the important factors for BE and states the significance of the relationships among the Enablers and Results, but there are no clear causal relationships that allocate the accurate score of weights to the different criteria based on statistical evidence. It is not obvious from the EFQM model how a change of a particular score of a criterion will impact others, and which other criteria will be affected and to what degree. This makes it difficult to predict how improvement efforts in some criteria will influence other criteria.

8 Kanji's Business Excellence Model for a European organization

Introduction

This chapter is concerned with the application of Kanji's Business Excellence Model (KBEM) (Kanji 1998*a*) for the purpose of measuring an organization's Business Excellence (BE). Kanji (1998*b*) defines Business Excellence Index (BEI) as follows:

> The Business Excellence Index (BEI) is a means of measuring customer's, employer's and shareholder's (stakeholder's) satisfaction simultaneously within an organization in order to obtain a comprehensive evaluation of the organizational performance.

The organization being studied is a large Information Technology (IT) company, company 'B'. The research provides pertinent information to the company's top management on how well key areas of the organization, that is, Critical Success Factors (CSFs), are being managed to achieve organizational goals. In addition, top management gains knowledge about the organization's current state of affairs, strengths and weaknesses that will assist them to take necessary actions to chart future progress.

Data about the efficiency and effectiveness of processes were collected in June 1999 via a questionnaire survey that was administered by mail. The mail survey method was selected because it was believed that suitable data could be obtained by using a concise structured questionnaire of measurement items that can be self-administered by respondents. In addition, the study population comprised of all divisions of company 'B' in Europe that could be conveniently reached by mail, which otherwise would have been impossible. The target respondents were represented by managers at all levels of management.

The measurement instrument consists of multiple-item scales representing each CSF and BE. Because CSFs and BE cannot be directly measured, groups of items that represent measurement scales serve as their measures.

Data analysis is performed with Partial Least Square (PLS) method and Excellence Seeker's Approach. The PLS method is used in conjunction with the *PLS-PC 1.8* software (Lohmoller 1984), which determines the values of several important variables: the strength of causal connections between independent and dependent variables, correlation matrix among variables, and reliability of measurement scales. The Excellence Seeker's Approach applies a variable assignment algorithm that maximizes improvements to key areas of the organization to further improve its BE. The Excellence Seeker's Approach is performed on the computer with a Quantitative Management software, *AB:QM Version 2.01* (Lee and Shim 1991). Other software used included *EQS* for Windows (Bentler and Wu 1995) for model validation and Statistical Package for Social Sciences Version 6.0 (*SPSS Version 6.0*) for frequency analysis to obtain descriptive statistics.

Background of company

It is a large international IT company based in Europe, with 21,000 employees worldwide. The company offers a wide range of products that include IT systems, infrastructure software and services. It has managed to enhance its competitiveness by forming alliances with strong partners, including accomplished multinationals in this area. At present, the company ranks third in systems integration and fifth in maintenance and support in Europe's information sector. Part of its success lies on its own strengths, that is, expertise in information systems (I/S) and innovation.

The majority of the company's customers are from Europe, which constitute 60 per cent of the total. Large contracts are received from major European companies. In order to provide efficient service to its relatively large foreign markets, the company has established an international network spanning some one hundred countries that is structured, inturn, into several geographic networks:

- North America
- Europe
- South America
- Asia, Africa, and Eastern Europe

Quality efforts the company has obtained on two distinct occasions, which coincide with changes in the company's leadership:

- 1985–1994 Crosby's approach to process improvements. Certification and training in improvement tools, ISO 9000;
- Mid-1998 Total Quality Management (TQM).

Only two of its companies have been reported to have adopted TQM, which indicates how scarcely TQM is being practised by the company. Nevertheless, in its policy statements, the company views quality as central to the retention of market share and for achieving competitive advantage.

In addition, the company believes that the focus of quality efforts is to create customer satisfaction. Concerning its future business outlook, the company foresees a growth in server and mainframe demands which is influenced by increasing Internet traffic volume.

Business excellence model

The Business Excellence Model (BEM), which was introduced by Kanji in 1998, shows causal relationships among the TQM CSFs and BE. The structure of the BEM is given in Figure 5.1.

The model is made up of fourteen CSFs. It begins with leadership (prime) that gives rise to four principles, that is, delight the customer, management by fact, people-based management, and continuous improvement. Each principle, in turn, gives rise to two core concepts. As shown in Figure 5.1, delight the customer gives rise to external customer satisfaction and internal customer satisfaction; management by fact to all work is process and measurement; people-based management to teamwork and people make quality; and continuous improvement to continuous improvement cycle and prevention. The combined effect of the variable relationships specified in the model contributes to BE.

The condensed business excellence model

For computational purposes, the number of variables and relationships in the BEM need to be reduced. In this research, every pair of core concepts of the model is combined so that only one core concept adjoins a principle (Figure 8.1). Nevertheless, the proposed model reduction does not result in

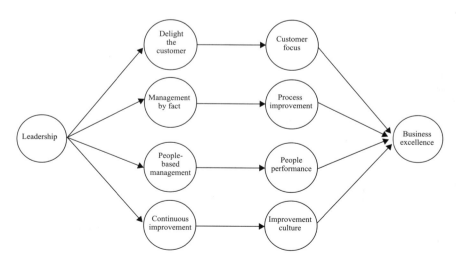

Figure 8.1 Kanji's Business Excellence Model (condensed).

loss of information because the same type and amount of data are collected to measure CSFs and BE.

Research design

The research design involves determining the method of study, the design of measurement instruments, and the selection of the sample. A causal research is conducted to test the causal relationships in the BEM using company B's data. Because CSFs and BE cannot be measured directly, their empirical content is measured via a measurement instrument that consists of multiple item scales. A ten-point rating scale is used in each questionnaire item. The source of data is a convenient sample of main companies that are located in Europe. The companies are represented by managers at various levels of management.

Data collection

Data were collected by mail survey in June 1999. Sixty copies of the measurement instrument were distributed to various company managers, including those in overseas branches, and divisions. Altogether thirty-six copies of the questionnaire were returned, giving a response rate of 60 per cent.

Data analysis

Profile of companies that responded

Tables 8.1–8.5 give the profile of the European network of the company according to type of business, location, type of managers responded, company size, and number of years established.

Correlation matrix

Pearson correlation coefficient is computed to show the association among all variables in the model. The correlation matrix of variable mean scores is

Table 8.1 Respondent company's type of business

Type of business	No. of questionnaires returned	%
Manufacturing only	4	11.1
Trading only	10	27.8
Service only	9	25.0
Combination	10	27.8
No response	3	8.3
Total	36	100.0

Table 8.2 Respondent company's locations

Location	No. of questionnaires returned	%
France	18	50.0
Germany	2	5.6
Belgium	1	2.8
Sweden	1	2.8
No response	14	38.8
Total	36	100.0

Table 8.3 Level of managers that responded

Type of managers responded (level)	No. of questionnaires returned	%
Top	1	2.8
Middle	28	77.8
First-line	0	0
No response	7	19.4
Total	36	100.0

Table 8.4 Company size

Size (no. of employees)	No. of questionnaires returned	%
< 50	2	5.6
$50 \leq x \leq 100$	1	2.8
> 100	26	72.2
No response	7	19.4
Total	36	100.0

Table 8.5 Number of years established

Number of years established	No. of questionnaires returned	%
< 10	16	44.4
$10 \leq x \leq 50$	5	13.9
> 50	7	19.4
No response	8	22.2
Total	36	100.0

given in Table 8.6. It can be seen in the table that independent and dependent variables (in boxes) are correlated. For example, the correlation of leadership with delight the customer is $r = 0.593$. This implies that every independent variable explains the existence of its corresponding dependent variable. This finding sets the stage for a confirmatory analysis of causal connections in the model, which will be discussed in a later section.

Table 8.6 Correlation matrix of BEM for company 'B'

Variable	1*	2	3	4	5	6	7	8	9	10
1*	1									
2	0.593	1								
3	0.727	0.703	1							
4	0.657	0.542	0.622	1						
5	0.623	0.559	0.707	0.784	1					
6	0.741	0.514	0.562	0.618	0.646	1				
7	0.783	0.540	0.627	0.677	0.611	0.729	1			
8	0.636	0.637	0.811	0.595	0.725	0.640	0.576	1		
9	0.718	0.506	0.774	0.697	0.789	0.670	0.802	0.791	1	
10	0.469	0.586	0.623	0.654	0.673	0.627	0.661	0.730	0.727	1

*1. Leadership; 2. Delight the customer; 3. Customer focus; 4. Management by fact; 5. Process improvement; 6. People-based management; 7. People performance; 8. Continuous improvement; 9. Improvement culture; 10. Business excellence.

Table 8.7 Mean values of CSFs and BE

Critical success factor and business excellence	Mean score
Leadership	4.49
Delight the customer	5.73
Customer focus	5.63
Management by fact	5.18
Process improvement	4.86
People-based management	4.90
People performance	5.21
Continuous improvement	5.64
Improvement culture	4.55
Business excellence	5.30

Variable mean scores

The variable mean scores (Table 8.7) provide a rough indication of organizational performance in terms of fulfilment of CSFs and BE. The mean scores are derived from means of individual questionnaire items (Appendix A). Individual item mean scores have a range of 4.36 for everyday leadership to 6.08 for customer feedback.

Arbitrarily, a minimum score of 7.5 out of a possible 10 can be considered as a high score. The company's scores are somewhat average and none exceed the minimum cut-off point of 7.5. Leadership, which has been shown in previous research to be *the* most crucial factor that influences the success of continuous improvement processes, has the lowest mean score in this case. The low CSF scores are consistent with a low score for BE. Thus, the organization has to work on its CSFs to improve its BE. This may mean a change in the existing ways of doing things, that is, quality culture, for the organization. However, the low score for improvement culture may prove to be a hindrance to the companies efforts for change.

Further analysis of the CSFs will provide more information for deciding what actions to take to improve the organization's performance.

Path coefficients

The correlation analysis is taken a step further by conducting a confirmatory analysis on the causal connection (linear relationship) between independent and dependent variables by using a statistical technique known as PLS. The *PLS-PC 1.8* software is used to apply the PLS method on the computer. The linear relationships among variables are represented by a system of linear regression equations. The corresponding regression coefficients (path coefficients) are determined simultaneously by analysing the correlation matrix of mean scores of the CSFs and BE.

The path coefficients are values that show the strength of relationships among independent and dependent variables. Causal connections are established when the values of path coefficients are significantly greater than zero. Specifically, in any symmetrical relationship of the model, its path coefficient represents the amount of change in the dependent variable that is caused by one unit of change in the independent variable, assuming other factors are constant. Therefore, a path coefficient can be taken as one unit contribution of an independent variable on an independent variable. Table 8.8 contains the path coefficients for all causal connections in the BEM for the organization.

The path coefficients in Table 8.8 are all greater than zero, suggesting that causal connections exist among variables as specified in the BEM.

Table 8.8 Path coefficients of CSFs and BE

Relationships	Inner coefficient
Leadership – delight the customer	0.597
Delight the customer – customer focus	0.669
Leadership – management by fact	0.656
Management by fact – process improvement	0.783
Leadership – People-based management	0.740
People-based management – people performance	0.729
Leadership – continuous improvement	0.638
Continuous improvement – improvement culture	0.794
Customer focus – business excellence	0.131
Process improvement – business excellence	0.258
People performance – business excellence	0.229
Improvement culture – business excellence	0.237

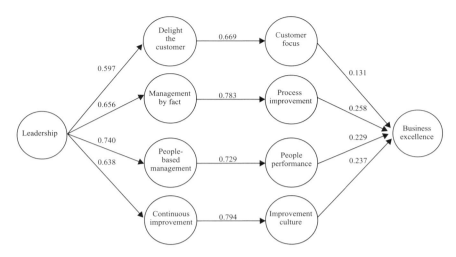

Figure 8.2 Structural parameters.

Figure 8.2 is a structural diagram of the BEM labelled with the path coefficients.

Model validity

The eqs software is used to test the goodness of fit of the model by employing the χ^2 goodness of fit test. Without going into detail, the software computes the χ^2 statistic and compares this value with tabled values of $\chi^2(df)$ to determine the probability of exceeding it. If the model fits the data well, this probability should exceed a standard cut-off in the χ^2 distribution (such as 0.05 or 0.01). However, χ^2 statistic is sensitive to sample size. Consequently, the normed fit index (NFI) (Bentler and Bonnet 1980) and the comparative fit index (CFI) (Bentler 1988) are used as alternative indicators for model fit. A model has a good fit with the data if NFI and CFI are greater than 0.9.

For company 'B', the probability value for χ^2 statistic is 0.04746. This probability is slightly below the standard cut-off point of 0.05. However, the NFI and CFI exceed 0.9, that is, 0.966 and 0.979, respectively. Therefore, it can be concluded that the model has a good fit with the data.

A further support for the validity of the BEM is given by the small values of standardized residuals (highest being 0.09), from the analysis of the data. This implies that the model has a good fit with the data. The distribution of the standardized residuals is symmetrical and centred on zero, which lends support to model accuracy.

Unit contribution of critical success factors

All variables in the BEM are dependent variables except leadership, which is an independent variable. All dependent variables are directly connected to only one independent variable except BE, which is directly connected to four independent variables. In PLS, functional equations are formulated for every causal connection. These equations take into account path coefficients and variable mean scores. The equations only describe relationships between variables that are directly connected. Similarly, path coefficients only show the effect of change of a variable to another that is causally connected under the assumption that all other factors are unchanged. Thus in the BEM, BE is taken into account by a functional equation that contains the variables, customer focus, process performance, people performance and improvement culture, which are the corresponding independent variables.

The BEM has four paths going through it, each starting from leadership and ending with BE (Figure 8.3). It is possible to calculate the contribution of each variable toward BE from the value of path coefficients. It can be seen in Figure 8.2 that, for every unit change of leadership, the variable management by fact increases by 0.656 unit. Furthermore, management by fact is followed by process performance and finally BE (path 2). The increase in process performance would be $0.656 \times 0.783 = 0.4203$ unit and consequently BE would have increased by $0.4203 \times 0.258 = 0.133$ unit, which represents the unit contribution of leadership towards BE.

The unit contribution of leadership can also be calculated from the other three paths of the model. This would yield unit contributions of 0.052 for path 1, 0.124 for path 3, and 0.120 for path 4. The highest of the calculated unit contributions is selected as the unit contribution of leadership. Similarly, the unit contributions of other CSFs can be determined using the same approach.

Knowledge about unit contributions of variables in the BEM is useful for the organization's continuous development in all its key areas. The variables can be ranked in terms of their unit contributions from highest to lowest to indicate their relative importance (Table 8.9).

Based on its unit contribution, leadership seems to be a lesser factor for the company and is followed by customer focus and delight the customer, which are the bottom two factors in terms of unit contributions. This is a serious

Path 1	Leadership	–	delight the customer	–	customer focus	–	business excellence
Path 2	Leadership	–	management by fact	–	process improvement	–	business excellence
Path 3	Leadership	–	people–based management	–	people performance	–	business excellence
Path 4	Leadership	–	continuous improvement	–	improvement culture	–	business excellence

Figure 8.3 The four paths through the Business Excellence Model.

Table 8.9 Unit contribution of CSFs to BE

Relationship	Rank	Unit contribution
Process improvement	1	0.258
Improvement culture	2	0.237
People performance	3	0.229
Management by fact	4	0.202
Continuous improvement	5	0.188
people-based management	6	0.167
Leadership – business excellence	7	0.133
Customer focus	8	0.131
Delight the customer	9	0.090

Table 8.10 Indices of CSF and BE for the company

Critical success factor and business excellence	Index %
Leadership	39
Delight the customer	52
Customer focus	51
Management by fact	46
Process improvement	43
People-based management	43
People performance	47
Continuous improvement	53
Improvement culture	42
Business excellence	48

threat to the success of TQM because leadership is the prime that directs all other key organizational areas and that TQM is primarily concerned with customer satisfaction.

Business excellence index

As discussed earlier, mean scores only provide rough estimates of how well an organization is doing in terms of key organizational areas. The mean scores are raw scores, in the sense that they do not reflect the influence of independent variables on dependent variables. To do this, a mathematical function for determining CSF and BE indices is formulated. The function takes into account path coefficients associated with questionnaire items (outer coefficients) and their mean scores. Table 8.10 shows the indices of CSFs and BE for the organization and Figure 8.4 charts the indices.

Similar to mean scores, an arbitrary percentage of 75 for indices is chosen as the cut-off point. Excellently managed CSFs have indices greater than the cut-off. Likewise, the BE indices of excellent organizations also have high index

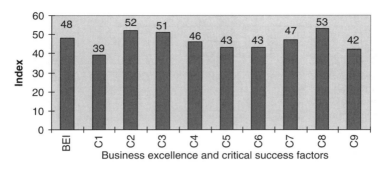

Figure 8.4 Indices of CSFs and BE.

Notes: BEI = Business Excellence Index. C1 = Leadership; C2 = Delight the customer; C3 =
Customer focus; C4 = Management by fact; C5 = Process improvement; C6 = People-
based management; C7 = People performance; C8 = Continuous improvement ; C9 =
Improvement culture.

values. As shown in Table 8.10, all CSF and BE indices for the organization
are less than 75, which is similar to the mean scores of Table 8.7. Likewise,
leadership has the lowest index value.

Forces of Kanji's Business Excellence

The ranking of CSFs for BE in Table 8.9 can help top management in planning
for resource allocation to key organizational areas and ultimately achieve
improved BE. A target level of BE can be fixed and one or more selected
factors with the highest unit contribution can be increased to achieve the
desired total contribution to BE. This procedure will inevitably depend on
some technical constraints and other considerations. The procedure which
provides the forces of BE is called the Excellence Seeker's Approach.

Excellence Seeker's Approach

The Excellence Seeker's Approach involves the use of an optimization algorithm, that is, variable assignment method, for determining which indices
to increase and by how much to achieve a given target level of business
excellence. The steps involved in the algorithm are:

1   Choose an upper limit for increasing each CSF, say 75 per cent.
2   Determine the maximum possible increase in factor index by subtracting
    current index from the upper limit and multiply the result by factor unit
    contribution given in Table 8.9. For example, the leadership index can
    be increased as much as

$$(75\% - 39\%) \times 0.133 \cong 5\%$$

3 Choose a target level for business excellence, say 75 per cent.
4 Determine the required increase in BEI by subtracting current level from target level.
5 Select the factor with the highest unit contribution (from Table 8.9).
6 Make the largest possible increase to index to achieve target BEI.
7 If target level is reached, stop. If not, repeat step 1 by selecting another factor with the next highest unit contribution.

Business excellence as a requisite

As an illustration, assume that the company fixed the BE target level and upper limits for CSFs to 75 per cent. Given this target level and constraint, the required indices (performance level) for every CSF can be determined. The new indices were computed using a Quantitative Management software, *AB:QM Version 2.01* (Lee and Shim 1991), which applied the assignment method. The result is shown in Table 8.11.

Several observations can be made about the result:

- The above result is achieved entirely from the company's current performance. If its BE was originally 75 per cent, its CSF indices would have been higher.

Table 8.11 Revised indices of CSF and BE

Critical success factor and business excellence	Upper limit	Original index BE = 48	Target business excellence index (%)					
			65	75	80	85	90	95
Leadership	75	39	39	39	39	39	75*	75
Delight the customer	75	52	52	52	52	52	52	75*
Customer focus	75	51	51	51	51	51	51	75*
Management by fact	75	46	46	70*	75*	75	75	75
Process improvement	75	43	75*	75	75	75	75	75
People-based management	75	43	43	43	43	75	75	75
People performance	75	47	52*	75*	75	75	75	75
Continuous improvement	75	53	53	53	75*	75	75	75
Improvement culture	75	42	75*	75	75	75	75	75

*New index for a higher target level.

- With the assignment method, CSFs with larger unit contributions are selected first, followed by other factors in descending order. The result suggests that, under present leadership conditions, the company can develop short-, medium-, and long-term plans that specify which CSFs needed improvements, over the range of target BE indices of 65–85 per cent. Beyond these levels, for example, 90 and 95 per cent, a change in the present state of leadership is necessary. However, in reality, the role of leadership is a requisite for instituting changes in key areas of organizations. Thus, it would be difficult to increase BE without leadership involvement.
- Target BE levels below 95 per cent could be achieved without the need to improve all CSFs to their pre-determined upper limits.

The initial instrument has been refined by means of an iterative procedure that selects measurement items based on whether they provide a good measure of variables. Specifically, items that correspond to sufficiently large values of outer coefficients and as a whole provide a reliable measure of the variables are selected by the procedure. However, by the same token, this procedure may have deleted certain 'good' items that are relevant to the organization. For example, some items that are believed to be important for the organization's success are later found to be irrelevant. Examples of items that have been removed due to lack of strength within the company are:

For leadership

- Top-management involvement
- Manager's involvement
- Institutional goal definition
- People management

For customer focus

- Service obligation
- Customer-perceived quality
- Customer satisfaction
- Competitor's customer satisfaction
- Customer–supplier relationship
- Task coordination
- External customer focus
- Employee job requirements

These and other factors are undoubtedly important concerns for managers for managing the quality of their organizations. From a total of fifty-seven items altogether in the initial instrument, thirty of them have been preserved and twenty-seven removed due to their very weak contribution for this analysis.

Based on the information in Table 8.11, it is possible to narrow down the improvement process to specific activities. However, the organization's management would have to choose its target level of BE that will specify which CSFs require improvements. Assuming that the organization has opted for a BE level of 75 per cent, the CSFs of interest are:

- management by fact
- process improvement
- people performance
- improvement culture

The subsequent analysis would be to examine the item mean scores of these CSFs given in Appendix A. Here, the aim is to increase the mean scores further to achieve target indices for corresponding CSFs. The new mean scores are determined with the Excellence Seeker's Approach using an algorithm that takes into account the BEI formula. Tables 8.12–8.15 give the results of improving management by fact, process improvement, people performance, and improvement culture respectively.

Leadership as a requisite

So far, the proposed solution for improving the organization's BE was obtained entirely with the analytical procedure, that is, Excellence Seeker's Approach, without any intervention from the model user. The result is optimal insofar as the BE target levels are concerned. However, as discovered earlier, the leadership index remained unchanged at 39 per cent over a wide range of target levels of 65–85 per cent. The indices at the higher end of this

Table 8.12 Mean scores associated with management by fact

Item	Target critical success factor index	
	47% Old mean	75% New mean
Performance measurement	4.97	7.79
Use of measurement information for product improvement	5.39	7.75

Table 8.13 Mean scores associated with process improvement

Item	Target critical success factor index	
	43% Old mean	75% New mean
Staff recruitment process	5.06	6.74
Assessment and benchmarking	4.67	5.46

Table 8.14 Mean scores associated with people performance

Item	Target critical success factor index	
	47% Old mean	75% New mean
Cross-function teamwork	5.58	6.06
Individual group teamwork	5.97	6.60
Managerial training	4.33	4.95
Training resources	4.92	5.43
Empowerment	5.22	5.44

Table 8.15 Mean scores associated with improvement culture

Item	Target critical success factor index	
	42% Old mean	75% New mean
Presence of quality culture	4.58	4.94
Employee suggestion	3.58	3.72
Problem-free process design	5.47	5.81

range represent significantly high target levels for the organization. Only at 90 and 95 per cent target levels does it become necessary for leadership to be increased to its upper limit. However, it is believed that any substantial change in key organizational areas and BE requires a change in the functioning of leadership. Therefore, it is believed that leadership should be improved to a reasonable level in order to achieve a more desirable solution.

Table 8.16 gives the result of using the variable-assignment method to improve CSFs with a fixed leadership level of 75 per cent over a range of BE target levels of 65–95 per cent.

It can be seen in Table 8.16 that by improving leadership, the solution for improvement is better than if leadership were simply allowed to take any value up to 75 per cent (Table 8.11). For example, only two factors were required to be improved in Table 8.16 for BE target level of 65 per cent compared to three in Table 8.11. For a target level of 75 per cent four factors need to be improved, including leadership. They are:

- Leadership
- Process improvement
- People performance
- Improvement culture

It is not necessary to improve management by fact as in the previous solution. The variable-assignment method is used to determine new item

Table 8.16 CSF and BE indices (leadership fixed at 75% level)

Critical success factor and business excellence	Upper limit	Original index BE = 48	Target business excellence index (%)					
			65	75	80	85	90	95
Leadership	–	39	75	75	75	75	75	75
Delight the customer	75	52	52	52	52	52	52	75*
Customer focus	75	51	51	51	51	51	51	75*
Management by fact	75	46	46	46	70*	75*	75	75*
Process improvement	75	43	75*	75	75	75	75	75
People-based management	75	43	43	43	43	43	75	75*
People performance	75	47	47	75*	75	75	75	75
Continuous improvement	75	53	53	53	53	75*	75	75
Improvement culture	75	42	75*	75	75	75	75	75

*New index for a higher target level.

Table 8.17 Mean scores associated with leadership

Item	Target critical success factor index	
	43% Old mean	75% New mean
Institution's quality values	5.06	7.77
People management	4.67	7.89

mean scores for leadership that correspond to a leadership index value of 75 per cent (Table 8.17). The new item mean scores for process performance, people performance, and improvement culture are the same as in the previous solution.

Conclusions

The research has been focussed on the internal assessment of a company's organizational performance in terms of nine key areas that contribute to BE according to KBEM. As it was shown by suitable statistical tests that the model has a good fit with the company's data, it was possible to use it as a reliable and valid tool for assessing the company's organizational performance. In its annual company report, various achievements have been portrayed in terms of its

- size of employment;
- financial performance such as sales;
- research and development – large number of highly skilled research engineers;
- product lines such as computers, servers, software, and smart cards;
- market share – growth in some areas.

Top management's concern for quality has been limited to the following areas:

- employee involvement;
- customer satisfaction, for example, customer satisfaction surveys;
- quality assurance, for example, certification with the ISO 9000 quality system.

Indeed, the company's top management believes that ISO 9000 certification is the foundation of any quality policy that is aimed at maintaining and improving production processes on an on-going basis. However, by definition, quality assurance involves the documentation of an organization's quality objectives and specifications of processes, to which actual processes are being compared. Thus, regardless of the quality of the company's output, if its actual processes have been performed as planned then the organization is said to have demonstrated a conformance to specified quality standards. A quality assurance system, therefore, does not necessarily result in products or services of desirable quality but rather assures that an organization has adhered to a documented quality blueprint. In addition, ISO 9000 quality system has a problem of lack of control on how it is being practised by certifying bodies in different countries.

There is hardly any indication of the company's commitment to TQM although it has been reported that quality teams and quality task forces have been formed in many parts of the organization. In this respect, company 'B' could be missing the opportunities that TQM could offer, such as effective leadership, customer delight (*highly* satisfied customers), everyone's participation, continuous improvement, prevention (rather than remedy), excellent customer–supplier relationships, and BE. Many large international corporate giants, such as Motorola, IBM, Ford, Matsushita, Toyota, Nissan, Xerox, and others, have been able to improve their business competitiveness substantially, which were the direct consequences of TQM processes that they have undertaken.

It is not clear as to how TQM has been or is being implemented in this company. Based on the findings of the present research, several conclusions can be drawn about its performance on the nine key areas of BEM:

- At a general level, the company's performance has been somewhat modest in all its CSFs (index = 39–53 per cent) and BE (index = 48 per cent).
- Its poorest performance is leadership, which has an index score of 39 per cent. This should be improved substantially if a speedier progress is to be achieved. In TQM, the various types of managers would be working in teams to look at improvement opportunities. Teams may not necessarily be comprised of only managers (like in quality councils). For example, in quality improvement teams, the bulk of the membership is employees while managers are responsible for managing team processes. Another important aspect of leadership is empowerment, which is the autonomy given to employees in performing their tasks to encourage innovation, create job satisfaction, reduce bureaucracy, improve quality of decisions, create better solutions to problems and improve job performance.
- Other below-average performances are management by fact (46 per cent), process improvment (43 per cent), people-based performance (43 per cent), people performance (47 per cent), and improvement culture (42 per cent). While the company's use of financial measures is very impressive, the use of non-financial measures on factors pertaining to leadership, people, processes, internal and external customer satisfaction, and affinity towards quality improvement should also be regularly practised.
- People are the most flexible assets of an organization. They can learn and acquire new skills, perform various roles, be given many kinds of responsibilities, located at various work stations and work at varying pace. On people management, TQM process focuses on four aspects:

  - education on TQM principles and concepts
  - training on the use of TQM tools
  - empowerment
  - reward

- The improvement process covers two areas: improvement of processes, and improvement of products and services. In TQM, the improvement process is never-ending because TQM is concerned with achieving a constantly moving target of customer needs, technological developments in processes and products, increase in various types of costs, new materials, and new markets. The improvement concept is closely related to prevention, in that prevention is one way to move towards improvement by way of driving out failures that threaten the smooth running of a system. If done continuously, failure removal will breed a culture of continuous improvement over time. Of equal importance is the need for information on how well processes are running, and products and services are performing. The measurement function should provide this information so that it could be used to plan improvements to chart future progress.

- At a narrower level, the company's improvement strategy should be centred on the improvement of all activities listed in Appendix A that are found to be relevant by the iterative procedure used and consider carrying out activities listed in Appendix B that are found irrelevant by the same procedure. The improvement of activities should relate to amount of increase of their mean scores. The approach of computing the mean scores was illustrated in the previous section.

To obtain a sharper snapshot of the company's performance, a much larger and more representative sample such as the one that is produced by a stratified or clustered sampling design is desired which would provide an excellent data set for use with the BE methodology.

The results of the empirical analysis have demonstrated that the BEM is useful for the continuous improvement of the company's BE. The model has several notable strengths:

1 Simple – in terms of concepts and conceptual network;
2 Easy to use – in terms of model parameters and outputs;
3 Generic – can be applied in different contexts;
4 Robust – it efficiently yields different outputs when inputs are changed;
5 Complete – it includes all TQM factors and utilizes a measurement instrument which is flexible, that is, can be expanded;
6 Valid – its validity has been statistically proven;
7 Achieves its objectives – by being able to measure all CSFs and their contributions towards BE.

Appendix

Appendix A

Business excellence questionnaire

Directions: *please cross the appropriate box to indicate how you would rate the extent to which your unit practices total quality management, critical success factors and evaluate business excellence.*

1. LEADERSHIP

The extent to which:	Very little								Very much	
	1	2	3	4	5	6	7	8	9	10
Top management assumes responsibility for quality performance										
Major departments' heads participate in quality improvement process										
The unit's quality goals are clearly defined										
The unit's quality values are adopted and reinforced throughout the unit										
The quality values are integrated into day-to-day leadership										
The people are feeling well managed and motivated										

2. DELIGHT THE CUSTOMER

The extent to which the unit:	Very low								Very high	
	1	2	3	4	5	6	7	8	9	10
Determines current and future customer requirements and expectations										
Provides effective management in order to achieve customer loyalty										
Uses information gained from customers to improve customer services										

Appendix A (continued)

2.1 CUSTOMER SATISFACTION (EXTERNAL)

The extent to which the unit:	Hardly								Always	
	1	2	3	4	5	6	7	8	9	10
Is committed to its explicit and implicit promise underlying its services to customers										
Handles complaints, resolves them, and uses complaint information for quality improvement and for prevention of recurrence of problems										
Uses methods for determining external customer's perceived quality										
Uses methods for determining external customer's perceived value										
Uses methods for determining external customer's satisfaction										
Compares its customer satisfaction results with that of competitors										

2.2 INTERNAL CUSTOMER SATISFACTION

The extent to which:	Very low								Very high	
	1	2	3	4	5	6	7	8	9	10
There are strong employee interaction with internal customers and suppliers										
There exist methods to improve coordination of interdependent tasks										
The unit focuses on external customers when tasks are being performed										
The unit provides what is needed by employees for them to perform their jobs										

3. MANAGEMENT BY FACT

The extent to which the unit:

	Very low								Very high	
	1	2	3	4	5	6	7	8	9	10
Has performance measurement system that evaluates its quality improvement process										
Disseminates performance measurements to those that require them										
Uses the performance measurements to improve its products and services										

3.1 ALL WORK IS PROCESS

The extent to which the unit:

	Very low								Very high	
	1	2	3	4	5	6	7	8	9	10
Has processes that are designed to meet all the quality requirements										
Assess the quality of its processes										
Has procedures to improve the quality of its products and services										
Has effective policy for recruitment and admission of employees										
Has effective policy for recruitment of highly outstanding employees										
Has effective policy for maintaining highly outstanding employees										

3.2 MEASUREMENT

The extent to which:

	Very low								Very high	
	1	2	3	4	5	6	7	8	9	10
The unit collects a wide range of complete and accurate performance indicators										
Has appropriate methodology for comparing or assessing quality										
Compares current performance of organization with that of competitors										
Compares current performance of organization with that of world market leaders										
Has applied assessment criteria to its external suppliers										

Appendix A (*continued*)

4. PEOPLE-BASED MANAGEMENT

The extent to which:

	Very low								Very high	
	1	2	3	4	5	6	7	8	9	10
Feedback is provided to employees on their performance										
The unit's overall human resource management effort supports its quality objectives										
Means are available for all employees to contribute effectively to meeting the unit's quality objectives										

4.1 TEAMWORK

The extent to which:

	Very low								Very high	
	1	2	3	4	5	6	7	8	9	10
Teamwork is encouraged for employees to communicate to others about their jobs										
Teams are used to solve cross-functional problems										
Action-teams are used to solve local problems										

4.2 PEOPLE MAKE QUALITY

The extent to which:

	Very low								Very high	
	1	2	3	4	5	6	7	8	9	10
Quality related training is given to managers										
Quality related training is given to employees										
There are resources available for employee training										
Managers remove the barriers that prevent people from improving quality, e.g. lack of training, poorly defined jobs, etc.										
People are proud to work for the unit										
Promotes innovation by empowering individuals within the organization										

5. CONTINUOUS IMPROVEMENT

The extent to which:	Very low								Very high	
	1	2	3	4	5	6	7	8	9	10
The unit reacts to trends in its customer satisfaction and indicators of adverse customer response										
Quality improvement methods are used to improve all services										
The unit compares current quality levels of service features with those of competitors										

5.1 CONTINUOUS IMPROVEMENT CYCLE

The extent to which:	Very low								Very high	
	1	2	3	4	5	6	7	8	9	10
The unit has quality culture of continuous improvement										
An active employee suggestion scheme is used										

5.2 PREVENTION

The extent to which:	Very low								Very high	
	1	2	3	4	5	6	7	8	9	10
Improved customer services are introduced to drive out failures										
Processes are designed to prevent potential problems										

Appendix A (*continued*)

6. BUSINESS EXCELLENCE

The extent to which the unit:

	Very low									Very high
	1	2	3	4	5	6	7	8	9	10
Has strong financial performance										
Has high customer demand										
Achieves its goals										
Has performed recruitment and admission of employees effectively										
Has achieved the desired product and services outcome										
Has performed recruitment of highly outstanding staff										
Has been able to maintain outstanding staff										

Name:

Organizational unit: Example: ERA/AL/V

Unit function: Example: Design, Business

Approximate number of subordinates:

Appendix B

Leadership excellence questionnaire

Organizational Values

The extent to which:	Very little								Very much	
	1	2	3	4	5	6	7	8	9	10
Leaders develop shared meanings and interpretations of reality										
Leaders use the organizational principles to guide decision-making										
Leaders put in place reinforcement systems that are consistent with organizational values and principles										

Vision

The extent to which:	Very little								Very much	
	1	2	3	4	5	6	7	8	9	10
Leaders create a compelling vision of the future of the organization										
Leaders communicate the vision effectively										
Leaders inspire confidence in vision										

Mission

The extent to which:	Very little								Very much	
	1	2	3	4	5	6	7	8	9	10
Leaders identify the organization's purpose										
Leaders generate commitment among organizational members for the chosen purpose										

Appendix B (*continued*)

Strategy

The extent to which:	Very little								Very much	
	1	2	3	4	5	6	7	8	9	10
Leaders develop policies and strategies consistent with the organization's mission, vision and values										
Leaders anticipate and guide change										
Leaders monitor resources and organizational performance and use feedback to review strategies for customer satisfaction										

Key Issues

The extent to which:	Very little								Very much	
	1	2	3	4	5	6	7	8	9	10
Leaders align the organization's structure to support delivery of its policy and strategy										
Leaders give subordinates authority to act and make decisions										
Leaders communicate and build supportive relationships with peers and subordinates in order to motivate people										

Leadership Excellence

The extent to which:	Very little								Very much	
	1	2	3	4	5	6	7	8	9	10
Leaders are accessible, actively listening and responding to people										
Leaders promote discussion, feedback and involvement										
Leaders encourage continuous improvement through innovation and continuous learning										
Leaders identify best practices in leadership										

Appendix C

Business scorecard questionnaire

Organizational Value

The extent to which:	Very little								Very much	
	1	2	3	4	5	6	7	8	9	10
The Organization communicates what it stands for										
The Organization develops a strategy aligned with its values										
The Organization builds a sense of community surrounding the values										

Process Excellence

The extent to which:	Very little								Very much	
	1	2	3	4	5	6	7	8	9	10
The Organization delivers what it promises										
The Organization collects and disseminates a wide range of complete and accurate performance indicators										
The Organization compares its process performance with that of its best competitors										
The Organization uses processes measurements to improve its activities										

Appendix C (*Continued*)

Organizational Learning

The extent to which:

	Very little								Very much	
	1	2	3	4	5	6	7	8	9	10
The Organization uses performance indicators and other forms of feedback to improve the products and services provided										
The Organization regularly introduces new and innovative products and services										
The Organization leaders are accessible, actively listening and responding to people										
The Organization has a culture of continuous improvement										
The Organization works in partnership with its stakeholders										

Delight the Stakeholders

The extent to which:

	Very little								Very much	
	1	2	3	4	5	6	7	8	9	10
The Organization listens to its stakeholders needs and requirements										
The Organization provides relevant and reliable information to its stakeholders										
The Organization has an ethical conduct and effectively deals with complaints										

Stakeholders Value Excellence

The extent to which:

	Very little								Very much	
	1	2	3	4	5	6	7	8	9	10
The Organization has a good overall image										
The Organization cares about its stakeholders										
The Organization provides good value for money for its stakeholders										
The Organization has strong financial performance										
The Organization has good quality reputation										

Appendix D

Individual item mean scores

Dimension	Label	Variable	Mean score	Number of questions providing weak relationships
1. Leadership	L4	Institution's quality values	4.61	4
	L5	Everyday leadership	4.36	
2. Delight the customer	DC1	Customer requirements	6.00	
	DC2	Customer loyalty	5.64	0
	DC3	Customer services	5.56	
3. Customer focus	C2	Handling customer complaints	6.03	8
	C4	Customer perceived value	5.17	
4. Management by fact	F1	Performance measurement	4.97	1
	F3	Use of measurement information for product improvement	5.39	
5. Process improvement	Pr4	Staff recruitment process	5.06	6
	Pr6	Assessment and benchmarking	4.67	
6. People-based management	Pm2	Human resource management	4.83	1
	Pm3	Employee quality involvement	4.97	
7. People performance	P2	Cross-function teamwork	5.58	
	P3	Individual group teamwork	5.97	
	P4	Managerial training	4.33	3
	P6	Training resources	4.92	
	P9	Empowerment	5.22	
8. Continuous improvement	C1	Customer feedback	6.08	1
	C2	Quality improvement methods	5.19	
9. Improvement culture	I1	Presence of quality culture	4.58	
	I2	Employee suggestions	3.58	1
	I4	Problem-free process design	5.47	
10. Business excellence	X1	Organizational performance	5.33	
	X2	World leader's performance	5.56	
	X3	Financial performance	5.03	
	X4	Customer demand	5.69	1
	X5	Goal achievement	5.47	
	X7	Staff maintenance	4.89	
	X8	Supplier assessment criteria	5.14	

Appendix E

Questions providing extremely weak relationships

Leadership
- Top-management involvement
- Manager's involvement
- Institution's goal definition
- People management

Customer focus
- Service obligation
- Customer perceived quality
- Customer satisfaction
- Competitor's customer satisfaction
- Customer-supplier relationship
- Task co-ordination
- External customer focus
- Employee job requirements

Management by fact
- Measurement information

Process improvement
- Quality process design
- System for product design
- Process assessment
- Staff maintenance process
- Performance indicators
- Quality assessment methodology

People-based management
- Performance feedback

People performance
- Employee training
- Quality improvement barriers
- Institutional pride

Continuous improvement
- Service competitiveness

Improvement culture
- Failure removal through improved services

Business Excellence
- Staff recruitment

Appendix F

Sequence for obtaining Kanji's Business Excellence Model

Kanji's Business Excellence Model (KBEM) uses a structural equation modelling approach. A few books and articles present the concepts associated with structural equation models and discuss the steps in applying this relatively complex statistical approach (for a basic understanding see, for example, Chapter 12 in Hair *et al.* (1997)).

Given below is a brief explanation on the issues of Structural Equation Modelling (SEM) and steps for the measurement of KBEM Index.

- *Latent variables* correspond to concepts and cannot be measured directly. They are operationalizations of constructs in a structural equation model. In KBEM case, the prime, principles and core concepts are all latent variables. Since they cannot be directly observed, they must be represented by manifest variables.
- *Manifest variables* are, therefore, observed values for specific items or questions which are used as indicators of latent variables. In KBEM, a set of manifest variables were identified to adequately cover the domain of each construct. The manifest variables correspond to the questionnaire items.

- Sometimes the set of manifest variables that represent one particular latent variable is referred to as a *measurement scale*. Measurement scales must obey certain conditions. Apart from adequately representing the domain of the concept (validity), scales are expected to be unidimensional (representing a single construct) statistically reliable (stable and consistent, for which, in the KBEM approach, Cronbach's coefficient α is calculated).
- That is obviously different from the simple notion of *scale* as the range of values a variable can assume. In KBEM questionnaire each item is answered on a one-to-ten scale.
- The weights in the structural equation model are usually designated as *path coefficients* and represent the strength of the relationships among different variables. In a structural equation model, both inner and outer coefficients are estimated.
- *Inner coefficients* reflect the strength of causal relationships among variables. They are the coefficients of the equations linking latent variables and each inner coefficient represents the amount of change in an effect variable that results from a unit of change in a cause variable. The coefficients in KBEM are expected to be all positive, showing that all Critical Success Factors (CSFs) contribute to Business Excellence (BE) and reinforce each other.
- *Outer coefficients* correspond to the weights of the manifest variables. The higher they are, the more relevant they become in explaining the correspondent manifest variable.
- *Indices* are the scores obtained for each manifest variable, based upon the correspondent manifest variables and the path coefficients in the model.

The steps for the measurement of index in KBEM require the following sequence:

1 Develop the theoretically based model: any structural equation model must have a strong theoretical foundation. Relevant constructs are identified, logical causal connections proposed and the specification error considered. In KBEM the CSFs were carefully identified and are consistent with the thinking of the most prominent quality management researchers.
2 Construct a path diagram which depicts in a diagram a series of causal connections that represent the predictive relationships among constructs. This corresponds to the usual way KBEM is pictured in the papers, as a series of interrelated constructs.
3 Convert the path diagram into a set of structural and measurement models. At this stage, the model is specified through a series of equations that defines (1) the structural equations linking constructs; (2) the measurement model specifying which variables measure which constructs; and (3) a set of matrices indicating any hypothesized constructs among constructs or variables. Before applying any software or making any calculations in

the KBEM, the set of indicators (manifest variables) for each latent variable is decided. This means that by then the questionnaire made up of the selected indicators for each construct of KBEM is ready.

4 Administer the questionnaire and obtain the measurement items from results of the questionnaire.

5 Estimate the proposed model, running the equations on computer to get estimates for the path coefficients and the factor indices. SEM uses the variance–covariance or the correlation matrix as its input data. Once the input data type is selected, it is necessary to decide how the model will be estimated. In the KBEM case, the correlation matrix is used and the estimates calculated according to Partial Least Squares (PLS). The software used is the *SAS* or a special program developed for the MatLab package that is, KW management improvement software. The estimates for all coefficients are calculated simultaneously.

6 The results for the model estimation must be carefully analysed. Sometimes it is necessary to identify/correct offending estimates. Since KBEM is a theoretical model with sound theoretical justifications, these situations seldom occur.

7 Assess goodness-of-fit. Besides evaluating overall model fit, it is necessary to analyse whether or not the measurement of each construct fits the requirements of unidimensionality and reliability. Briefly, Cronbach's α is used as a reliability measure, while outer coefficients and r^2 must be analysed to assess the power of explanation of each measurement scale and of the structural model as a whole.

8 Interpret and eventually refine the model.

Appendix G

Statistical calculations in Kanji's Business Excellence Model

Reliability

Coefficient α is the basic formula for determining the reliability based on internal consistency. It should be applied to all new measurement methods. The test proves if the measurement is too short or if the items have too little in common:

$$\alpha = r_{kk} = \left[\frac{k}{(k-1)} \right]^* \left[1 - \left(\frac{\sum \sigma_i^2}{\sigma_y^2} \right) \right]$$

r_{kk} = reliability of the whole test (correlation of the whole test)
k = number of test items
$\sum \sigma_i^2$ = sum of the variance of all individual items in a test
σ_y^2 = variance of a sum of items

Latent-variable partial least squares

Here x is leadership, y_i's are principles, z_i's are core concepts, and **b** is business excellence (see Figure A.1 for principles and core concepts). The latent variables, x, y_i, z_i and **b**, which are not directly measurable, are derived by linking them with directly measurable manifest variables. In the diagram, for example, the exogenous variable x has a causal relationship with endogenous variable y_i and has a structural coefficient γ_i. Here, the letter ε_i is a disturbance variable and δ_{ij} is used to indicate the effect of a disturbance variable on an endogenous variable. Variable x can have linkage with one or more manifest variables ς_i. The resulting equation is $y_3 = \varsigma_i x + \gamma_3 + \delta_{33}\varepsilon_3$. Other endogenous variable will have similar equations.

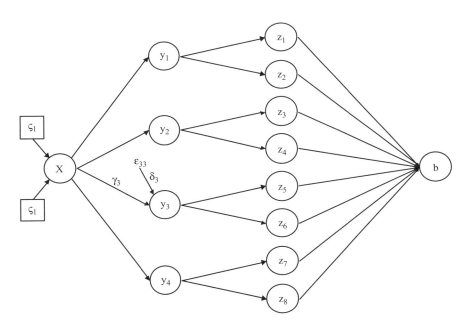

Figure A1 Latent-variable structural model for Kanji's Business Excellence Model.

Appendix H

MBNQA scoring guidelines

Score	Approach/deployment
0%	• no systematic approach evident; anecdotal information
10–20%	• beginning of a systematic approach to the basic purposes of the Item
	• major gaps exist in deployment that would inhibit progress in achieving the basic purposes of the Item
	• early stages of a transition from reacting to problems to a general improvement orientation
30–40%	• an effective, systematic approach, responsive to the basic purposes of the Item
	• approach is deployed, although some areas or work units are in early stages of deployment
	• beginning of a systematic approach to evaluation and improvement of basic Item processes
50–60%	• an effective, systematic approach, responsive to the overall purposes of the Item
	• approach is well-deployed, although deployment may vary in some areas or work units
	• a fact-based, systematic evaluation and improvement process is in place for basic Item processes
	• approach is aligned with basic organizational needs identified in the other Criteria Categories
70–80%	• an effective, systematic approach, responsive to the multiple requirements of the Item
	• approach is well-deployed, with no significant gaps
	• a fact-based, systematic evaluation and improvement process and organizational learning/sharing are key management tools; clear evidence of refinement and improved integration as a result of organizational-level analysis and sharing
	• approach is well-integrated with organizational needs identified in the other Criteria Categories
90–100%	• an effective, systematic approach, fully responsive to all the requirements of the Item
	• approach is fully deployed without significant weaknesses or gaps in any areas or work units
	• a very strong, fact-based, systematic evaluation and improvement process and extensive organizational learning/sharing are key management tools; strong refinement and integration, backed by excellent organizational-level analysis and sharing
	• approach is fully integrated with organizational needs identified in the other Criteria Categories

Score	Results
0%	• no results or poor results in areas reported
10–20%	• some improvements *and/or* early good performance levels in a few areas
	• results not reported for many to most areas of importance to the organization's key business requirements
30–40%	• improvements *and/or* good performance levels in many areas of importance to the organization's key business requirements
	• early stages of developing trends and obtaining comparative information
	• results reported for many to most areas of importance to the organization's key business requirements
50–60%	• improvement trends *and/or* good performance levels reported for most areas of importance to the organization's key business requirements
	• no pattern of adverse trends and no poor performance levels in areas of importance to the organization's key business requirements
	• some trends *and/or* current performance levels – evaluated against relevant comparisons *and/or* benchmarks – show areas of strength *and/or* good to very good relative performance levels
	• business results address most key customer, market, and process requirements
70–80%	• current performance is good to excellent in areas of importance to the organization's key business requirements
	• most improvement trends *and/or* current performance levels are sustained
	• many to most trends *and/or* current performance levels – evaluated against relevant comparisons *and/or* benchmarks – show areas of leadership and very good relative performance levels
	• business results address most key customer, market, process, and action plan requirements
90–100%	• current performance is excellent in most areas of importance to the organization's key business requirements
	• excellent improvement trends *and/or* sustained excellent performance levels in most areas
	• evidence of industry and benchmark leadership demonstrated in many areas
	• business results fully address key customer, market, process, and action plan requirements

Appendix I

EFQM RADAR model

The assessors use the RADAR logic to allocate points to each of the sub-criteria in the European Foundation for Quality Management (EFQM) Excellence Model. RADAR consists of four elements: Results, Approach, Deployment, Assessment and Review and is based on the logic that an excellent organization will:

- Determine the Results it intends to achieve as part of its policy and strategy making process. These results will reflect present and future needs of stakeholders.
- Plan and develop an integrated set of sound Approaches to deliver the required results.
- Deploy the approaches in a sound way to ensure full implementation.
- Assess and Review the approaches and deployment by monitoring and analysing the results achieved and ongoing learning activities. Finally identify, prioritize, plan and implement improvements where needed.

Assessors score each result sub-criterion by consideration of the excellence and scope of the results presented. The excellence of the results takes account of:

- Positive trends and/or sustained good performance
- Comparisons with internal targets
- Comparisons with external organizations – including, as appropriate, competitors, industry averages and 'best-in-class' organizations
- The extent to which the results presented are caused by the approaches and deployment described in the enabler criteria.

The scope of the results takes account of:

- The extent to which the results cover all relevant areas of the organization
- The extent to which a full range of results, relevant to the sub-criterion, is presented
- The extent to which the relative importance of the results is understood and presented.

Taking account of all of the above factors, the assessors use the RADAR scoring matrix to allocate a percentage score to the excellence of results and scope and derive an overall percentage score to each of the results sub-criteria. Assessors score each enabler sub-criterion by consideration of Approach, Deployment and Assessment and Review.

Approach takes account of:

- The soundness of the method or process described – the extent to which it has a clear rationale and is focused on stakeholder needs
- The extent to which the method or process described is integrated – supports policy and strategy and is linked to other approaches where appropriate and is fully integrated into daily activities.

Deployment takes account of:

- The extent to which the approach has been implemented across different areas and layers of the organization
- The extent to which the deployment of the approach is systematic.

Assessment and Review takes account of the steps the organization takes to assess and review the approach and the deployment of the approach. Assessors will consider:

- The measurements that are taken
- The learning activities that are followed
- The improvements that have been identified, prioritized, planned and implemented.

Taking account of all the above factors, the assessors use the RADAR scoring matrix to give percentage scores to Approach, Deployment, Assessment and Review and derive an overall percentage score to each of the enabler sub-criteria. Details of the RADAR card are presented in the EFQM Excellence Model brochure. Percentage scores are converted into points according to the weights allocated to the criteria and sub-criteria.

References

Ackoff, R. A. (1994) *The Democratic Corporation*, Oxford: Oxford University Press.

Andrews, J. P. and Field, R. (1998) 'Regrounding the concept of leadership', *Leadership & Organization Development Journal*, 19(3): 128–36.

Anthony, N. R., Dearden, J. and Vancil, R. F. (1976) *Management Control Systems: Text and Cases*, Homewood, IL: Irwin.

Atkinson, P. E. (1990) *Creating Culture Change: The Key to Successful Total Quality Management*, Bradford, UK: IFS Publications.

Atuahene-Gima, K. (1996) 'Differential potency of factors affecting innovation performance in manufacturing and services firms in Australia', *Journal of Product Innovation Management*, 13: 35–52.

Bartlett, C. and Goshal, S. (1997) 'The myth of the generic manager: new personal competencies for new management roles', *California Management Review*, 40(1): 92–116.

Bendel, T., Kelly, J., Merry, T. and Sims, F. (1993) *Quality Measuring & Monitoring*, London: Century Business.

Bentler, P. M. (1988) 'Comparative fit index in structural models', *Psychological Bulletin*, 107: 238–46.

Bentler, P. M. and Bonnet, D. G. (1980) 'Significance tests and goodness of fit in the analysis of covariance structures', *Psychological Bulletin*, 88: 588–606.

Bentler, P. M. and WU, E. J. C. (1995) EQS for Windows, Encino, Calif: Multivariate Software, Inc., Software.

Bergendahl, S. and Wachtmeister, A. (1993) 'Creating an index', *Managing Service Quality*, May, 19–22.

Blackburn, R. and Rosen, B. (1993) 'Total quality and human resources management: lessons learned from Baldrige Award-winning companies', *Academy of Management Executive*, 7: 49–65.

Borbely, J. (1981) 'The critical success factors method: its application in a special library environment', *Special Libraries*, 72(3): 201–8.

Boynton, A. C. and Zmud, R. W. (1984) 'An assessment of critical success factors', *Sloan Management Review*, Summer, 21(4): 17–27.

Brown, M. (1994) 'Is your measurement system well balanced?', *The Journal for quality and Participation*, 17(6): 6–11.

Burello, L. C. and Zadnik, D. J. (1986) 'Critical success factors of special education administrators', *Journal of Special Education*, 29: 367–77.

Butler, A., Letza, S. and Neale, B. (1997) 'Linking the balanced scorecard to strategy', *Long Range Planning*, 30(2): 242–53.

Cardona, P. (2000) 'Transcendental leadership', *Leadership & Organizational Development*, 21(4): 201–7.

Caruana, A. and Pitt, L. (1997) 'INTQUAL – an internal measure of service quality and the link between service quality and business performance', *European Journal of Marketing*, 31(8): 604–16.

Chadwick, L. (1991) *The Essence of Management Accounting*, Hemel Hempstead: Prentice Hall.

Churchman, C. W. (1968) *The Systems Approach* chap. 3. New York: Delacorte Press.

Clayton, M. (1995) 'Encouraging the *kaizen* approach to quality in a university', *Total Quality Management*, 6(5–6): 593–601.

Clemmer, J. (1990) *Firing on All Cylinders*, London: Judy Piatkus Publishers Ltd.

Coate, E. (1993) 'The introduction of total quality management at Oregon State University', *Higher Education*, 25: 303–20.

Collier, J. and Esteban, R. (2000) 'Systemic leadership: ethical and effective', *The Leadership & Organization Development Journal*, 21(4): 207–15.

Cooper, R and Kaplan, R. (1998) 'The promise – and peril – of integrated cost systems', *Harvard Business Review*, 76: 109–19.

Cooper, R. G. and Kleinschmidt, E. J. (1995) 'Benchmarking the firm's critical success factors in new product development', *Journal of Product Innovation Management*, 12: 374–91.

Craig, R. J. (1994) The No-nonsense Guide to Achieving ISO 9000 Registration, New York: Asme Press.

Crosby, P. B. (1979) *Quality is Free*, New York: McGraw Hill.

Crosby, P. B. (1996) *Quality Is Still Free*, New York: McGraw-Hill.

Dahlgaard, J., Larsen, H. Z. and Norgaard, A. (1997) 'Leadership profiles in quality management: A Danish perspective', *Total Quality Management*, 8(2–3): 16–30.

Dale, B. and Cooper, C. (1994) 'Introducing TQM: the role of senior management', *Management Decision*, 32(1): 20–6.

Darling, J. (1999) 'Organizational excellence and leadership strategies: principles followed by top multinational executives', *Leadership & Organization Development Journal*, 20(6): 309–21.

DeCosmo, R. D., Parker, J. S. and Haverly, M. A. (1991) 'Total Quality Management Goes to Community College' in 'Total Quality Management in Higher Education', L. A. Sherr and D. J. Teeter, (eds) *New directions for Institutional Research*, 71, Fall.

Deming, W. E. (1981) 'Improvement of quality and productivity through action by management', *National Productivity Review*, 1:12–22.

Deming, W. E. (1982) *Quality, Productivity, and Competitive Position*, Cambridge, MA: MIT Center for Advanced Engineering Study.

Deming, W. E. (1986) *Out of the Crisis*, MIT Press.

Deming, W. E. (1994) *The New Economics*, Cambridge, MA: MIT Centre for Advanced Engineering Study.

Dering, N. (1998) 'Leadership in Quality Organizations', *Journal for Quality and Participation*, January–February, 32–5.

Dervisiotis, K. N. (1995) 'The objective matrix as a facilitating framework for quality assessment and improvement in education', *Total Quality Management*, 6: 563–70.

Dixon, J. R., Nanni, A. and Vollmann, T. E. (1990) *The New Performance on the EFQM Model for Business Excellence*, EFQM, Brussels.

Doherthy, G. D. (1993) 'Towards total quality management in higher education: a case study of the University of Wolverhampton', *Higher Education*, 35(3): 321–39.

Drucker, P. F. (1964) *Managing for Results*, New York: Harper Row.

Eccles, R. (1991) 'The performance measurement and manifesto', *Harvard Business Review*, 69: 131–8.

Edgeman, R. and Scherer, F. (1999) 'Systemic leadership *via* core value deployment', *Leadership & Organization Development Journal*, 20(2).

EFQM (1999) *EFQM Excellence Model*, EFQM, Brussels.

EFQM (1999) *The EFQM Excellence Model: Public and Voluntary Sector* EFQM, Brussels.

EFQM website 2000 at *http://www.efqm.org/*

Egan, G. (1994) *Re-engineering the Company Culture*, New York: Egan Hall.

Elzinga, J., Horak, T., Lee, C. and Bruner, C. (1995) 'Business process management: survey and methodology', *IEEE Transactions on Engineering Management*, 42(2): 119–28.

Epstein, M. and Manzoni, J. (1998) 'Implementing corporate strategy: from tableaux de bord to balanced scorecards', *European Management Journal*, 16(2): 190–203.

Feigenbaum. A. V. (1991) *Total Quality Control*, 3rd edn, New York: McGraw-Hill.

Ferguson, C. R. and Dickson, R. (1982) 'Critical success factors for directors for the eighties', *Business Horizons*, May–June, 14–18.

Fiedler, F. E. (1967) 'A theory of leadership effectiveness', McGraw-Hill, London.

Fornell, C. (1992) 'A national customer satisfaction barometer: the Swedish experience', *Journal of Marketing*, 56: 6–21.

Garvin, D. A. (1988) *Managing Quality*, New York: Free Press.

Garvin, D. A. (1991) 'How the Baldrige award really works', *Harvard Business Review*, November–December, 80–93.

Gass, G. L., Bentson, R. and McMackin, G. (1987) 'White collar productivity', *Management Accounting*, September, 33–8.

Geanuracos, J. and Meikejohn, I. (1993) *Performance Measurement: The New Agenda*, Business Intelligence, Ltd.

Geddes, R. (1993) 'The total quality initiative at south Bank University', *Higher Education*, 25(3): 341–61.

Georgiades, N. and MacDonell, R. (1998) *Leadership for Competitive Advantage*, John Willey & Sons.

Gering, M. and Rosmarin, K. (2000) 'Central beating', *Management Accounting*, 78(6): 25–35.

Ghobadian, A. and Woo, H. (1996) 'Characteristics and shortcomings of four major quality awards', *International Journal of Quality*, 13(2): 55–65.

Gowan, J. R. and Matthieu, G. R. (1996) 'Critical success factors in information system development for a flexible manufacturing system', *Computers in Industry*, 28: 173–83.

Grady, M. W. (1991) 'Performance measurement implementing strategy', *Management Accounting*, June, 49–53.

Graetz, F. (2000) 'Strategic change leadership', Management Decision, 38(8): 550–62.

Graves, F. (1987) 'Measuring the quality of health care for decision support', *Quality Progress*, May, 37–8.

Hackman, J. R. and Wagerman, R. (1995) 'Total quality management: empirical, conceptual, and practical issues', *Administrative Science Quarterly*, 40: 309–42.

Hepworth, P. (1998) 'Weighing up – a Literature review of the "Balanced Scorecard"', *Journal of Management Development*, 17(8), 559–563.

Hersey, P. and Blanchard, K. H. (1993) 'Management of organizational behaviour: utilizing human resources', Prentice-Hall, London.

Hofer, C. W. and Schendel, D. E. (1979) *Strategic Management: a New View of Business Policy and Planning*, Boston: Little, Brown and Co.

Hogan, T. J. (1992) The application of the Malcolm Baldrige National Quality award criteria to the evaluation of quality in collegiate administration services', PhD dissertation, Ohio University, Athens.

Horner, M. (1997) 'Leadership theory: past, present and future', *Team Performance Management*, 3(4): 270–87.

Howell, R. A. and Soucy, S. R. (1987*a*) 'Cost accounting in the new manufacturing environment', *Management Accounting*, August, 42–8.

Howell, R. A. and Soucy, S. R. (1987*b*) 'Operating controls in the new manufacturing environment', *Management Accounting*, October, 25–31.

Howell, R. A. and Soucy, S. R. (1988) 'Management reporting in the new manufacturing environment', *Management Accounting*, February, 22–9.

Hroned, S. M. (1993) *Vital Signs: Using Quality, Time & Cost Performance Measurements to Chart Your Company's Future*, New York: Amacom.

Imai M. (1986) *Kaizen: The Key to Japan's Competitive Success*, New York: McGraw-Hill, 243–5.

Ishikawa, K. (1985) *What is Total Quality Control? The Japanese Way*, Englewood Cliffs, NJ: Prentice Hall.

Jenster, P. V. (1987) 'Using critical success factors in planning', *Long Range Planning*, 20: 102–3.

Johnson, H. T. and Kaplan, R. S. (1987) *Relevance lost: The Rise and Fall of Management Accounting*, Massachusetts: Harvard Business School.

Johnson, S. (1998) 'Identification and selection of environmental performance indicators: application of the balanced scorecard approach', *Corporate Environmental Strategy*, 5(4): 35–41.

Jung, D. and Avolio, B. (1999) 'Effects of leadership style and followers' cultural orientation on performance in group and individual task conditions', *Academy of Management Journal*, 42(2): 208–18.

Kakabadse, K. and Kakabadse, N. (1997) 'Best practice on the Australian Public Services (APS): an examination at discretionary leadership', *Journal of Management Psychology*, 12(7).

Kanji, G. K. (1990) 'Total Quality Management: the second industrial revolution', *Total Quality Management*, 1(1): 3–12.

Kanji, G. K. (1995) 'Quality and statistical concepts', in G. K. Kanji (ed.) *Total Quality Management: Proceedings of the First World Congress*, London: Chapman & Hall, pp. 1–10.

Kanji, G. K. (1996) 'Implementation and pitfalls of total quality management', *Total Quality Management*, 7: 331–43.

Kanji, G. K. (1997) 'Quality culture and business excellence', in S. Naharandi and M. Saadat (eds) *Proceedings of the International Symposium on Manufacturing Management*, ISMM '97, Auckland, November, 18–21.

Kanji, G. K. (1998*a*) 'An innovative approach to make ISO 9000 standards more effective', *Total Quality Management*, 9(1): 67–78.

Kanji, G. K. (1998*b*). 'Measurement of business excellence'. *Total Quality Management*, 9(3).

Kanji, G. K. (2000*a*) 'A European application of the Business Excellence Index', *Quality Progress*, December, 109–14.

Kanji, G. K. (2000*b*) 'Take a Test Drive for Business Excellence', *Proceedings of the ASQ Congress.*

Kanji, G. K. and Asher, M. (1993) *Total Quality Management Process: A Systematic Approach*, Madras: Productivity Press.

Kanji G. K. and Asher M. (1996) '100 methods for Total Quality Management', London: SAGE.

Kanji G. K. and Tambi A. (1999) 'Total Quality Management in UK higher education institutions', *Total Quality Management*, 10(1): 129–53.

Kanji, G. K. and TAMBI, A. M. A. (1999) 'TQM in US higher education-best on quality', *IAQ Book Services*, 10, Wisconsin, US: ASQ Quality Press, (to be published).

Kanji, G. K. and Wallace, W. (2000) 'Business excellence through customer satisfaction', *Total Quality Management*, 11(7): 979–98.

Kanji, G. K. and Wong, A. (1999) 'Business Excellence for supply chain management', *Total Quality Management*, 10: 1147–68.

Kanji, G. K. and Yui, H. (1997) 'Total quality culture', *Total Quality Management*, 8: 417–28.

Kanji, G. K. and Mouraesä, P. (2001) 'Measuring leadership excellence', *Total Quality Management*, 12(6): 701–18.

Kaplan, R. S. (1984) 'The evolution of management accounting', *The Accounting Review*, LIX(3): 390–418.

Kaplan, R. S. and Norton, D. P. (1992) 'The balanced scorecard – measures that drive performance', *Harvard Business Review*, January–February, 71–9.

Kaplan, R. and Norton, D. (1996) *The Balanced Scorecard – Translating Strategy into Action*, Harvard Business School Press, Harvard.

Kenny, T. (1994) 'From Vision to reality through Values', *Management Development Review*, 7(3): 17–20.

Kets de Vries, M. and Loper, M. (1994) 'The leadership mystique', *Academy of Management Executive*, 8(3): 73–89.

Korpela, J. and Tuominen, M. (1996) 'Benchmarking logistics performance with an application of the analytic hierarchy process', *IEEE Transactions of Engineering Management*, 43(3): 323–33.

Kotler, P. and Armstrong, G. (1996) *Principles of Marketing*, 7th edn., Englewood Cliffs, N. J: Prentice-Hall.

Kotter, J. (1990) 'What leaders really do', *Harvard Business Review*, May–June, 103–11.

Kristensen, K., Kanji, G. K. and Dahlgaard, J. J. (1993*a*) 'Measurement of customer satisfaction', *Total Quality Management*, 3: 123–8.

Kristensen, K., Kanji, G. K. and Dahlgaard, J. J. (1993*b*) 'Quality cost and total quality management', *Total Quality Management*, 3: 211–22.

Kristensen, K., Matrensen, A. and Gronholdt, L. (1999) 'Measuring the impact of buying behaviour on customer satisfaction', *Total Quality Management*, 10(4–5): 602–14.

Lee, S. and Shim, J. P. (1991) AB: QM Version 2.01, Software.

Lee, S., Lo, K., Leung, R. and Ko, A. (2000) 'Strategy formulation framework for vocational education: integrating SWOT analysis, balanced scorecard, QFD methodology and MBNQA education criteria', *Managerial Auditing Journal*, 15(8) 407–23.

Leidecker, J. K. and Bruno, A. V. (1984) 'Identifying and using critical success factors', *Long Range Planning*, 17: 23–32.

Lengyel, C. (2000) 'Integration of the balanced scorecard system', *Proceedings of the 44th EOQ Congress*, Budapest, 1: 40–8.

Letza, S. (1996) 'The design and implementation of the balanced scorecard: an analysis of three companies in practice', *Business Process Reengineering & Management Journal*, 2(1): 59–76.

Lohmoller, J. B. (1984) PLS-PC 1.8, software.

Loomba, A. and Johanessen, T. B. (1997) 'Malcolm Baldrige National Quality Award: critical issues and inherent values', *Benchmarking for Quality Management & Technology*, 4(4): 59–77.

Lynch, R. L. and Cross, K. F. (1995) *Measure Up! - Yardsticks for Continuous Improvement*, Cambridge: Basil, Blackwell.

Lynch, R. (2000) 'Corporate strategy', Pitman, Harlow (2nd edition).

Mangelsdorf D. (1999), 'Evolution from quality management to an integrative management system based on TQM and its impact on the profession of quality managers in industry', *The TQM Magazine*, 11(6): 41–2.

Martinsons, M,. Davison, R. and Tse, D. (1999) 'The balanced scorecard: a foundation for the strategic management of information systems', *Decision Support Systems* 25: 71–88.

Mauro, N. (1999) 'The Deming leadership model and profound knowledge: a global prescription', *Cross Cultural Management*, 6(3): 13–24.

McAdam, R. and O'Neill, E. (1999) 'Taking a critical perspective to the european business excellence model using a balanced scorecard approach: a case study in the service sector', *Managing Service Quality*, 9(3): 191–7.

McAdam, R. and Welsh, W. (2000) 'A critical review of business excellence quality model applied to further education colleges', *Quality Assurance in Education*, 8(3): 120–30.

McCamus, D. R. (1991) 'Performance and the quality voyage', *CMA Magazine*, 64(10): 8–12.

McClintock, C. J. (2000) Performance Indicators in Lisburn Borough Council, MSc. thesis, Faculty of Business and Management, University of Ulster.

McNair, C. J. and Leibfried, K. (1992) *Benchmarking: A Tool for Continuous Improvement*, New York: Harper Business.

Mello, J. (1999) 'Refraining leadership pedagogy through model and theory building', *Career Development International*, 4(3): 163–9.

Mills, T. (1995) 'Measuring business excellence', in: G. K. Kanji (ed.) *Total Quality Management: Proceedings of the first world congress*, Cornwall: Chapman & Hall.

Mintzberg, H. (1994) *The Rise and Fall of Strategic Planning*, Prentice-Hall, New York.

Mooraj, S., Oyon, D. and Hosteller, D. (1998) 'The balanced scorecard: a necessary good or an unnecessary evil?', *European Journal of Management*, 17(5):481–91.

Morden, T. (1997) 'Leadership as vision', *Management Decision*, 35(9), 668–676.

Morgan, G. (1988) *Riding the Waves of Change*, London: Sage.

Nadler, D. and Tushman, M. (1990) 'Beyond the Charismatic leader: leadership and organizational change, *California Management Review*, Winter, 77–97.

NIST (1994) *1994 Application Guidelines: Malcolm Baldrige National Quality Award*, Gaithersburg, MD, US.

NIST, (1999) 'Criteria for Performance Excellence', *Baldrige National Quality Program 2000*.

NIST (2000) *Baldrige National quality Program 2000 – Critera for Perfomance Excellence*, Gaithersburg, MD, US.

Nørreklit, H. (2000) 'The balance on the balanced scorecard – a critical analysis of some of its assumptions', *Management Accounting Research*, 11: 65–88.

Northouse, P. (1997) *Leadership: Theory and Practice*, Sage Publications.

Nunnally, J. C. (1978) *Psychometric Theory*, 2nd edn., New York: McGraw-Hill.

Oakland, J. (1993a) *Total Quality Management, the route to improving performance*, 2nd edn.

Oakland, J. S. (1993b) *Total Quality Management* 2nd edn. Oxford: Butterworth-Heinemann Ltd.

Oakland, J. (1999) *Total Organizational Excellence: Achieving World-Class Performance*, Oxford: Butterworth-Heinemann.

Odiorne, G. S. (1997) 'Measuring the unmeasurable: setting standards for management performance', *Business Horizons*, July–August.

Parasuraman, A., Berry, L. L. and Zeithaml, V. A (1991) 'Understanding, measuring, improving service quality: findings from a multiple research program' in S. Brown *et al.* (eds) *Service Quality: Multidisciplinary and Multinational Perspectives*, Lexington, MA: Lexington Books.

Parasuraman, A., Zeithaml, V. A. and Berry, L. L. (1988) 'SERVQUAL: a multi item scale for measuring consumer perception of service quality', *Journal of Retailing*, 64: 12–40.

Peters, T. (1997) *The Circle of Innovation: You Can't Shrink your way to Greatness*, New York: Alfred A. Knopf.

Peters, T. and Watermans, J. (1982) *In Search of Excellence: Lessons from America's best run companies*, 1st edn., Harper and Row.

Porter, L. and Tanner, S. (1996) 'Assessing business excellence' in R. McAdam and W. Welsh (2000) 'A Critical Review of Business Excellence Quality Model Applied to Further Education Colleges' *Quality Assurance in Education*, 8 (3):120–30.

Porter, L. J. and Tanner, S. J. (1998) *Assessing Business Excellence – a guide to self-assessment*, Oxford: Butterworth-Heinemann.

Powell, T. L. (1995) 'Total quality management as competitive advantage: a review and empirical study', *Strategic Management Journal*, 16: 15–37.

Prabhu, V. and Robson, A. (2000a) 'Achieving service excellence – measuring the impact of leadership and senior management commitment', *Managing Service Quality*, 10(5): 307–17.

Prabhu, V. and Robson. A. (2000b) 'Impact of leadership and senior management commitment on business excellence: an empirical study in the North East England', *Total Quality Management*, 11(4–6): 399–409.

Rai, A., Borah, S. and Ramaprasad, A. (1996) 'Critical success factors for strategic alliances in information technology: an empirical study', *Decision Sciences*, 27(1): 141–54.

Reavill, L. R. P. (1998) 'Quality assessment: total quality management and the stakeholders in the UK higher education system', *Managing Service Quality*, 8(1): 55–63.

Ridgeway, V. F. (1956) 'Dysfunctional consequences of performance measurements', *Administrative Science Quarterly*, September, 240–7.

Rockart, J. F. (1982) 'The changing role of the information systems executive: a critical success factors perspective', *Sloan Management Review*, Fall, 24(1): 3–13.

Rowden, R. (2000) 'The relationship between charismatic leadership behaviours and organizational commitment', *Leadership & Organizational Development Journal*, 21(1): 30–5.

Rowlands, K. (1998). 'Total quality management at the Dell Primary School', *Total Quality Management,* 9 (4–5): 223–9.

Saberwhal, R. and Kirs, P. (1994) 'The alignment between organisational critical success factors and implementation technology capability in academic institutions', *Decisions Sciences,* 25(2): 301–31.

Saraph, J. V., Schroeder, R. G. and Benson, P. G. (1989) 'An instrument for measuring the critical factors of quality management', *Decision Sciences,* 20: 810–29.

Schein, E. H. (1985) *Organisational Culture and Leadership: A Dynamic View,* San Francisco: Jossey–Bass.

Schoderbek, P. P., Schoderbek, C. G. and Kefalas A. G. (1990) *Management Systems: Conceptual Considerations,* 4th edn., Boston: R. D. Irwin Inc.

Seddon J (1998) 'The Vanguard Guide to Business Excellence' in R. McAdam and W. Welsh (2000) 'A critical review of business excellence quality model applied to further education colleges'. *Quality Assurance in Education,* 8(3): 120–30.

Sellenheim, M. R. (1991) 'J. I. case company: performance measurement', *Management Accounting,* September, 50–3.

Senge, P. (1990) 'The leader's new work: building learning organizations', *Sloan Management Review,* Fall, 7–22.

Senge, P. M. (1993) *The Fifth Discipline: The Art and Practice of the Learning Organisation,* London: Century Business.

Seymour, D. (1993) *On Q: Causing Quality in Higher Education,* New York: Macmillan.

Shriberg, A., Lloyd, C., Shriberg, D. and Williamson, M. (1997) *Practicing Leadership: Principles and Applications,* John Wiley & Sons.

Sink, D. S. (1991) 'The role of measurement in achieving world class quality and productivity management', *Industrial Engineering,* June, 23–8.

Smith, M. (1990) 'The rise and rise of the NF1', *Management Accounting,* May, 24–6.

Smith, G. F. (1993) 'The meaning of quality', *Total Quality Management,* 4(3): 235–44.

Smith, P. and Peterson, M. (1988) *Leadership, Organizations and Culture,* Sage Publications.

Snee, R. D. (1993) Creating robust work processes, *Quality Progress,* 26(2): 37–41.

Sowards, D. (1992) 'TQM is a journey: so where do we begin?', *Industrial Engineering,* January, 24–8.

Spanbauer, S. J. (1989) *Measuring and Costing Quality in Education,* Appleton, Wisconsin: Fox Valley Technical College Foundation.

Stogdill, R. M. (1991) *Handbook of Leadership: A Survey of Theory and Research,* The Free Press, London.

Stoner, A. F., Freeman, R. E. and Gilbert Jr., D. R. (1995) *Management,* 6th edn., Englewood Cliffs, N. J: Prentice-Hall Inc.

Taguchi, G., Elsayed, E. and Hsang, T. (1988) *Quality Engineering in Production Systems,* New York: McGraw-Hill.

Tawse, E. L. and Keogh, W. (1998) 'Quality in the leisure industry: an investigation', *Total Quality Management,* 9(4–5): 219–22.

The European Foundation for Quality Management (1994) *Self-Assessment 1995 Guidelines, based on the European Model for Total Quality Management 1995,* Brussels.

Thompson, J. (1997) *Strategic Management: Awareness and Change,* 3rd edn., International Thomson Business Press.

Thornberry, N. (1997) 'A View about 'Vision' ', *European Management Journal,* 15(1): 28–34.

Tsang, A. (1998) 'A strategic approach to managing maintenance performance', *Journal of Quality in Maintenance Engineering*, 4(2): 87–94.

Udo, G. J. and Ehie, C. I. (1996) 'Critical success factors for advanced manufacturing systems', *Computers and Industrial Engineering*, 3(1–2): 91–4.

Vroom, V. H. and Yetton, P. W. (1973) *Leadership and Decision Making*, University of Pittsburgh Press, Pittsburgh.

Walker, K. (1996) 'Corporate performance reporting revisited – the balanced scorecard and dynamic management reporting', *Industrial Management and Data Systems*, 26(3): 24–30.

Wells, R. (1998) 'E-Quality leadership', *Total Quality Management*, 9(4–5): 230–6.

Williams, J. J. and Ramprasad, A. (1996) 'A taxonomy of critical success factors', *European Journal of Information Systems*, 5: 250–60.

Yang, H. (1996) 'Key information management issues in Taiwan and the US', *Information and Management*, 30: 251–67.

Zairi, M. (1992) *TQM-Based Performance Measurement*, TQM Practicioner Series, Letchworth, UK: Technical Communications.

Zairi, M. (1994*a*) *Measuring Performance for Business Results*, London: Chapman and Hall.

Zairi, M. (1994*b*) 'Leadership in TQM Implementation: Some case examples', *The TQM Magazine*, 6(6): 9–16.

Zairi, M. (1995) 'Leadership in TQM implementation: some case examples', *American Journal of Management Development*, 1(1): 37–44.

Zairi, M. (1999). 'Managing excellence leadership', *The TQM Magazine*, 11(4): 215–20.

Zink K. J. and Schmidt A. (1998) 'Practice and Implementation of Self Assessment', *International Journal of Quality Science*, 3(2): 147–70.

Zink, K. J., Hauer, R. and Schmidt, A. (1994) 'Quality assessment: instruments for the analysis of quality concepts based on EN 29000, the Malcolm Baldrige Award and the European Quality Award', *Total Quality Management*, 5(5): 32.

Index